The People's War

The People's War

Responses to World War II in the Soviet Union

Edited by Robert W. Thurston
and Bernd Bonwetsch

University of Illinois Press

Urbana and Chicago

Library of Congress Cataloging-in-Publication Data
The people's war : responses to World War II in the Soviet Union /
edited by Robert W. Thurston and Bernd Bonwetsch.
p.   cm.
Includes bibliographical references and index.
ISBN 978-0-252-02600-3 (acid-free paper)
1. World War, 1939–1945—Soviet Union. I. Thurston, Robert W.
II. Bonwetsch, Bernd, 1940–
D764.P45   2000
947.084'2—DC21   00-008493

c 6 5 4 3 2

For Jakob Bonwetsch, who knows how much he means to us.
B.B.

For Alexander, who has brought us much joy and pride.
R.T.

Contents

Maps appear on pages 15, 76, and 165

Acknowledgments

This book has a long history. Many people and institutions have helped in its creation, and they deserve great thanks. The project grew out of a casual and then increasingly intense interchange of materials, views, and people between Miami University in Oxford, Ohio, and the Ruhr-Universität in Bochum, Germany. In 1992 Bernd Bonwetsch, Beate Fieseler, and Susanne Conze on the German side and Robert Thurston on the American side obtained grants from the Deutscher Akademischer Austauschdienst (DAAD) and the German-American Commission on Collaborative Research of the American Council of Learned Societies. Funds from these sources, along with additional support from the Ruhr-Universität and the International Research and Exchanges Board in Washington, D.C., enabled us to hold a conference in Bochum in July 1993 that brought together most of the contributors to this book. Funds from the DAAD and the German-American Commission also made possible visits by the editors to each other's universities and by Robert Thurston to Moscow. We are deeply grateful for the financial assistance from all of these sources.

Jeri Schaner, the head secretary of the history department at Miami University, did her usual magnificent and efficient work with correspondence and in helping to prepare some aspects of the manuscripts. Without her help this project would have been much more difficult. Thanks also to cartographer Denis Mullally, who drew the maps that appear in the book.

The German editor wishes to thank the American editor for his work in translating and editing some of the contributions. The American editor wishes to thank the German editor for all of his work on the articles, his many suggestions and corrections as the manuscript took shape, finding the photographs, arranging the conference in Bochum, and general support, good cheer, and good beer. Beate Fieseler did much to make the conference run smoothly and to arrange Robert Thurston's visit to Bochum.

The participants in the Bochum conference have waited with grace and patience to see their work in print, and the editors thank them for their willingness to go along with us through a long process. We hope that they are pleased with the results.

❖ ❖ ❖

Portions of Robert W. Thurston's chapter first appeared in his book *Life and Terror in Stalin's Russia* (New Haven, Conn.: Yale University Press, 1996), 199–266, and are reprinted with the permission of Yale University Press. Portions of Richard Stites's chapter first appeared in his essay "Introduction: Russia's Holy War," in *Culture and Entertainment in Wartime Russia*, ed. Richard Stites (Bloomington: Indiana University Press, 1995), 126–39, and are reprinted with the permission of Indiana University Press. An earlier version of Mark Von Hagen's chapter first appeared as "Soviet Soldiers and Officers on the Eve of the German Invasion: Towards a Description of Social Psychology and Political Attitudes" in *Soviet Union/Union Soviétique* 18:1–3 (1991): 79–101 and is reprinted here with the permission of Charles Schlacks Jr., publisher.

The People's War

Introduction

Bernd Bonwetsch and Robert W. Thurston

Germany and the Soviet Union were locked in a fight to the death on the eastern front during World War II. Seventy to eighty percent of all German field troops engaged in the war served on that front, and Hitler's forces suffered by far the largest share of their killed, wounded, and missing while fighting the Red Army.[1] On the Soviet side the old estimate of twenty million civilian and military dead has proven to be merely a widely repeated figure unsupported by reliable data. But surely the toll was huge; recent estimates range up to twenty-seven million. About one-third of all Soviet deaths were military.[2] The Germans came not merely to conquer but to brutalize or destroy entire nations. Rarely has war been conducted so mercilessly.[3]

The Second World War has been the subject of thousands of books, and new works appear almost weekly.[4] The eastern front has had its share of these studies. The present volume, however, offers new departures, sources, voices, and analyses. Although the story of economic policy and the combat itself has been told and retold virtually day by day, the human experience of the war in the USSR has not been adequately covered.

What the authors of the present collection have wanted to know above all might be summarized this way: what was the war really like and what did it mean for ordinary Soviet people? Given the wide variety of popular responses to the war and to the Stalinist leadership during it, what can we say about the nature of Soviet society during, before, and after the fighting? How did the state interact with society during this immense struggle, when its power to rule by coercion was much reduced, and when its stability and performance depended more than ever on consent and voluntary cooperation? No study can hope to answer such vast questions, but our contributions add considerably to our knowledge of the *people's* war; it is their experience and their points of view, in all their tangled and sometimes contradictory complexity, that we explore.

"People" here does not imply the old Soviet use of that term; *narodnaia* (popular) usually meant something heroic and pure by definition, as if nothing that came from the salt of the earth could ever be bad. This concept was central to Soviet ideology, which boasted that a state ruled by the people had been created in the USSR. "Bosses come and go, but the people remain," Stalin said in a speech of October 1937.[5] In February 1942, in an address aimed at ordinary Germans but surely heard by few of them, he said that "Hitlers come and go, but the German people . . . remain."[6] These are indications of where virtue, by Soviet lights, could be found. Stalin's remarks might be interpreted as full of concern for average citizens, yet the abstract concept of "the people" suggests that they are one entity with one voice. That voice, the Soviet leader implied, was purely loyal vis-à-vis the regime, as was the regime to the citizens.

This purported unanimity and solidarity of state and society is a dehumanizing pretense, as are the statues of brawny workers and soldiers still encrusting ex-Soviet buildings. Such figures, which were repeated endlessly in paintings, films, and literature, are not real people but superhuman heroes. Whole towns were proclaimed hero-cities (*goroda-geroi*) for their participation in the war, a level of abstraction unmatched in other countries. This is not to say that genuine heroes did not appear during 1941–45; under the extreme demands of battle, wartime production, or civil defense they did come forward by the thousands. But older Soviet studies went beyond the inflation of ordinary experience conferred by the term "hero" to suggest that the entire war experience in the USSR was one of inexhaustible heroism, blemished only slightly by occasional acts of treason and collaboration. For decades the dark side was not mentioned at all. Such starkly dichotomized treatments echoed ancient Russian traditions of describing national behavior as either purely virtuous or utterly sinful.[7] Earlier Soviet studies therefore tended to cheapen what real people actually went through, extending ironically to the true heroism that did occur.

In recent years, writers in the former Soviet Union have begun to explore the war in more down-to-earth terms. This has probably been more true of fiction than of historical studies, which once induced the writer and war veteran Viktor Astaf'ev to say that he took part in a war entirely different from that depicted by official historiography.[8] (Until *Saving Private Ryan* appeared in 1998, Western film treatments of the war often elicited the same response from the people who actually fought it.) Writing history in the former Soviet Union is now mostly free of ideological restraints, although the financial situation of historians and publishing is often perilous. Scholars like Margarita Zinich can now explore the "everyday life of the horrible war years."[9] We wish to augment such beginnings and to help restore the range and validity of human experience during one of history's most savage periods.

We have not been particularly interested in the course of combat itself, except as it relates to the questions and issues surrounding everyday life. Many books and articles cover the major battles of the eastern front, for instance the ones at Stalingrad in 1942–43 and at Kursk in the summer of 1943. There are also multivolume works that discuss military operations in great detail.[10] But many such investigations give the impression of a dry and faceless war: commanders gave orders, certain units moved in certain directions—or failed to—while certain enemy units moved to oppose them. The war becomes almost a classroom exercise, drained of its massive pain and destruction, emotion and anxiety, hope and sometimes even joy. When in the old USSR someone like the prominent war historian Aleksandr Samsonov tried to give a touch of realism and feeling to all the dying, he was reproached for "slander," "degrading heroes," and telling "trench truths."[11]

Western studies depended heavily on Soviet works and official information and in many respects could not overcome their shortcomings, but nevertheless some authors wrote brilliantly on the war. Two works that come immediately to mind are Alexander Werth's *Russia at War* and Harrison Salisbury's deeply moving *The 900 Days: The Siege of Leningrad*,[12] both of which combine the skills of journalism and scholarship. In studies like these, astonishing dimensions of patriotism, sacrifice, and suffering become palpable. For the purely military side of the war, John Erickson's *The Road to Stalingrad* and *The Road to Berlin* have long been of great value.[13] As useful as these and other books are for beginning to understand the war as it touched actual people, much has been left out. Werth's and Salisbury's works also tend to emphasize the political and the heroic, and they were written long before key evidence became available. Other recent studies have addressed the nature of the war for ordinary citizens,[14] but have not concentrated on that experience in as much depth, nor marshaled as much detailed evidence, as the contributors to this volume.

Existing treatments of a particularly gruesome topic, the German occupation, are mostly discussions of the invaders' policies and practices. We have histories of the Germans in the Soviet Union but not a history of the Soviet Union under German occupation.[15] While the first subject is essential in producing a picture of what happened, it does not explore the rich variety of ordinary citizens' responses to the unbearable and often fatal pressures with which they tried to cope. Our knowledge of this area has depended mainly on German documents, some of which are now being published in Russia.[16] Uwe Gartenschläger relies mainly on this kind of source but has unearthed rare materials and has used them to present a chilling picture of life in occupied Minsk from 1941 to 1944.

Hans-Heinrich Nolte details the calculated, cold, and haughty destruction of a Jewish town by the Germans. Nolte depicts the valor and creativity of Jewish resistance against hopeless odds and succeeds in making the meaning of genocide hauntingly clear.

Russian archives have yielded considerable material on the home front, particularly in Leningrad (now known by its pre-1914 name of St. Petersburg) and Moscow. The Russian historians Andrei Dzeniskevich, Mikhail Gorinov, and Gennadi Bordiugov have brought years of study to bear on these regions. The American Richard Bidlack has sifted through a mass of information on life in occupied Leningrad to illuminate survival strategies in that most tragic of all locales. How did people cope with shortages of everything, especially food, and still produce crucial armaments? These articles are compelling looks at civilian life behind the front lines.

The same feast of new material has appeared for most of the subjects covered in this volume. Mark Von Hagen has pored over reports of morale and behavior within the Red Army in the late 1930s, and he has much to say about a number of issues, especially the attitudes of rank-and-file troops toward their superiors and the regime. New conclusions are now possible about the behavior of the Red Army in the early fighting, when crushing defeats at the hands of the Germans were officially explained as defeatism or cowardliness on the part of generals and other high officers. The chapter by Robert W. Thurston explores the behavior and morale of ordinary Red Army troops during the initial stages of the German invasion as well as the thorny web of factors leading to the decisions of ex-prisoners either to remain in the West or return to the USSR after the fighting ceased.

Other contributors pay particular attention to the cultural side of the war. Aileen G. Rambow delves into the poetry of besieged Leningrad, as professional writers and ordinary citizens strove to give their immense losses some greater meaning. Richard Stites brings his unmatched knowledge of Soviet cultural life to a study of wartime entertainment and the responses it evoked among performers and listeners. Bernd Bonwetsch sums up the experience of Soviet intellectuals during the war and explains why, despite the horror of the period, they saw it as a time of relative freedom.

Women have been among the most important icons of the war, both in Soviet propaganda produced during the war and in published works afterward. Icons are stylized and purified representations, however, not pictures of people caught in a vast mix of bullets, blood, dirt, and feelings. Beate Fieseler and

Susanne Conze redress the prettified traditional views of women in the war, which dehumanize participants by mentioning only a narrow range of their experience, in a discussion of women's myriad roles in combat and other spheres of activity.

This fullness of human experience and choices is important to an understanding of Soviet history not only during the war but before and after it as well. A one-dimensional portrait of the USSR from 1941 to 1945—whether it be the iconography of women, descriptions of X German unit facing Y Soviet force, or the heroism of Leningrad's people—contributes to the general mythology of the USSR's past that is now prevalent in both East and West. Brought to the public in many books and films,[17] a common image of Soviet history is that the omnipotent state, led by dictators of varying viciousness, throttled and murdered the helpless people.

While no one denies that massive crimes and repression, probably unprecedented in history, took place in the USSR during World War II, numerous western scholars have begun to offer a new picture. They argue that, powerful as it was, the Soviet state was far from able to achieve all its aims and goals. Much was beyond its control; it was perhaps not even particularly separated from Soviet society.[18]

To come closer to an accurate picture of the Stalinist USSR it is necessary not only to describe the command structures and repressive power of the state but also to show how people reacted to them, interacted with them, cooperated with them, opposed them, and adapted or ignored central policy in their own ways. Research into these topics has so far dealt with the prewar years; here we carry the investigation into the most difficult period of Soviet existence, when the authorities could hardly rule by coercion alone.

Considerations of space and the contributors' particular interests have meant that our collection emphasizes certain aspects of the war. While some articles devote attention to the fate and behavior of non-Russian nationalities within the USSR, outside of the Jews those groups are not the direct focus of our work. The disparate reactions to the German invasion and the war as a whole among various nationalities within the USSR is a huge topic that deserves a great deal of attention in its own right. To give only one example of how tangled this issue can be, consider Ukraine. Before the war it was the site of four major religions (Orthodoxy, Catholicism, Judaism, and the Uniate Church), with some Muslims scattered about; fiercely independent Cossack traditions; different historical legacies in the different regions of the country that had long been part of the old Austro-Hungarian and Russian Empires, and then from 1919 to 1939 under capitalist Poland and the socialist Soviet Union; different alphabets and languages; a volatile ethnic mix involving Ukrainians, Russians, Jews, Tatars, and other immigrating nationalities; grinding poverty, pollution, and endemic daily violence in the mining and industrial areas; a struggle to define identities and loyalties that raged almost unabated from the late nineteenth century on; and immense tragedy at the hands of various forces in the "Russian" Civil War of 1918–20, collectivization of the peasantry in the late twenties, a devastating famine in 1932–33, and the Stalinist Terror of 1936–38.[19] This almost impenetrable swirl of influences and events, in which Ukrainians repeatedly took different sides, sometimes changing positions in rapid succession, makes the question of why anyone reacted in a certain way to the German invasion extremely difficult to answer.

The gruesome fighting between Russia and Chechnya in 1994–95 and again in 1999–2000, as the smaller nation tried to break away from the larger nation's control, further reminds us that ethnic conflicts existed long before the Soviet Union did and will last long after its demise. The Chechens had bitter memories of the Russian conquest of their territory in the nineteenth century, for example, while the Kazakhs, Kirghiz, and Turkmen of Central Asia rose against the tsarist regime when it attempted to introduce conscription among them in 1916.[20] Other nationalities in the prerevolutionary empire felt long-standing resentment toward the Russians and the government dominated by them. This sentiment forms part of the background to the welcome given to the Germans by some members of Soviet minorities, who seized the chance to express their displeasure with any Russian government. However, there is no question that the harsher aspects of Soviet rule produced yearning among some of the USSR's inhabitants for liberation from abroad; several of the chapters in this volume touch on this issue. Stalin, in his usual style, reacted with great severity to the disloyalty shown by members of minorities with mass arrests and deportations of entire ethnic groups; the literature on this subject is extensive.[21] This volume provides a look at the complexity of feelings among the three nationalities that were most intensely involved in the war on Soviet soil: the Russians, Jews, and Germans. Their stories are perhaps only slightly less complicated than those of other Soviet groups.

It will be apparent that the authors participating in this volume are by no means of one mind. Many differences exist in tone, emphasis, and even basic assessments of Stalinism. Readers can only benefit from this range of views as they move toward their own conclusions. In two respects, however, the contributors are united: they wish to put the Soviet people back into their war and to grapple with the complex, uneven, contradictory, and often dismaying qualities that a subject of such immense proportions deserves.

Notes

1. Burkhart Mueller-Hillebrand, *Das Heer, 1933–1945: Die Entwicklung des organisatorischen Aufbaues*, vol. 3, *Der Zweifrontenkrieg: Das Heer vom Beginn des Feldzuges gegen die Sowjetunion bis zum Kriegsende* (Frankfurt am Main, 1969), 124 and 174. Of course, the percentage of German troops engaged on the eastern front was extremely high into 1942–43, before western Allied troops expanded operations into Italy and finally into France.

2. John Erickson, "Soviet War Losses: Calculations and Controversies," in *Barbarossa: The Axis and the Allies*, ed. John Erickson and David Dilks (Edinburgh, 1994). On Soviet military losses see *Grif sekretnosti sniat: Poteri vooruzhennykh sil SSSR v voinakh, boevykh deistviiakh i voennykh konfliktakh: Statisticheskoe issledovanie*, ed. G. V. Krivosheev (Moscow, 1993). This source appears to exaggerate German losses relative to Soviet ones.

3. The exhibition *Crimes of the Wehrmacht* has finally brought this behavior to the attention of the general public in Germany. More than a million people to date have visited the exhibition. See the catalog *Vernichtungskrieg: Verbrechen der Wehrmacht, 1941 bis 1944*, ed. Hamburger Institut für Sozialforschung (Hamburg, 1996); *Vernichtungskrieg: Verbrechen der Wehrmacht, 1941–1944*, ed. H. Keer and K. Naumann (Hamburg, 1995).

4. In March 2000 a search of materials in English on the Soviet-German war held by libraries at Ohio colleges and universities turned up almost four thousand titles. There are tens of thousands of other volumes in both Russian and German. Asked to find web pages using the words "Russia" and "World War II," a standard Internet search engine located 98,100 sites.

5. Iosif Stalin, *Sochineniia*, vol. 14, ed. Robert H. McNeal (Stanford, Calif., 1967), 254.

6. Joseph Stalin, *The Great Patriotic War of the Soviet Union* (New York, 1945), 44.

7. See the intriguing article on this Russian tradition by Ju. M. Lotman and B. A. Uspenskij, "The Role of Dual Models in the Dynamics of Russian Culture," in *The Semiotics of Russian Culture*, ed. Ann Shukman, Michigan Slavic Contributions, no. 11 (Ann Arbor, Mich., 1984). For a discussion of official commemoration and private memory of the war, see Bernd Bonwetsch, " 'Ich habe an einem völlig anderen Krieg teilgenommen': Die Erinnerung an den 'Großen Vaterländischen Krieg' in der Sowjetunion," in *Krieg und Erinnerung*, ed. H. Berding, K. Heller, and W. Speitkamp (Göttingen, 2000).

8. "Istoriki i pisateli o literature i istorii: Materialy konferentsii," *Voprosy istorii* no. 6 (1988), 33. For an example of vivid fiction on the war, see Vasilii Grossman, *Life and Fate*, trans. Robert Chandler (New York, 1987). Writers such as Vladimir Tendriakov, Valentin Rasputin, Vasilii Grossman, and above all Vasilii Bykov had long presented the war in ways that allowed veterans to identify with at least some of its aspects.

9. M. S. Zinich, *Budni voennogo likholetia, 1941–1945*, 2 vols. (Moscow, 1994).

10. *Istoriia Velikoi otechestvenoi voiny Sovetskogo Soiuza*, 6 vols. (Moscow, 1960–65);

Istoriia vtoroi mirovoi voiny, 1939–1945, 12 vols. (Moscow, 1973–82). For a recent western example of traditional military history, see David M. Glantz and Jonathan M. House, *When Titans Clashed: How the Red Army Stopped Hitler* (Lawrence, Kans., 1995).

11. Viktor Kulish, "K voprosu ob urokakh i pravde istorii," *Nauka i zhizn'* no. 12 (1987), 15.

12. Alexander Werth, *Russia at War, 1941–1945* (New York, 1964); Harrison Salisbury, *The 900 Days: The Siege of Leningrad* (New York, 1969).

13. John Erickson, *The Road to Stalingrad: Stalin's War with Germany*, vol. 1 (London, 1975); *The Road to Berlin: Stalin's War with Germany* (Boulder, Colo., 1983).

14. *World War 2 and the Soviet People*, ed. John Garrard and Carol Garrard (New York, 1993), concentrates more on images of the war than experience of it; John Barber and Mark Harrison, *The Soviet Home Front, 1941–1945: A Social and Economic History of the USSR in World War II* (London, 1991).

15. Alexander Dallin, *German Rule in Russia, 1941–1945: A Study of Occupation Policies*, 2d ed. (Boulder, Colo., 1981); Gerald Reitlinger, *The House Built on Sand: The Conflicts of German Policy in Russia, 1939–1945* (New York, 1960).

16. See for example "Okkupatsiia," *Neizvestnaia Rossiia XX vek* no. 4 (1994), 231–365.

17. An example of a film in this genre is *Stalin* (London, 1990). A general history of the Soviet Union that follows these lines is Mikhail Heller and Aleksandr M. Nekrich, *Utopia in Power: The History of the Soviet Union from 1917 to the Present*, trans. Phyllis B. Carlos (New York, 1986).

18. For recent arguments along these lines, see Robert W. Thurston, *Life and Terror in Stalin's Russia, 1934–1941* (New Haven, Conn., 1996); Nellie Hauke Ohr, "Collective Farms and Russian Peasant Society, 1933–37," Ph.D. dissertation (Stanford University, 1990); J. Arch Getty, introduction to *The Road to Terror: Stalin and the Self-Destruction of the Bolsheviks, 1932–1939* (New Haven, Conn., 1999).

19. On Ukraine to 1941 see Hiroaki Kuromiya, *Freedom and Terror in the Donbas: A Ukrainian-Russian Borderland, 1870s-1990s* (Cambridge, 1998). For an example of the literature on nationalities and the war, see Harry Gordon, *The Shadow of Death: The Holocaust in Lithuania* (Lexington, Ky., 1992); Peter Lawrence, "Why Lithuania? A Study of Active and Passive Collaboration in Mass Murder in a Lithuanian Village, 1941," in *Why Germany? National Socialist Anti-Semitism and the European Context*, ed. John Milfull (Oxford, 1993). Considerable collaboration between Lithuanians and Germans occurred; it had to do above all with Lithuanian anti-Semitism and anger over being forcibly incorporated into the Soviet Union in 1940.

20. On Chechnya, see Anatole Lieven, *Chechnya: Tombstone of Russian Power* (New Haven, Conn., 1998). For a brief treatment of the long history of Chechen-Russian tensions, see Carlotta Gall and Thomas de Waal, *Chechnya: Calamity in the Caucasus* (New York, 1998). On the Kazakh-Turkmen-Kirghiz revolt of 1916, see Martha Brill Olcott, *The Kazakhs*, 2d ed. (Stanford, Calif., 1995), esp. 118–26. Hundreds of thousands of Kazakhs and Kirghiz were treated harshly and resettled into a barren region after the revolt.

21. For documents on Soviet treatment of nationalities considered guilty of collaboration, see N. F. Bugai, ed., *L. Beriia–I. Stalinu: "Soglasno Vashemu ukazaniiu . . ."* (Moscow, 1995). See also A. M. Nekrich, *The Punished Peoples: The Deportation and Fate of Soviet Minorities at the End of the Second World War,* trans. George Saunders (New York, 1978); Robert Conquest, *The Nation Killers: The Soviet Deportation of Nationalities* (London, 1970).

Part 1

How Soviet Citizens Lived and Died during the War

1

Living and Surviving in Occupied Minsk

Uwe Gartenschläger

What was life actually like in the occupied areas of the Soviet Union in the midst of a cruel war of annihilation? How could individuals or social groups bear the pressure of permanent menace, and how did they react in this situation? On the German side, how could human beings commit such acts of cruelty as described by the survivors of those years? To answer these questions, a local perspective seems best, because its manageable scope allows access to people's concrete life and environment. With regard to the occupied areas of the Soviet Union, only a few investigations of this type have appeared.

Sources for this study are documents from the German Federal Archive in Koblenz and the Center for State Judicial Administrations in Ludwigsburg. The *Minsker Zeitung* (Minsk times), a daily newspaper published by the German civil occupation administration, was helpful in reconstructing the invaders' mentality. Memoirs by Germans and Belorussian Jews who survived the war were also useful. Additionally, I have been able to use some Belorussian publications from the last few years.

This chapter concentrates on a description of the living conditions and experiences of the people of Minsk between 1941 and 1944. Three groups can be clearly distinguished: Belorussians/Russians, Jews, and Germans. Only in rare cases, for example in the Jewish resistance, did the circumstances of these ethnic groups overlap. The first section of this chapter outlines the situation at the beginning of the war and German strategy in the campaign against the Soviet Union, with particular regard to Belorussia.

A woman from Minsk described how she learned that war had begun: "We were awakened by the outrageous crashes of bombs dropped by fascist planes that destroyed the train station nearby. Buildings collapsed, clouds of black smoke covered the whole sky. We didn't really perceive all this. It seemed like

Farewell to those forced to go to Germany to work. Place and date unknown. (1-229; courtesy of the Lithuanian Archive of Picture and Sound, Vilnius)

watching a horror movie or having a nightmare: You rub your eyes and the vision is gone."[1] On 22 June 1941 the city was hit by the first in a series of massive bombing raids that were to continue until the German occupation on the 28th. Only seven days after the war began, the first capital of a Soviet republic was in German hands. The soldiers entered a city that was 80 percent destroyed,[2] its infrastructure broken thoroughly. Of 240,000 inhabitants, about 200,000 had stayed.

By 24 June, leading party and Soviet officials had escaped the city, which had become a no-man's-land. Marauders roamed the streets: "They dragged anything they could find from warehouses, shops, factories. A lot was taken from the warehouses on Dolgobrodskaya Street, where flour, cereals, and butter were kept; in the cellars, wine. There were many drunken people wandering the streets."[3] Witnesses report that the citizens of Minsk were very unhappy with the authorities.[4]

Until the first of September Minsk remained under a German military administration that left few traces. This was due to its short life span and lack of personnel and competence. In any event, this organization's primary goal was

USSR Border Pre-September, 1939
USSR Border Mid 1940

to oversee the flow of supplies to the front. The military administration cooperated closely with operational forces of the *Schutzstaffel* (SS)—elite and supposedly completely politically dedicated German units—stationed in Minsk
since early July. Such cooperation had a negative impact on relations with the
population. In particular, the creation of a prison camp for all men between

eighteen and forty-five years of age—about thirty thousand persons—pro-voked hatred. Together with one hundred thousand Soviet troops captured in the Minsk "pocket," they were interned under inhuman conditions in a two-square-kilometer open field on the outskirts of the city.[5] The operational forces "combed" the prison camp periodically, searching for Jews,[6] Soviet commis-sars, functionaries, and so-called criminals, who were shot when found. The SS routinely reported a daily murder toll in the four-figure range; members of the Jewish "intelligentsia"[7] were frequently mentioned among the dead.

The beginning of the war was a shock for the people of Minsk. Those who could not escape to the Soviet hinterland now faced a severe struggle for sur-vival. All energies were consumed by basic tasks like finding food, fuel, and a place to stay in an almost completely destroyed city. At first the Germans not-ed neither acts of resistance, except for listening to illegal Soviet radio stations, nor any willingness to collaborate. The occupiers especially complained about the lack of readiness among the city's residents for so-called spontaneous pogroms against the Jewish inhabitants.[8] In the *Minsker Zeitung*, a German soldier described the collective state of shock: "In the yawning debris that's full of heat, people—in most cases poorly dressed women—are digging in the ashes for their belongings. Many others have given up the futile search. They are just standing beside their former homes—silently and bowed down."[9]

It is well known that from the very beginning the war against the Soviet Union was planned as one of expropriation and annihilation, which made this theater of the fighting fundamentally different from all the others. Apart from this general definition, which was undisputed by all institutions and influen-tial groups in the Third Reich, the goals and plans of individual participants varied considerably. Contrary to the campaigns in Poland or France, the army (*Wehrmacht*) confined itself mainly to military aspects of the war, while in the planning stage the SS and police command set a high value on ideological aims (labeled "the fight against bolshevism and Jewry"). The minister for conquered East European territories (*Ostminister*), Alfred Rosenberg, pursued a vague strategy of "divide and conquer" by proposing the support of certain nation-alist movements in the Soviet republics. The commissioner of the four-year plan for the German economy developed projects for the effective and merci-less expropriation of the *Ostgebiete* (eastern regions). When the war began, a coherent strategy did not exist with regard either to the German institutions involved or to the form of their actions. The stereotype of the "four pillars in the administration of the East" (army, SS, civil administration, and four-year plan) had little to do with the reality and contradictions of German behavior.

In Belorussia, yet another factor contributed to this situation: the Germans' lack of interest in the region. They considered it merely a transit area that had to be conquered on the way to Moscow. Only a few Germans occupied themselves with its history or political relevance. Personnel sent to Minsk tended to be those who had failed elsewhere. In April 1943 *Generalkommissar* Wilhelm Kube complained in the presence of regional commissars from the Generalkommissariat of White Russia (Belorussia): "I request [that you] not sift out the personnel so that the best stay in Riga [the capital of Latvia] and the shabby remainder is sent here, so that Minsk is viewed as a sort of detention colony."[10]

During the Minsk occupation the lack of preparation resulted in vehement struggles for power. This was true not so much for rival institutions—although, of course, their Berlin headquarters tried to exert influence at the local level—but for individual persons. The controversy between the head of the security police, Eduard Strauch, and Generalkommissar Kube may serve as an example. Once Strauch boasted of having "hunted down" a Belorussian emigrant who was Kube's protégé.[11] He arranged for the murder of Kube's German-Jewish hairdressers behind his back.[12] Kube in turn initiated a campaign against the murder of German Jews by Strauch's SS, using Strauch's dubious biography as an argument.[13] The German occupying forces in Minsk, as was typical of the situation in Eastern Europe, were hardly monolithic in attitudes or structures of power. Although in some circumstances these divisions enabled local residents to play one authority against another, differences among the Germans also proved occasionally to be even more murderous than their everyday behavior.

The following section describes the challenges of daily life in occupied Minsk for the three ethnic groups involved, starting with the largest one, Belorussians and Russians. It seems justified to consider them as one group because although some of the National Socialists on the scene advocated their separation, in reality this goal had no practical significance. Neither did such a division exist for Belorussians and Russians themselves.

Regardless of ethnic or religious background, the most important problem for the local population was obtaining food. The Germans systematically stripped the villages of produce, while local manufacture of consumer goods all but ceased because of the devastation caused by the battle for Minsk and because the invaders had little interest in the local economy beyond what it could contribute to their military needs. The official food supply system relied heavily on cafeterias and a card system for basic products and was thus centered at the workplace. In addition, some communal kitchens were set up.[14] Although we do not have exact data on the rations that were distributed, they certainly did not suffice to sustain life.[15] People were therefore forced to make use of other sources. Apart from growing fruits and vegetables on the sites of destroyed buildings,[16] food could be procured through barter with local farmers and theft from German offices.[17] The black market also played an important role. It was obviously tolerated by the occupying force, but the high prices prevented most people from buying there: while the average monthly salary was about 30–50 RM, a kilogram of butter cost about 32 RM, a kilogram of bread cost 3.50 RM.[18] An impressionistic article in the *Minsker Zeitung* described it this way: "The black market—men and women swarm all over the place and crowd in the narrow area. Between them children of all sizes. . . . Bartering everywhere. Goat-meat, or maybe it is veal, without wrapping in someone's naked hand. Another has wrapped the meat in a half-page of the *Minsker Zeitung*. Standing or sitting, people buy, sell, and trade things. . . . In a man's hand, a cheap watch is dangling from an even cheaper chain. . . . All this swarming makes us dizzy."[19] Throughout the occupation finding food remained a precarious activity. It is hard to estimate what this meant individually, but in general those without special connections, skills, luck, or items to trade fared poorly or simply starved.

Housing, health care, and cultural needs also remained areas of tremendous difficulty. Above all, employment represented a central condition for survival. To have a job was important for two reasons: first, it provided some access to food and guaranteed a certain basic support for nonworking family members. Second, anyone who worked was entitled to a certificate of employment. This document had to be carried at all times by persons fit to work and had to be produced on demand.[20] It protected its bearer from being deported to Germany to work, something that the people of Minsk dreaded: "After having discussed the situation with my mother, I decided to go to the exchange, where supposedly they found people work. At the labor exchange, which was on Volodarsky Street (where there's a map factory today) a lot of us young girls gathered."[21] Therefore, after waiting awhile, most of the people of Minsk tried to get jobs at the administration of the occupying force, a Wehrmacht office, the German railways, or some private company. Conditions were extremely bad, wages were low, and the workers had no protection against the arbitrariness of their bosses. Working time was ten to twelve hours a day, in the last stage up to sixteen hours,[22] even if productivity was low. Malnutrition and poor pay contributed to this level of performance, along with the passive resistance of many persons who, by dawdling and sabotage, successfully obstructed the wheels of the German war effort. It soon became clear that each Soviet citizen had to choose between resistance or collaboration; an attitude of indifference could not be maintained in view of the growing pressure from both the German and the Soviet sides.

A clear definition of collaboration is not easy to make. It can be described as any activity that goes beyond a necessary minimum enforced by the occupiers. Under the circumstances, however, people often had to choose between collaboration and death. This was the case, for example, with the underground fighter Kovalev who was taken prisoner by the Germans and offered the choice between helping them and execution. Kovalev later became the key figure in an intense German propaganda campaign.[23] Yet in most cases collaborators were recruited from the German administration, especially among the so-called *fremdvölkische Hilfspolizisten* (foreign ethnic auxiliary police force) and the *Ordnungsdienst* (order service). The Minsk case does not support the assertion that collaborators were predominantly recruited from victims of Stalinism, criminals, and uprooted prisoners of war.[24]

There were not only individuals but, at least in the beginning, also an institution that the Germans could win over for cooperation: the Orthodox Church. The SD (*Sicherheitsdienst*, security service) described a Minsk clergyman as "the best propagandist for the German issue. His services are pure thanksgiving services dedicated to the Führer, his numerous visitors cross themselves in front of the Führer's portrait in his room."[25] A similar enthusiasm appears in German reports on numerous church services and in clerics' calls to oppose "bandits," that is, partisans.[26] The church's attachment to the occupants in the early stages can certainly be explained by the severe repression suffered under Stalin and by the limited support that the Germans gave to the Orthodox Church. The situation later changed, thanks to Stalin's more conciliatory strategy toward the church. Finally, relations between the German occupying force and Orthodox clerics greatly deteriorated over the question of the independence of the Belorussian church. The ecclesiastical leadership, with its traditional Russian background, entirely rejected this division. The role of the Orthodox Church in the occupied areas is a painful chapter in the history of the war that needs further inquiry.

The Germans had little success using Russian emigrés for their purposes. Since most had left the country immediately after the October Revolution, they could not establish meaningful contacts with the population and were viewed with distrust. A Belorussian emigré who worked for the SD wrote, "People see a 'foreigner' in everyone who is dressed better. When a spy, wearing an urban outfit, mingled with the population and talked to them in Russian or Belorussian, he was met with cold rejection."[27] The same fate befell Belorussian puppet organizations founded by the Germans, like the White Ruthenian Self-help Association. Managed for the most part by emigrés and lacking any real power, such groups quickly disappeared. The *Weissruthenisch Jugendwerk* (White Ruthenian youth association), founded by the occupiers in June 1943 and organized according to the Hitler Youth principle that "youth leads youth," represented the only exception. Since it appears to have been quite popular—the Germans claimed thirty to fourty thousand members—the Communist underground youth organization (*Komsomol*) waged a large-scale campaign against the organization.[28] Again, joining the youth association may have been an act of "collaboration," or it may have been a means of staying alive.[29]

The longer the occupation continued, the more people decided to participate in the resistance. The German politics of occupation, with its grotesque cruelty and contempt for humanity, hardly left another choice. Besides hunger and diseases, people were worn down by the day-to-day terror: executions of hostages, hard labor camps, deportations, and lawlessness. A report from the Ministry of Propaganda graphically described the attitude of the Minsk population: "If I stay with the Germans I will be killed by the Bolsheviks when they come. Should the Bolsheviks not come I'll get killed by the Germans sooner or later. Therefore, staying with the Germans means certain death, joining the partisans most probably salvation."[30]

There were three distinctive moments in the history of the Minsk underground:[31] two crushing German raids in March and September of 1942, each of which practically annihilated the underground, and the successful establishment of a permanent city party committee of partisans in September 1943. This sequence of events illustrates two important tendencies: first, the underground's vulnerability to German counteractions decreased; second, cooperation with partisan units around the city became increasingly close. An example was the coordinated murder of Generalkommissar Kube in September 1943.[32]

The Minsk underground was basically communist from the beginning. During the first months ordinary party members dominated. Their belief in the power of the Communist Party went so far that it prompted them to call the association they established at the end of 1941 "the complementary party committee."[33] This designation assumed that there was a regular party committee on the scene, but of course none existed. It was not until 1942 that agents sent from the Soviet hinterland took over a more substantial role. The party rank and file, however, remained important. This was also true for young people who, especially after the devastating German raids, were the first to take new action, often in the form of small, symbolic gestures of defiance. Therefore the stress on the role of the Komsomol underground in Soviet historiography seems quite justified.

Under adult leadership, Komsomol members acted as messengers or scouts, especially in the later phases of the occupation. Throughout the German presence youngsters carried out propaganda work, especially in fighting the influence of the White Ruthenian youth organization.

In 1941 about half of the Minsk population were Jews.[34] They were just as unprepared for the war as the Gentiles were. Although many Jews escaped, by the time of the German occupation there were still seventy to eighty thousand left in the city and its outskirts, many of them having returned from a failed flight. A powerful train of events then gripped them. Already in July a barbed-wired ghetto was installed, all Jews had to wear yellow patches, and the *Einsatzgruppen* (action groups, a curious term for execution squads) began to kill Jewish intellectuals. At the end of July, Jewish work gangs were established, a Jewish "Order Service" guarded the ghetto, and a Jewish Council carried out certain administrative functions.[35] Thus stable structures for the control of the Jewish population had been created as early as August 1941. Events had overrun the unsuspecting people.

Permanent terror was a characteristic of ghetto life.[36] There was not even a minimal degree of reliable rules. Day by day people had to face death; spontaneous acts of murder and cruelty by the Germans were normal. In addition, unannounced pogroms took place, for example in November 1941 (six thousand dead), in March 1942 (three thousand dead), and in July 1942 (nine thousand dead).[37]

This kind of terror produced a constant climate of fear. For instance, an SS troop leader once gave an order to shoot every seventh Jewish employee of a Minsk depot because a gun was allegedly found there.[38] For "simple convenience," as a survivor put it, SS members killed all the inmates of a ghetto hospital in the summer of 1943, when the Soviet army was temporarily expected to march in. On the retreat, the Germans did not want to burden themselves with the sick.

These conditions, combined with the desperate supply and housing situation, had a devastating impact on the ghetto dwellers' state of mind. Many got tired of life, while others lost any moral bearings. In order to arrange for comfortable final days, some took to robbing living and dead people alike. The survivors' reports also indicate a strong sense of solidarity among the majority of the Jews, however, one of whom recalled that, "We were, to put it succinctly, one great family."[39] Religious feasts were rediscovered, and sometimes being Jewish was stressed more strongly than before the war. Many Jews of Minsk actively took part in the resistance.[40]

The Germans had chosen Minsk, like Riga, as a location to exterminate German, Austrian, and Czech Jews. They arrived in two groups: about seven thousand Jews from northern Germany in November 1941, and about thirteen thousand Jews from all parts of the (enlarged) "Greater German" Reich between May and October 1942.[41] While the first group was imprisoned in a special ghetto and experienced living conditions similar to those of the Minsk Jews, members of the second group were, with few exceptions, immediately shot or gassed in specially constructed railroad cars. The German Jews in Minsk found their situation even more precarious than that of the natives, because they neither spoke Russian nor had contacts with the Belorussian population. Therefore only about ten German Jews survived the stay in Minsk.[42] For that matter, probably at most only a few hundred Soviet Jews from the area survived; they were the ones who avoided death on the spot or deportation to the extermination camps by fleeing to the partisans.

The third group in the city was the Germans. Most of them were poorly educated and prepared; few knew Russian or had any knowledge of the area's culture. In addition, because of Belorussia's low ranking in National Socialist plans, Germans made Minsk only their third or fourth choice for a place of service.

Arriving Germans reproduced the stereotypes learned in the Third Reich. Through this filter they perceived the people of the home of "Bolshevism" as "proletarianized," which meant reduced to the mental level of drones. To the Germans, new buildings represented "Bolshevik construction grotesques."[43] Another distinctive aspect of the invaders' response to local conditions was a feeling that the Germanic was naturally superior to the Slavic. A reporter wrote that, "It is certainly not easy for us who have no organ for seeing through the soul of the East European to ignore his animal nature. Beyond the observations that we make with respect to sanitary facilities, hygienics, road construction, organization, and some other areas of civilization, we must arrive at a broader understanding of this type of human being."[44] The emotional gap was intensified by the experience of coming from the apparently intact home country to a city that was nearly totally destroyed. The head of the NS *Frauenschaft* (womens' association) called it a "tantrum of ruins."[45]

The enigmatic, threatening world of Minsk was contrasted with the familiar home. The *Deutsche Zeitung im Ostland* (German times in the east) took up this feeling:

> Moonlight over Minsk—moonlight over a German city, one thinks instinctively. The blue flower of romanticism is blossoming: pointed gabled roofs, well-known

streets and corners, childhood memories are rapidly passing by and leave a slight longing. But what can it mean to us—we have to face rough reality. . . . In a ghost-like fashion, burned, blackened ruins reach out for the sky. . . . Suddenly, out of the blue, a girl's gentle voice is sounding in the night: Ah, this same moon is shining right on my bed, illuminating it all over! And now, my beautiful, soft bed stands all alone there! . . . For a moment, the feeling of being so far away, at a forward post, depresses us.[46]

Many Germans tried to contact Jews from their home towns who had been deported to Minsk. They recruited their domestic servants from this circle, or simply went into the ghetto to have a talk.[47] The Minsk newspaper reported on a planting campaign of "German sunflowers,"[48] and the Nazi Party organized *Heimatabende* ("homeland nights").

A striking aspect of the occupation was the Germans' great freedom in arranging their everyday life. The network of hierarchies and orders seems to have been so loose that individuals made various uses of their time. They began to pursue their own interests and hobbies. An army member started on his own, despite some serious resistance, to sift through the Minsk archives.[49] An employee of the civil administration conducted social work with youths.[50] Generalkommissar Kube, too, indulged his own interests: in the midst of the war he initiated historical excavations, discovering "hill graves" of "prehistoric relevance."[51] He had his own play, *Tortila*, which dealt with the "German heroic spirit and German womanhood," performed at the Minsk theater.[52]

But this freedom of action was felt much more drastically when it was coupled with moral indifference and inhumanity. Predominantly biased or inexperienced people had suddenly become the masters of life and death. In addition, most of them were well aware that they owed their belated careers to National Socialism and, consequently, were willing to act in its spirit. This background produced a low level of behavior not only toward the native population but within the German community in Minsk.

Descriptions of social manners and colloquial language often mention constant choleric shouting and yelling. Even the SD referred to a "rough tone" common not only in communicating with Jews and Belorussians but also among the German occupants themselves. During a "companionship festivity," for example, the head of the police, Carl Zenner, was said to have "slapped in the face an administration official who got on his nerves."[53]

Private property was not respected. Especially while marching in and withdrawing, looting by soldiers, officers, and civil servants occurred.[54] Corruption was widespread in many offices. Underground fighters reported that the valuable employment certificates were traded for food. Physical cruelty was the custom during interrogations.

Not everyone felt up to these murderous actions. Some Germans suffered nervous breakdowns, especially in the beginning, while others asked to be posted back from Minsk. Those who stayed were a "heap of depraved subjects with mercenary manners"[55] who took real pleasure in killing people. Of many examples, only the murder of the first Jewish Council by the SS Group Leader Kurt Burkhardt shall be mentioned here:

> Accompanied by kicks and whip lashes, they had to jump from the car one af-ter another, lie down with their faces to the ground and align their feet. Then Burkhardt placed himself behind the feet and began by shooting the first man on the right wing. Then, in a big curve, he walked around the bodies on the ground in order to shoot the man on the left. In another big curve, he returned to the second from the right, shot him, and repeated [the process] by going back and forth until the last one was shot. Apparently he wanted to increase the stress and agony of the poor victims by this circuitous route.[56]

Gradually, a great indifference toward human life spread among the Germans. Sick persons were shot for "pure indolence." A police official wrote an *L* for "liquidate" into each file submitted to him.[57]

Sporadically, the situation in Minsk led some Germans to question their own ideology. This was caused in particular by the Jews who had been deported from Germany and who suddenly appeared to many hard-core anti-Semites (like Generalkommissar Kube) to be more German or "Aryan" than the Be-lorussians. The invaders' racial anti-Semitism began to fall apart. Kube wrote: "I am certainly tough and ready to help solve the Jewish question, but people of our own cultural background are, after all, different from the native brut-ish hordes."[58] However, statements like this had no further effect on the fate of the German Jews.

For Minsk, as for all cities of the Soviet Union that fell under enemy con-trol, the German occupation was a disaster. It came close to totally destroying the city; many thousands of inhabitants died, more from indirect effects of German rule than from combat and executions, while the Jewish population was nearly eliminated.

The occupation was a complete failure from Nazi Germany's point of view as well. This was due in part to the lack of preparation by the invaders, who were profoundly ignorant of the area. Once they arrived, it is hard to detect any aim of the occupation other than maintaining control. Even that goal was hampered by the many differences among the (temporary) conquerors and the poor quality of the personnel involved.

The people of Minsk found it extremely difficult to react to the occupation, surprised as they were by the suddenness of the German onslaught and the brutality of the new order; after the signing of the Nazi-Soviet Nonaggression Pact in August 1939, the Soviet press devoted little attention to German anti-Semitism. To stay neutral in this situation proved impossible for the local people. In view of the cruelty of the occupiers, the majority of those who clung to life in Minsk participated in some fashion in the resistance. As this happened, the German overlords hardly acted like a master race.

Notes

This chapter is based on research for a master's thesis submitted to Professor Manfred Alexander at the University of Cologne in 1989, "Minsk during the German Occupation, 1941 to 1944," and my further researches.

1. Z. A. Karenkova, "Fedor iz Kamennoi ulitsy," in *V lesakh Belorussii*, ed. Historisches Institut beim ZK der KPB und Institut für Marxismus-Leninismus beim ZK der SED, (Minsk, 1977), 236.

2. These figures are naturally estimates. They appear for example in the *Deutsche Zeitung im Ostland*, 20 Feb. 1942.

3. V. I. Sajcuk, cited in Galina Knatko, "Minsk v gody okkupacii," *Narodnaya Gazeta*, 1 July 1993, 13. See also Anna Bogdanova, "Zarpoje leto sorok pervogo," *Prava Celoveka* no. 3 (May 1997).

4. See for example Hersh Smolar, *The Minsk Ghetto* (New York, 1989): "On the walls of burned out buildings in the occupied city I saw later rhymed anti-Ponomarenko slogans, one of which ended with the words: PANTILEIMON—DUSHA Z TIEBA WOK! (Pantileimon—May Your Soul Depart From You)." Pantileimon K. Ponomarenko was the chief of the Belorussian Communist Party at the time.

5. On the prison camp see Adelheid L. Rüter-Ehlermann, H. H. Fuchs, and C. F. Rüter, *Justiz und NS-Verbrechen (Ju-NSV)*, vol. 9 (1972), 13; *Ereignismeldungen UdSSR*, nos. 19 and 21, Federal Archive, Koblenz (FA), R58/241. See also Knatko, "Minsk v gody okkupacii," 11.

6. Obviously, some local people helped the Germans identify Jews among the prisoners. See Smolar, *Minsk Ghetto*, 15.

7. On the fate of the "intelligentsia," see Rostislav Platonov, "Minsk okkupirovannyj—Novye archivnye svidetel'stva," *Minsk Respublika*, 18 June 1994, 7.

8. *Ereignismeldung UdSSR*, no. 43, FA, R58/215, 170.

9. *Minsker Zeitung (MZ)*, 28 and 29 June 1942. The *MZ* is more or less complete at the Institut für Weltwirtschaft, Kiel.

10. "Protokoll eines Vortrages Kubes vor Gebietsträgern und Hoheitsträgern," Minsk, dated April 1943, FA, R93/20, 9. During the war only one publication dealt with Belorussia: Eugen Frhr. von Engelhardt, *Weißruthenien* (Berlin, 1943).

11. Helmut Heiber, "Aus den Akten des Gauleiters Kube," *Vierteljahreshefte für Zeitgeschichte* 1 (1956), 82.

12. *Ju-NSV,* vol. 19 (1978), 260–61.

13. Heiber, "Aus den Akten," 72, 79.

14. Knatko, "Minsk v gody okkupacii," 13.

15. German sources for February 1942 figure the daily allowances per person at 15 grams of butter, 10 grams other fat, 30 grams of yeast or syrup, and 80–500 grams of low quality bread. *Ereignismeldungen UdSSR,* nos. 50, 92, and 162, FA, R58/217, 220, 224.

16. See especially an article in the *MZ* from 17 May 1942, "Gärtchen hinter dem Haus—Minsker Familien sorgen für ihren Kochtopf" (Gardens behind the house—Minsk families take care of their cooking pots).

17. Besides hospitals and canteens, mainly companies were concerned. See *Ereignismeldungen UdSSR,* nos. 176 and 180, FA, R58/221, 36, 77.

18. Knatko, "Minsk v gody okkupacii," 12.

19. *MZ,* 25 Nov. 1943.

20. The certificate of employment was introduced in August 1942. Those without such a certificate could either be sent to the local SS labor camp or be deported to Germany. See *MZ,* 8 Aug. 1942; *Ereignismeldung UdSSR,* no. 148, FA, R58/221, 123.

21. Bogdanova, "Zarpoje leto sorok pervogo."

22. *Ereignismeldung UdSSR,* no. 165, FA, R58/220, 359; *Vsenarodnaja Bor'ba protiv nemecko-fasistiskich zachvatcikov,* vol. 3 (Minsk, 1983), 177.

23. "Meldung aus den besetzten Ostgebieten," FA, R58/223. See also a long article in the *MZ,* 23 Jan. 1943, "Ich bin überzeugt, daß Deutschland siegen wird" (I am sure that Germany will win); Kovalev reportedly was brought to Germany later. See Historisches Institut des ZK der KPB und Historisches Institut der Akademie der Wissenschaften der BSSR, ed., *O partijnom podpol'e v gody Velikoj Otecestvennoj vojny* (Minsk, 1961), 17.

24. This is claimed by Nicholas P. Vakar, *Belorussia: The Making of a Nation* (Cambridge, Mass., 1956), 179. Hans-Heinrich Wilhelm stresses the "retaliation hysteria" of many victims of Stalinism, due to which in the first weeks of the occupation numerous real or alleged communists were killed. Helmut Krausnick and Hans-Heinrich Wilhelm, *Die Truppe des Weltanschauungskrieges: Die Einsatzgruppen der Sicherheitspolizei und des SD, 1938–1942* (Stuttgart, 1981), 490.

25. *Ereignismeldung UdSSR,* no. 91, FA, R58/217, 226. See also "Wehrmachtsbefehlshaber Ostland an Reichskommissar Ostland," 22 Aug. 1942, FA, R90/126, 471.

26. For example in the *MZ,* 24 and 25 May 1942, under the headline "Deutschland hat uns befreit" (Germany has freed us).

27. "Wehrmachtsbefehlshaber Ostland an Reichskommissar Ostland," 22 Aug. 1942, FA, R90/126, 473.

28. For this organization see H. D. Handrack, *Das Reichskommissariat Ostland* (Hannoversch-Münden, 1981), 185–86; *MZ,* 23 June, 20 July, 24 Aug., 2 Sept. 1943, and 28 Mar. 1944; "Vortrag Abteilungsleiter Schulz vor Hoheitsträgern in Minsk," FA, R93/5, 5–10.

29. A Soviet view of collaboration can be found in Rostislav Platonov, "Minsk okku-pirannyj—Novye archivnye cvidetel'stva," *Respublika*, 21, 25, and 28 July 1994. The Germans were extremely unsuccessful in recruiting collaborators among the Soviet-educated Minsk population; one of the reasons for this was the poor quality of their propaganda. See Johannes Schlootz, ed., *Deutsche Propaganda in Weißrußland, 1941–1944* (Berlin, 1996), 57–63.

30. Alexander Dallin, *Deutsche Herrschaft in Rußland, 1941–1945* (Dusseldorf, 1958), 231.

31. To date, there is practically no research on the history of the Minsk underground. Some traces can be found in the *Ereignismeldungen UdSSR* and the *MZ*. See also Witalij Wilenchik, *Die Partisanenbewegung in Weißrußland, 1941–1944* (Berlin/Wiesbaden, 1984). The emphasis of this book lies significantly on the rural areas, however. In spite of being biased, the following works from the Soviet side provide useful details: M. N. Goranskij, *Minsk—gorod-geroj* (Minsk, 1978); I. G. Novikov, *Minsk—gorod-geroj* (Minsk, 1986).

32. See the "Schlußbericht der großen Sonderkommission," FA, R90/3. This astonishingly detailed report illustrates how well the SD knew the organization of the Minsk underground even until the end of 1943.

33. Wilenchik, *Partisanenbewegung in Weißrußland*, 167.

34. To reconstruct the Jewish population data in Minsk before and during the war, see especially *JuNS-V*, vol. 19 (1978), 192–205; Jewish Black Committee, ed., *The Black Book* (New York, 1946), 335, 453.

35. For the organization of the ghetto, see "Bericht der Militär-Verwaltungsgruppe Feldkommandantur 812," 20 July 1941, FA, R43II/691, 40; *Ereignismeldung UdSSR*, no. 31, FA, R58/215, 9.

36. Among the most valuable sources on life in the Russian section of the ghetto are the memoirs of Anna Krasnoperko, which have been published in Russian and German. Anna Krasnoperko, "Pisma moej pamjat," in *Drushba narodov*, Aug. 1989; A. Krasnoperko, *Briefe meiner Erinnerung* (Villigst, 1991).

37. For a description of the pogroms from the Jewish point of view see Krasnoperko, *Briefe*, 25–29, 56–57; R. A. Cernoglasova, ed., *Tragedija evreev belorussii v 1941–1944 gg.* (Minsk, 1997), 95–96, 123–27.

38. Karl Loewenstein, "Minsk—im Lager der deutschen Juden," supplement to the periodical *Das Parlament* 45/46 (7 Nov. 1956), 711.

39. Ibid., 715.

40. Smolar, *Minsk Ghetto*, provides an impressive account of their activities.

41. For the first group, see Loewenstein, "Minsk," 707; *Ju-NSV*, vol. 9 (1972), 13. The second group is examined in *Ju-NSV*, vol. 19 (1978), 195–96.

42. This is Loewenstein's estimate in "Minsk," 705. The number may have been somewhat higher.

43. See the article "Sozgorod," in the *MZ*, 10 Mar. 1943. Remarkable is the author's comparison to Frankfurt am Main and Nuremberg, which is complete historical nonsense.

44. "Vertraulicher Bericht des wissenschaftlichen Referenten Dr. H. Weidhaas über seine Erfahrungen und Tätigkeiten während der nach Weißruthenien unternommenen Reise," Apr. 1944, FA, R90/127, 11.

45. GKW an RKO, Abteilung Frauen, 8 Aug. 1942, FA, R9/229. See also the expression *Steppensender* (steppe radio) for the Minsk radio station in the *MZ*, 15 May 1942.

46. *Deutsche Zeitung im Ostland*, 10 Oct. 1941.

47. Examples can be found in Loewenstein, "Minsk," 711; *Ju-NSV*, vol. 9 (1972), 16.

48. *MZ*, 24 and 25 Mar. 1942.

49. "Bericht Staatsarchivrat Dr. Mommsen," 20 Sept. 1942, FA, R93/5, 2.

50. See for example a long article in the *MZ*, 23 June 1942.

51. *MZ*, 19 Sept. 1942.

52. For a review, see the *MZ*, 18 Aug. 1942. See also Boris Drewniak, *Das Theater im NS-Staat* (Dusseldorf, 1983), 138.

53. *Ju-NSV*, vol. 19 (1978), 551.

54. On the withdrawal, see Galina Knatko, "Poslednjaja nedelja okkupacii," *Narodnaja Gazeta* (Minsk), 28–30 June 1993.

55. Krausnick and Wilhelm, *Die Truppe*, 557–58.

56. Loewenstein, "Minsk," 711.

57. *Ju-NSV*, vol. 9 (1972), 14.

58. "Generalkommissar Weißruthenien an Reichskommissar Ostland vom 16.12.1941," FA, R90/146, 558–59.

2

Destruction and Resistance:
The Jewish Shtetl of Slonim, 1941–44

Hans-Heinrich Nolte

A Strange Encounter

There were ancient links between the Germans and the Jews of Slonim who were murdered by them; after all, those Jews spoke Yiddish, which originally developed from the German language. But what connected twentieth-century Germans with a distant group of people in a country characterized by woods and swamps, without big wheat fields or oil wells? Could the Jews of Slonim have expected to face mass murder, which was committed mainly between summer 1941 and summer 1942? Could they have prepared for it or worked to avoid it?

The Jews could not possibly have predicted their own murder. Their encounter with the Germans of the Third Reich was not only terrible but strange as well. A community existing for centuries was extinguished in little more than a year, by people who knew almost nothing about their victims.

❖ ❖ ❖

Slonim is situated some three hundred kilometers east of Warsaw and two hundred kilometers west of Minsk, in what is today Belarus (Belorussia). Slonim's heyday was during the seventeenth and eighteenth centuries, when it was part of the Commonwealth of Poland and Lithuania and became a meeting site for assemblies of nobles. One of the local princes built a canal nearby that connected the Neman and Pripiat Rivers, making Slonim an important shipping point for wood and agrarian products. A Jewish community developed in the town, and in 1642 an impressive synagogue was founded.

A long series of events contributed to Slonim's relative decline. After the partitions of Poland among its neighbors in the late eighteenth century, when the Russian Empire absorbed Belorussia, the princes left the town. Vilna became the provincial capital. Between 1872 and 1880 the junction of new rail-

A Jew—note the Star of David sewn onto his jacket—selling bread on the street in occupied Kaunas, Lithuania. (A81-P67; courtesy of the Lithuanian Archive of Picture and Sound, Vilnius)

ways in the area was located some fifty kilometers to the east of Slonim, at the village of Baranovichi. In view of these developments Slonim stagnated or even decayed, but for the same reasons it remained overwhelmingly Yiddish. In 1885, 18,381 of the town's 22,350 inhabitants were Jewish. By 1897 the population had declined to 15,993, of whom 65 percent were Jewish. Slonim was still an "old" kind of Polish/Lithuanian town, populated by Jewish traders and artisans, Russian bureaucrats and soldiers, Polish nobles and clerics, and a small pocket of Tatars, but few Belorussian peasants turning into proletarians. The Jewish population dwindled, however, as young people left for Warsaw, Lodz, or America.[1]

In 1921, following the Russian Civil War and the Polish-Soviet War, Belorussia was partitioned between the resurrected country of Poland and the Soviet Union. Slonim became part of Poland, making it more than ever a peripheral town.[2] By 1931 its population had fallen to 15,251 inhabitants, of whom 8,605 were Jewish.[3]

Anti-Semitism had existed in the area for centuries. Eastern European Jews had been forced to emigrate from Western Europe in the late medieval–early modern period, mostly from Germany, and they kept the late medieval German language—with added Hebrew and Slavic words—as Yiddish, just as they had kept the names of German towns as family names (Oppenheimer or Wormser, for example). In the old Polish-Lithuanian Commonwealth Jews were tolerated because with their handicraft and trading capacities they helped to modernize the Polish economy, and because as non-Christians they were not permitted to become citizens of the largely autonomous Polish towns, which meant that they posed no political or social threat to the nobility. As pawnbrokers, moneylenders, leaseholders on estates, and innkeepers they often took the brunt of peasant resentment in agrarian uprisings. During tsarist times, Jews were made into scapegoats for the difficulties of modernization; the regime considered both capitalism and socialism to be "Jewish." By the late nineteenth century, pogroms against the Jews broke out, and during the Civil War of 1918–19 Ukrainian nationalists were the first to systematically murder all Jews of certain villages. In the new Polish Republic, Jews stood in the path of the creation of a homogenous nation-state; their schools often were not acknowledged as state schools and had to be paid for privately, they found it difficult to enter public service, and eventually a quota system was introduced in the universities to keep down the percentage of Jewish students.[4]

On the other side of the border, in the Soviet Republic of Belorussia, the situation for Jews was quite different. Soviet communism promised equality but demanded secularization. Cheder (Jewish elementary schools) and yeshivas were closed, believers sent to the Gulag, and after 1928, when religious persecution began to increase, institutional Judaism was almost eradicated. Yiddish secular schools had opened in 1918, but during the 1930s most of them were closed in favor of schools using the languages of the various Soviet republics.

However, the Communist Party did not bar Jews from its membership; on the contrary, throughout the history of the USSR Jews were overrepresented in the party. About .0072 percent of all Soviet citizens were party members in 1927, but .0155 percent of all Jews, or roughly twice as many per capita, were communists. The percentage of Jews in administrative posts was even higher: in 1926 the Soviet Belorussian population was 8.2 percent Jewish, but in the republic's economic administration the figure was 49.3 percent, in administration of justice 42.1 percent.[5]

Thus when Slonim became part of Soviet Belorussia following the division of Poland between Germany and the Soviet Union in September 1939, local Jews, except perhaps for some Orthodox believers, were not alarmed.[6] Soon many Jews from the German-occupied territories west of the Bug River fled across the border, mostly to towns where they had relatives. Other Jews who had left earlier now returned, and the Soviet tally of Slonim's population taken later in the year showed 26,700 Jewish inhabitants.[7]

If after 1917 the Soviet system offered equal chances to Jews who endorsed communist ideals, the National Socialist system in the 1930s was on its way to the complete destruction of Jewry. However, this course was not automatic; it seems unlikely that anti-Semitism was much stronger in Germany before 1933 than it was in France, Poland, or the United States.[8] The Nazi Party did not get its votes so much for anti-Semitism as for the authoritarian promise to end unemployment and parliamentary debates, perceived by many Germans as a waste of time or worse. The party itself believed in anti-Semitism, however, and the majority of the population did not care when communists, leftists, pacifists, Jews, Sinti (a branch of the "Gypsies"), or homosexuals were harassed, removed to prison or camps, and later murdered. Ernst Fraenkel sketched a convincing model for the results in governing with his notion of the "double state," in which the Nazis used *Massnahmen* (mass measures of persecution and destruction) against marginal groups outside societal norms, but operated according to popular standards for "normal" citizens.[9]

While authoritarian, anticommunist politics and the fight for the full restoration of national sovereignty were popular among a broad sector of the old elites, anti-Semitism in the form of the belief that "the Jews are our [German] misfortune" was typical for Nazi Party members in particular. When arguing to his generals for mass murder of the Jews, Hitler attacked communism and the "Asiatic" character of Russia, but when arguing in front of party members, he attacked "world Jewry."[10]

This difference affected German politics in occupied Poland. The *Sicherheitspolizei* (the *Sipo*, or security policy) formed six *Einsatzgruppen* (activity groups) to destroy "elements fighting the Reich and Germans," a broad term indeed, behind the front line. Comprised of twenty-seven hundred men mostly drawn from the *Schutzstaffel* (SS), the elite units that served as combat troops and ran the concentration camps, the Einsatzgruppen quickly began to murder the old Polish elites and the country's Jewish population. At first some *Wehrmacht* (regular army) officers and military police arrested SS men who shot Jews or Polish priests, but a special amnesty ended the judicial inquiries against these murderers. General Johannes Blaskowitz, the German commander in the eastern theater, protested against the killings, but army leadership was not willing to risk a political fight with the Führer, and Blaskowitz, like other officers, lost his assignment.[11] Nevertheless, the Nazi Party was not interested in intensifying the conflict within German ranks in this situation, and mass murder in Poland stopped—for the moment. Adherence to "normal" behavior seemed to have gained some ground.

However, when planning the attack on the Soviet Union,[12] Nazi and Wehrmacht leadership formally organized the "double-state." On 28 April 1941, the commander in chief of the army, Field Marshal Walther von Brauchitsch, accepted the special obligation of the Einsatzgruppen to fight movements hostile to the Reich behind the front lines, as long as opponents were not wearing enemy uniforms. He further agreed that the Einsatzgruppen would be supplied by the Wehrmacht but would receive their "operational directives" from Heinrich Himmler,[13] the chief of the Sipo and *Sicherheitsdienst* (SD) and Hitler's specialist in the destruction of the Jews. An order issued in May officially ended the obligation of military justice to prosecute crimes committed by Germans against civilians in the territories of the USSR slated for conquest.[14] Soldiers could either act according to the rules of civilized behavior they had been taught earlier, or they could applaud and even join the special detachments in mass murder.

The Einsatzgruppen received direct orders to kill communists and Jews, but few communists were caught after the invasion, since they had been evacuated by the Soviets. Acting according to Nazi logic, the Einsatzgruppen started to kill all Jews in the countryside and to drive the rest into the ghettos in the towns. Step by step, the activity groups came close to fulfilling Hitler's order to exterminate all Jews, although such an order is not known in writing and most probably was never issued that way.[15]

The Wehrmacht leadership not only knew about the mass murder, some officers even defended the killings in front of the soldiers, for instance General Fritz Erich von Manstein on 20 November 1941.[16] As early as the postwar Nuremberg trials of German war criminals, cases of rearguard units of the Wehrmacht actively participating in these atrocities became known and documented.[17]

Of course it was impossible to hide the genocide from the German soldiers. More importantly, though, by fighting as well and advancing as fast as they could, the soldiers did their part in the job as planned. The Einsatzgruppen followed quickly, also as planned. In this way all German soldiers became accomplices of murder. This system necessarily developed into "cumulative radicalization and progressive self-destruction," as Hans Mommsen has argued.[18] Brutalization increased because, as Ian Kershaw has written, "opportunities presented themselves, and they were readily grasped."[19] That is exactly what happened in Slonim.[20]

Blitzmord (Lightning Death)

The murder of the Jewish population in Belorussia started almost immediately after German troops invaded the USSR.[21] Slonim fell three days after the attack began, on 25 June 1941, but rearguard actions of the Red Army continued in the area until 27 June. Eight days later, on 5 July, Slonim became the headquarters of Einsatzgruppe B. Later this outfit moved on to Minsk, and Slonim became the seat of *Einsatzkommando 9*, a subunit of Einsatzgruppe A.

The Einsatzgruppen, with their roughly three thousand men, received their weapons, gasoline, and other supplies from the Wehrmacht. Military police and Wehrmacht troops took part in many actions against the civilian population, but the Einsatzgruppen could not have committed their crimes without the help of anti-Semitic and nationalistic Ukrainians, Latvians, and other peoples. Only the Belorussians were rather slow to take part.

The main activity of the Einsatzgruppen at this stage was not directed against the compact Jewish population of a town like Slonim, but against the Jews in the surrounding villages. Units of the Wehrmacht also struck at Jews in these communities.[22] After entering Slonim, Einsatzgruppe B reported to Berlin that they had "worked the town through for safety measures," which meant that they had tried to collect and murder all communists. There was no immediate general activity against Jews in Slonim itself. This gave Jews in the countryside reason to hope that the town might be safer for them, and they crowded into it.

It is impossible to be sure of the number of Jews who lived and died in Slonim. Following a first massacre of around one thousand, local Jewish officials gave the figure of twenty-four thousand Jews in the district and town. The *Encyclopedia of the Holocaust* mentions twenty-two thousand killed, while Nachum Alpert notes twenty-five thousand.[23] Liuba Abramowich maintains that sixty thousand Jews were killed in the district and town.[24] The numbers chiseled on mass grave monuments around Slonim add to more than 43,529.[25] On some graves no figures are given, but it is not improbable that on some memorials dead are counted twice. Thousands of other Jews died from starvation, cold, or German search and destroy missions. Considering all these factors, about forty-five thousand murdered Jews in the town and region of Slonim, many of them returnees in 1939–41, seems a realistic guess for the final death toll.[26]

The high number of people who crowded into such a small town created difficult circumstances. Newcomers had to ask relatives or friends to make room. They lived on floors, often without any furniture. Whole families, including old people and children, often shared one room. Everyone tried to barter their possessions for food. Money, except for gold rubles, immediately lost all value.

For the Jews, German rule started with proclamations. In public Jews had to wear a visible yellow badge in the form of the star of David, and they were not allowed to use public transport or even the sidewalks. But soon the occupying authorities made it clear that these measures were far from their final program. On 17 July, Germans from the Einsatzkommando forced all young Jewish men they found on the streets to the marketplace. The invaders tore their victims' clothes and derided them. Rabbi Jehuda Leib Fain tried to intervene, thinking that he might command some influence with the Germans and be able to defend the young men. Instead he was insulted, and his beard was cut off and thrown to the ground. The rabbi then asked for permission to accompany the men, which he received. After being told that they would be put to work, the whole group had to climb onto trucks that took them some ten kilometers north of town, where a ditch had been dug near the village of Petrolevichi. All of these Jews, numbering more than a thousand, were shot and buried there.[27] In Slonim the Germans told people that the men had been taken to forced labor; later the authorities even pretended to transmit greetings from the victims. Few people believed these lies. But not much time was left to think about them.

The occupiers quickly organized a General Commissariat for Belorussia, with Minsk as its capital. Slonim and its surrounding area became a *Gebiet* (region) administered almost completely by members of the Nazi Party. They considered the area to be part of Germany's "wild east," where they had a perfect right to seek their fortunes. Some planned to set up large farms, but most were looking for quick enrichment and bribes from anyone who could be forced to pay.

The new regional commissar, Gerhard Erren, arrived in Slonim on 1 September. He had only a few people to help organize his administration, a problem aggravated because of his view that Belorussians were incapable even of handling clerical jobs. Only one of twenty-two pages in a report he filed in June 1942 was concerned with Jews; his main foci were economic and political. Regarding the Jews, Erren wanted to mark the victims, prepare them for an easy kill, and finally carry out mass murder. He wrote,

> On my arrival the district of Slonim had about 25,000 Jews, in the town of Slonim alone about 16,000, which meant more than two-thirds of the town population. It was impossible to organize a ghetto, because neither barbed wire nor possibilities for guarding were provided. Therefore from the beginning I prepared for a

large action. First of all expropriation was implemented. All German offices, including those of the Wehrmacht, were supplied with the collected furniture and tools, and we helped other districts to such a degree that now, when offices here are expanding, I feel a shortage myself. Materials unusable for Germans were sold to the population of the town, the gains going to the pay office. Then came the exact registration of the Jews according to number, age, and training, supplying them with special identity cards, and the allocation of separate living places to them. The action organized by the SD on November 11 liberated me of unusable gorgers, and the 7,000 Jews now living in Slonim all are engaged in work. Because they fear death constantly, they work willingly and will be supervised with extreme care for another diminution in the spring.[28]

Until the creation of the ghetto, the Jews were allowed to move around freely. At first only a relatively small part of the town was fenced in, while Jews living in other parts of the town were forced to move there. Part of Erren's reasoning was that he wanted to beautify the town: "The last great action concerning the Jews and the founding of the ghetto created so much room in formerly overcrowded Slonim that now I am able to resettle Aryans from surroundings unworthy of human beings. Tearing down dilapidated houses and construction of a fortified building for the SS has also started. I want to beautify the panorama of Slonim and create healthy living conditions."[29]

The establishment of the ghetto multiplied crowding and discomfort for the Jews, which were worsened because the whole moving process was supposed to be completed within two hours. The Germans now followed their standard procedure in occupied eastern territories by setting up an organization of Jews, the *Judenrat* (Jewish council). The Judenrat notified the Germans that twenty-four thousand Jews lived in the Slonim ghetto; Erren probably relied on that figure for his report of 1942. But the Judenrat had good reasons to conceal many, perhaps most of the Jews who had crowded into the town. Especially vulnerable were three categories of Jews: (1) those who had come as Soviet administrators when the USSR took over the area in 1939, many of whom were communists. The Germans would have killed such people instantly. (2) Those who had fled from Poland when it fell to the Reich; and (3) those who had fled from the countryside into Slonim, who were in danger of being sent back to face the Einsatzgruppen.

This first Judenrat was then forced to collect a special contribution of two million rubles in gold. After the council members had brought the money to the district commissariat, they were all murdered, including their families. As far as is known, their contribution went into private hands. One of the Germans in the blackmail business probably took the gold to Germany or put it into a Swiss bank, one of the "readily grasped" opportunities mentioned by Kershaw.[30]

This was hardly the only case of personal enrichment, since on one side a besieged population struggled to survive, while on the other side stood the German and native police and the SS, "at best" ardent anti-Semitic nationalists, but at worst simply thugs, thieves, blackmailers, murderers, and rapists. Some among them promised survival to young girls in return for sex, but did not keep their word.[31]

The authorities of the Reichskommissariat East drew the core of their personnel from local anticommunist and anti-Semitic nationalists. In October 1942 the Reichskommissariat directed 4,428 German police and SS, but 55,562 native-born police, consisting mainly of Latvians but with some Belorussians and Tatars. This meant that there were more than twelve native policemen for every German assigned to repression. Of course, Germans commanded the police, and where the fighting power of the partisans grew the Wehrmacht was called in.

In Slonim, the most important Germans were District Commissar Erren, "Plenipotentiary for the Solution of the Jewish Question" Dietrich Hick, and the director of the Central Trade Bureau, Rithmeyer. There were small units of the Wehrmacht in town stationed at the *Beutelager,* a sort of camp for booty from the Red Army, and at the railways.

The Nazis organized a second massacre of Jews on 14 November 1941. Police units from other places were brought in to help. As soon as Jews went out onto the streets, they were driven to the marketplace. Then the police entered some of the houses and drove out all the people, sometimes killing crying babies on the spot. The Jews were loaded onto trucks and carried to the village of Chepelovo, on the southern edge of Slonim.

Again ditches had been dug. The Jews were shot in front of the ditches and fell into them, or failing that were thrown in. The police were drunk and often failed to do their job properly, so a considerable number of the victims were only wounded when they fell into the ditches. Some of the SS and policemen took the opportunity to rape some of the girls and then shot them personally. Following the murder, the booty was distributed. Most of it went to Germans, but a considerable amount went to Belorussians, for instance to the mayor of the town. Names of the Germans and Belorussians involved are noted in an article of the communist underground paper of Baranovichi.[32] One of the German murderers, *Hauptsturmführer* (a mid-level rank in the SS) Forster, who boasted of having killed fifteen thousand Jews in Slonim, was promoted to commander of the ghetto Siauliai in Lithuania in September 1943.

During the night some of the wounded managed to climb from the graves and walk back to the town. Other Jews took some of the victims to the hospital. As soon as the Germans found out that some Jews had returned and even gone to the hospital, they tried to find and shoot them. But the news spread and Jews began to take defensive measures.

How many were murdered this time? Gerhard Erren gave the number of nine thousand, the figure that entered the *Black Book of Polish Jewry* published in New York in 1943.[33] The memorial at Chepelovo bears the number ten thousand. But there might have been more; there was no counting.

The massacre of 14 November made it unmistakably clear to the remaining Jews in the ghetto that they could not come to an arrangement with the Germans to save Jewish lives for any length of time. Death might fall on anyone at any time; the Jews' fate was completely in the hands of the occupation forces.

Resistance, Catastrophe, and One Victory: Summer 1942

Resistance seemed the only alternative, even under the extremely unfavorable conditions of the ghetto. One problem was that most young men were absent on service in the Red Army and were now fighting somewhere a thousand kilometers to the east, if they had survived thus far. The Germans had murdered other Jewish men, of course, during the massacre of 17 July.

However, there were still some young and middle-aged people left. They met at the workplace for Jews, the booty camp.[34] Here the Wehrmacht made Jews repair weapons abandoned by the Red Army as it retreated. Although the quality of Soviet weapons has not always been acknowledged, in fact it was generally high during the war. Russian tanks were superior to German ones and so was Russian artillery. Russian small arms were valued because they were considered to be highly reliable.

One of the Jewish repairmen at work on these weapons was Anshl Deliatitskii, a communist whose membership the Germans had not discovered.[35] Once he overheard four young people who worked with him planning to smuggle out rifles. They agreed to meet in the ghetto and later went on to found an underground movement based on five principles:

1. Any honorable Jew willing to fight the Germans might join, without regard to his political opinions.
2. The movement was to be organized in groups of five people.
3. Only one of these was to know someone of the next group, an old principle of Russian revolutionary organizations.

4. The weapons were to be brought to the woods, where contact with the partisans would be sought.
5. It was necessary to go on working for the Germans.

The underground movement grew fast. Pejsech Alpert, a trade union leader before the occupation, organized a meeting with Siama Shusterovich, David Epshtein, and Anshel Deliatitskii. Soon Abram Doktortshik, Dr. Abram Blumovich, Niania Tsirinskii, Wiltshinskii, and Matus Snovskii joined the leadership. All these were men. Tsirinskii in 1988 remembered seventy-two male and twenty-four female members of the Slonim underground movement by name,[36] which suggests a larger total membership.

Weapons were mostly smuggled out from the Beutelager after they had been dismantled. The parts were often carried out sewn to clothes, especially underwear. Some bigger parts were sometimes carried out in baskets. The Jews were searched when leaving the Beutelager, then they were marched to the ghetto together and checked again on entering it. Liuba Abramovich once carried grenades in a basket covered by dirty clothing. When she reached the ghetto, the guard ordered her to empty the basket. She answered laughingly, "well, excuse all this dirty women's underwear!" The German hit her and said, "Run off, dirty Jewess." That way the grenades entered the ghetto.

The next main problem was to establish contact with the Soviet partisans in the woods.[37] These fighters had already distributed leaflets in Slonim in the autumn of 1941.[38] At that time the partisans mostly consisted of Red Army soldiers who had not surrendered. They were loosely organized and had little contact with army headquarters in Moscow. Local communists took part. In Slonim, the partisan movement was founded by Aleksandr V. Fridrik, the former president of the rural soviet of Byten, a village some thirty kilometers to the south, surrounded by woods and close to the rail route from Berlin to Moscow. The soldiers joining him were led by a Red Army political commissar, G. A. Dudko. When Fridrik was killed in action in autumn 1941, Lieutenant G. A. Proniagin became commander of the unit, which now called itself the Shchors Brigade after a hero of the Russian Civil War. Proniagin later wrote about his time as commander of this unit, but because Soviet policy was to downplay contributions to the war effort by Jews, he had to omit much material on Jews or at least forego noting their religion.[39]

Fortunately, one of the Jewish arms repairmen made contact with Commissar Dudko of the Shchors Brigade. In March 1942 Dudko and Proniagin met with three representatives from the Jewish underground, Deliatitskii, Tsirinskii, and Kremen. The partisans wanted weapons, ammunition, medication, and flour, but they did not want people from the ghetto except for doctors, nurses, and radio technicians.

At this moment a quarrel about political options arose within the Jewish underground movement.[40] The majority, notwithstanding the skeptical reception by the Soviet partisans, decided to take to the woods and build their own partisan movement. This group would cooperate with but not join the existing partisans. Another large group of Slonim Jews, headed by David Epshtein, decided to remain in town and attempt to defend the ghetto when the Germans began the inevitable next massacre.

The first group carried more and more weapons and provisions to the woods through various channels. Liuba Abramovich remembered that from the ghetto the weapons were brought to a Jewish blacksmith, Matus Snovskii. Since he was working for the Germans, he was allowed to live outside the ghetto. He put the parts together. Then the weapons were brought to another of the Jews considered usable by the Germans, the joiner Sheliubskii, who had a closet in his workshop with a secret trapdoor leading to a small basement where weapons were stored. Partisans who came to fetch the arms might also be hidden in the basement if police were around. From the cellar a small subterranean path, covered with planks, led to a ditch from which it was possible to reach the outskirts of the town under cover.

Six radios were brought out, and there was even an (unsuccessful) attempt to smuggle out a small tank.[41] The risks rose, and one of the couriers, the kitchen worker Itshe Gratchuk, was uncovered by a Polish woman also working there. He managed to escape, but the Germans grew suspicious. A German Jew and former army officer, Erich Stein, was entrusted with overseeing the weapons at the Beutelager, because the Wehrmacht thought that as an ex-officer he might be trusted. But when Niania Tsirinskii of the underground movement addressed Stein, he found a sympathizer, which meant that carrying weapons out of the Beutelager could continue.

At this point a new Judenrat became involved as well. It provided false travel documents to villages near the planned site of the Jewish partisan base, the "wolves' den." Instead of going to work there, Jews carried clothing, medicine, weapons, and food.

By the end of May 1942, the German Central Trade Bureau for the East opened a store for harvesting machines in the old synagogue.[42] The company's Belorussian bookkeeper, Snovskii (no first name available; not to be confused with the Jewish blacksmith of the same name), brought in Niania Tsirinskii as a locksmith. Being an employee of a German firm gave Tsirinskii freedom to move around. The possibility of bringing things to the woods also increased since barter had replaced worthless paper money, which enticed peasants to town carrying sacks of food to trade for salt or valuables.

In May 1942 the first four Jewish partisans left for the woods, led by Itshe Gratchuk. More followed in June, and when forty-two had arrived, a separate Jewish group of the Shchors partisans was founded, called the Fifty-first Brigade. By July the brigade numbered 120 people, well armed with rifles, but also with some machine guns and grenades. The commander was Jakov Fedorovich, an officer who had escaped from German imprisonment.

Whether the Germans learned about leaks from the Beutelager and hence advanced their timetable for destruction of the shtetl of Slonim is not known. In any event, the third massacre started on 29 June 1942. The town was surrounded by SS and police troops. When the plenipotentiary Rithmeyer neared the gates of the ghetto, the chair of the Judenrat, Gershon Kwint, came out to meet him. Rithmeyer drew his pistol and shot him. Then the troops moved in.

They ran into fire from David Epshtein and his group, who had brought up a machine gun. Five Germans died and many more were wounded. When the troops overcame this resistance, the SS and police met silence. The SS demanded that the Jews should leave their houses to enter the trucks, but the people were not willing to obey. Since the November massacre they had built hideouts in artificial basements beneath the houses, in attics, or in double walls. They constructed concealed air supply passages to these sites and stored water and food. When SS and police entered the houses, they found few Jews. Most remained in the hideouts.[43]

Now the troops set fire to the houses and threw grenades into those where they assumed basements were hidden. Many people tried to escape to the river Shchara and the Oginskii Canal. But there the troops had set up machine guns to mow down the fleeing civilians. The ghetto was turned to ashes. For three days the ruins were searched. As many as thirteen thousand people were found and forced into trucks. Again they had to take off their clothes in Petrolevich, where they were searched for valuables. Then they were shot by Latvian volunteer SS and German SS units, commanded by Amelung. The Jews were all supposed to fall dead into ditches, but again the marksmen were drunk, and many Jews succeeded in crawling out of the ditches and fled; a few even reached Baranovichi. Some sadists voluntarily shot naked women in their bellies and then had them fall into the ditches.[44]

An SS Kommando unit involved in this slaughter counted "only" four thousand people murdered.[45] But Wilhelm Kube, the General Commissar for White Ruthenia (Belorussia), notified his superiors in July 1942 that eight thousand Jews had been killed.[46]

Somehow, several families survived in the ruins of the Slonim ghetto. Concealed by the smoke of the burning houses, some were able to flee at night to the woods. The family of a pharmacist named Milikowski was forced to leave their hideout ten days after the fire began because their water supply had run out. At least for the time being they were spared. Others, like the family of an engineer named Wolfstein, who had graduated from the Technical College of Danzig, succeeded in getting false passports.

Excepting such cases, the surviving Jews were those who had been considered "useful Jews," like doctors or skilled workers. They now lost the right to live outside the ghetto and were clumped together into a new, smaller ghetto to the north of the old one. It was, of course, terribly overcrowded.[47]

The remaining inhabitants of the Jewish shtetl of Slonim were annihilated by the fall of 1943 at the latest.[48] Taken to Zhirovichi, the victims were forced to enter a ditch and lie down. Then police units fired from both sides of the ditch until they reckoned that no one remained alive. Wehrmacht Lieutenant Munk and some soldiers participated voluntarily, hoping for—and getting—loot from the victims.[49]

Still, a considerable number of Jews from Slonim continued to fight.[50] On 2 August 1942, the Shchors unit learned that the Germans planned to destroy the ghetto of the little town of Kosov.[51] The group decided to intervene and attacked the German garrison successfully with the help of other partisan detachments. They captured weapons and ammunitions and set the ghetto population free. The Jews who were able to fight joined the Fifty-first Brigade, while others founded a special family camp in the woods near the brigade's position. A hospital was started, and a big kitchen was built. The family camp did repairs for the military unit, which in turn supported the families with food.[52]

Following the victory of Kosov the partisans liberated a zone with a radius of some thirty kilometers. The influx of Jews as well as Belorussians into family camps and partisan units was now huge, and the brigade itself came to number more than a thousand fighters. For the relatively small woods of the region they had grown too big. The Shchors unit was split, and on 18 August the main body started to move south in the direction of the Polesie, the woods and swamps on the Pripiat River. During the successful fighting along this march route no difference between Jewish and non-Jewish brigades can be noted in the unit's reports.[53] At the end of 1942, however, "the 51st brigade was disbanded and its members distributed among other groups," as Niania Tsirinskii wrote.[54] What happened?

The End of Brigade 51

Decades after the war a discussion took place in the Soviet newspaper *Izvestiia* about whether the Israeli government might award the title "Righteous Gentile among the Nations"[55] to the wartime commander of the Shchors unit, Proniagin, for his help to Jews during the fighting. In the course of the discussion, Liuba Abramovich, a Shchors veteran, told this story: the 51st Brigade was the best armed and most successful of the regional partisan groups and for that reason provoked envy among other fighters. When Commissar Dudko was wounded, Commissar Mersliakov took his place. Abramovich recalled that this new commander claimed that "Jews are the main people opposing Soviet policy, that they are panicking, and that they are cowards." Some gentile partisans took these words as guidelines for action. "A purge was started under the pretense of strengthening discipline in the unit by ejecting unsuitable ballast." Anti-Semitism surfaced in the following incidents:

1. A Jewish girl, against orders from Moscow, kept a ring from her mother thought to be made of gold. She was shot.
2. A Jewish fighter lost his rifle by accident and was shot.
3. Three scouts charged a Belorussian forest worker with spying for the Germans and shot him. Later it turned out that the forest worker was a friend of the commander and that the allegation was made by a provocateur from the German side. Of the three scouts, the one Jew was shot.
4. The local Komsomol leader wanted the wristwatch of a Jewish fighter, and when the man did not present it to him, he shot him.

Brigade 51 now gathered at the local partisan headquarters and demanded resolution of these grievances. No one would meet with them. The next day they were called together, surrounded by the other partisan groups, and forced to surrender their weapons. The commissar called their gathering of the day before "counterrevolution" and denounced them as "children of rich people with soft hands." Pejsach Alpert raised his hands to show his callouses, and the other men followed suit. But the group was dispersed. Abramovich concludes, "This was the destruction [of the unit]. They took the weapons from the fighters of Brigade 51 and forbade them to look for food in the surrounding villages."[56]

Abramovich argues that the official silence of the Soviet government about genocide of the Jews was considered by many as an indicator of how to behave, and that the chief of staff of the Belorussian partisans, Pantelei K. Ponomarenko, had issued an official order not to accept Jews in the partisan groups. When the Shchors unit was reorganized in September 1943, its new commander announced that Brigade 51 had been disbanded "because the majority of it consisted of Jews."[57]

But to what extent was the breakup of Brigade 51 a result of Soviet anti-Semitism, and to what extent was it due to other factors? The archives support Abramovich's claim that of the three partisans who shot the Belorussian forester and his family only the Jew was executed; however, he was also the only one who refused to acknowledge his guilt in the affair.[58] This was a grave violation of Soviet norms, which demanded direct and personal admission of mistakes, and it was probably this behavior rather than anti-Semitism that led his superiors to execute him.

Other factors in Brigade 51's demise had more to do with how the Jews in it behaved rather than who or what they were. The unit's early commander, Proniagin, fell in love with a Jewish refugee, and they lived in camp as man and wife.[59] Surely, in a field unit with few other women around, their relationship generated envy. When the members of Brigade 51 gathered at partisan headquarters to demand redress of grievances, an event called a "revolt" by a Russian journalist in 1995,[60] they were again violating Soviet norms.

The Jewish partisans from Slonim had grown up in an autocratic but basically "western" capitalist society. They were not members of the Communist Party, at least not of Stalin's party.[61] Moreover, they were not socialized in the way Soviet citizens had been since 1917. These cultural and political differences came to a boil under the severe conditions of partisan warfare, when food was extremely hard to find, sexual relations with women were rare or nonexistent, alcohol often seemed like the only escape, and death was always close.

This is not to say that anti-Semitism played no role in the breakup of Brigade 51. The report on its termination was destroyed by the summer of 1943,[62] indicating that the leadership was ashamed of what happened. The reported basis for the brigade's disbandment, that the Jews were "softhands," was an argument about class, not ethnicity. Later reports regularly mentioned Jewish partisans such as Natan Liker or Rachil Rosmarin for their heroism. But by the end of 1943 Soviet policy was to disband purely Jewish brigades, as part of an increase in control of all partisan units from Moscow. At the same time, the central authorities also tried to prevent acts of anti-Semitism among Soviet officials and troops.[63]

The Jews posed a special problem to the Soviet partisans. In the woods it was almost impossible to survive without weapons because the peasants, who themselves had little, would only sell food at gunpoint. But Jewish partisans had to feed the family camps as well as themselves. Moreover, their aims were not necessarily the same as those of other Soviet people. As long as ghettos existed, Jewish fighters wanted to liberate them.[64] When all ghettos were destroyed the Jews longed for vengeance, while the Red Army wanted to win the war. However, compromises were often found.[65]

Brigade 51 was dissolved above all because the Soviet officers did not know how to handle a group of people unaccustomed to *nachal'nichestvo*, the Soviet way of bowing to the bosses, or at least giving the appearance of doing so. Among Soviet partisans were some anti-Semitic people, and there was general uncertainty about Moscow's policy toward Jews, since Soviet propaganda did not talk about the Holocaust.[66] Yet other Jewish brigades survived, and there were many Jewish groups in mixed brigades. In any event, the Red Army gave the Jews of Eastern Europe the only realistic chance to defeat Nazism.

During the winter of 1942–43 several German units gathered to attack the partisans south of Slonim. The final report of the action, which deemed it a success, stated that 1,676 "bandits," 1,510 "sympathizers," 2,658 Jews, and 30 Roma ("Gypsies") were killed. "Bandit" was the German term for partisan. Since the troops were unable or did not take the time to establish during the fight which partisans were Jews, many of these were also Jews. The figure of 2,658 Jews refers to civilians, who must have been from the family camps. Most of these had probably escaped earlier from Slonim. "Sympathizers" indicates those Belorussian peasants who the Germans thought supported the partisans. Probably few people were alive in this region when the German troops left it.

A considerable part of the partisan units, however, succeeded in breaking through toward the south in the direction of Byten/Kosov. The Germans therefore followed with a second "action." Retreating, the partisans lost 97 fighting men. The German troops shot 785 Belorussian civilians considered to have helped the partisans, another 126 civilian Jews who did not succeed in evacuating to the south fast enough, and another group of 24 Roma.[67]

Despite this death toll, the German sweeps did not succeed in their main military aim, to destroy the fighting capacity of the partisans. Indeed, the fighters who had escaped were joined by more and more people who feared deportation to work in Germany. The uselessness of German antipartisan actions was underscored in a report written by Dr. Ludwig Ehrenleitner, Gerhard Erren's deputy, in March 1943. Ehrenleitner's evaluation of Erren was devastating, calling him a drunkard dependent on his secretary.[68] More important, Ehrenleitner noted two large regions still held by partisans close to Slonim. "The armament of the partisans generally is good, the leadership without doubt [is] in very good hands." He did not estimate the overall number of partisans, but thought that north of the town they numbered about fifteen hundred, "more than half of them runaway Jews."

Ehrenleitner found it "remarkable" that both partisan centers were in territory supposedly "cleared" months earlier by German actions, "during which the peasant population has been partly liquidated and partly transported into the Reich." To Ehrenleitner this proved "beyond doubt that the partisan problem [*die Bandenfrage*, the gang question] cannot be solved by police actions alone."[69]

Ehrenleitner may have exaggerated the number of Jewish partisans, but it is safe to conclude that although many had left the area with the Shchors unit and thousands had been killed during the winter campaigns, a sizeable group had survived to fight on. The Germans' ability to control the countryside was limited, and it was constantly eroded by hit-and-run partisan warfare. Little of the grain harvested in the region reached the Wehrmacht or the Reich.[70]

That the Jews of Slonim resisted with arms was nothing special in the region between the old Polish western border and the front line. Many Jewish groups took part in the partisan war, either in connection with the Red Army or with the Polish Communist People's Army.[71] As part of the broader Soviet resistance movement, Jews from Slonim played a considerable part in the liberation of Belorussia. The railways were blown up at more than a thousand places before the Soviet attack of June 1944. Since the railways were the only traffic system for supporting the Wehrmacht, this damage contributed significantly to the destruction of almost the whole *Heeresgruppe Mitte* (middle army group) the biggest defeat ever inflicted on the Wehrmacht. For several days the Germans attempted to defend a line running down the Shchara, but Slonim was soon liberated.[72] Now many small groups of German soldiers tried to make their way to the West through the same woods in which the partisans lived and fought. Various reports indicate that no Germans survived capture.[73]

The fate of some of the Germans responsible for the murders in Slonim is known. None of them belonged to any leading Nazi circle.[74] Dietrich Hick, the man in charge of the "Jewish Question," was killed in action in September 1944. Regional Commissar Erren managed to escape, but was put on trial in 1969 in Hamburg and received a sentence of life imprisonment, which he is serving today. The director of the Central Trade Bureau simply vanished.

Emptiness

The Jews of the Soviet Union were almost completely exterminated when they were engulfed by German occupation. On 22 June 1941 about 5.1 million Jews were living in the USSR. Of these, more than a million lived to the east of the farthest German advances, more than a million fled, and many were soldiers of the Red Army. About 2.7 million were brought under the power of the SS by the advances of the Wehrmacht; 2.6 million were murdered, and about a hundred thousand survived, some in the woods, others in hiding, some in concentration camps in the West. Shmuel Spector has come to the conclusion that some 650,000 Jews lived in Belorussia and Volhynia in 1941. Of these, about 47,500 managed to escape to the woods and about 12,000 managed to survive until the area was liberated by the Red Army. They constituted 1.9 percent of the area's prewar Jewish population—the highest percentage to survive in any territory conquered by Germany.[75] (This conclusion excludes the special cases of allies like Hungary, Slovakia, or Italy, and of Denmark, conquered but determined as a country not to allow the slaughter of Danish Jews.)

The 2.6 million Jews murdered east of the Bug River were killed in the cruellest way, by shooting and burning. No talk of "modernization" of murder, as is sometimes mentioned for the death camp at Auschwitz, is possible for this area. There may be something "modern" in the systematic character of the killings, but the way they were perpetrated was "old-fashioned" and disorderly, differing in this regard from killings by the NKVD, the Soviet security police.[76]

The genocide of Jews was part of the genocide of the population of Belorussia in general. This was a different kind of murder, not yet aimed at complete extinction in 1941–44; however, in the long run German policy was "Aryanization" and ethnic cleansing, to be achieved partly through murder and partly through expulsion of the indigenous population to the east. Most of the wartime assault on the Belorussian population took place during the ruthless fight against the partisans, but it also pointed toward emptying the country for future German settlement.[77]

Fundamentally, the National Socialists succeeded in killing the *jiddisches Folk*, the Yiddish-speaking people living between the German borders and the German eastern fronts. This ethnoreligious group used a language close to German, and its culture was close to German culture. The Reich almost completely destroyed this group. The town of Slonim serves as an example: it merited considerable space in nineteenth-century encyclopedias like Brockhaus and Maier, and it was still mentioned in encyclopedias of the 1920s and 1930s. Today there is no general German- or English-language encyclopedia with an entry entitled "Slonim." As a Yiddish shtetl it was destroyed. It does not have a place; its former space in our minds is empty.

In Germany and the West in general we are used to discussing the questions of "collective guilt" or "collective shame" for the horrors of World War II. In effect even now we are preoccupied with our own problems. For the history of the Yiddish people, and that of Eastern Europe in general, the point is much more fundamental.

What does genocide mean?

Emptiness.

Notes

1. On Slonim see Bronislaw Chlebowski, ed., *Slownik Geograficzny Krolewstwa Polskiego* (Warsaw, 1889); the Brokgauz-Efron *Enciklopediceskij Slovar* (Sankt Peterburg, 1900).

2. Jerzy Topolski, "Eastern Poland," in *Europäische Innere Peripherien im 20. Jahrhundert,* ed. Hans-Heinrich Nolte, Historische Mitteilungen der Ranke Gesellschaft Beiheft 23 (Stuttgart, 1997), 227–36.

3. *Glowny Urzad Statystyczny Rzespospolitej Polskiej,* ed. Drugu Powczechny Spis Ludnosci (Warsaw, 1938), 23.

4. In general see Léon Poliakov, *Histoire de l'Antisemitisme,* vols. 1–8 (Paris, 1955–77), used here in German translation, *Geschichte des Antisemitismus,* vols. 1–8 (Frankfurt, 1977–89). On Poland see Daniel Tollet, *Histoire des Juifs en Pologne du XVIe siècle a nos jours* (Paris, 1992); articles in *Polish Western Affairs* 64:1 (1993); Ute Caumanns and Matthias Niendorf, "Von Kolbe bis Kielce: Ein Heiliger, seine Presse und die Geschichte eines Pogroms," in *"Der Fremde im Dorf": Festschrift Rex Rexheuser,* ed. Hans-Jürgen Bömelburg and Beate Eschment (Lüneburg, 1998), 169–94. On Russia see Heinz-Dietrich Löwe, *Antisemitismus und reaktionäre Utopie* (Hamburg, 1978); Zvi Gitelman, *A Century of Ambivalence* (New York, 1988).

5. Zvi Gitelman, *Jewish Nationality and Soviet Politics* (Princeton, 1972); Nora Levin, *The Jews in the Soviet Union,* 2 vols. (New York, 1988); Hans-Heinrich Nolte, Beate Eschment, and Jens Vogt, *Nationenbildung östlich des Bug* (Hannover, 1994), esp. 118.

6. See also Daniil Klovskii, *Doroga iz Grodno* (Samara, 1994), 17–22: "nasha vlast prishla" (our authority arrived).

7. "Arkhitektura Belarusi," in *Belaruskaja Enciklopedyja* (Minsk, 1993), 411. The overall number of refugees is still a matter of debate. Shalom Cholawsky, *The Jews of Belorussia during World War II* (Amsterdam, 1998), 9, offers the figure of more than five hundred thousand. This is more probable than Emmanuil Joffe and Viacheslav Selemenev, "Jewish Refugees from Poland in Belorussia, 1939–1940," *Jews in Eastern Europe* 32 (1997), 45–60, who estimate two hundred thousand.

8. Ernst Frenkel, *The Dual State: A Contribution to the Theory of Dictatorship,* trans. E. A. Shils (New York, 1941).

9. The argument of Daniel Goldhagen, *Hitler's Willing Executioners: Ordinary Germans and the Holocaust* (New York, 1996), is not convincing to me.

10. Compare Hitler's lecture to generals on 3 March 1941, in Gerd R. Ueberschär and Wolfram Wette, eds., *"Unternehmen Barbarossa": Der deutsche Überfall auf die Sowjetunion, 1941* (Paderborn, 1984), 302–3, and Hitler's lecture to the "old guard" on 8 November 1940 and to the Nazi Party on 24 February 1941, in *Adolf Hitler: Der grossdeutsche Freiheitskampf* (n.p., 1941), especially 299–300, where "international Jewry" is called a "satanical power," and 430 (24 February 1941): "England and France wanted war, but it was less the people than tottering leading political and financial circles, behind which stood the last energetic strength of international Judaism, with its world-takeover plot, democracy, and Free Masonry." Nothing of this kind to the generals!

11. Helmut Krausnick, *Hitlers Einsatzgruppen* (Frankfurt, 1981, 1993), 26–88; Richard Breitmann, *Der Architekt der "Endlösung"* (Paderborn, 1996), 141–54.

12. My argument is further developed in Hans-Heinrich Nolte, *Der deutsche Überfall auf die Sowjetunion, 1941* (Hannover, 1991).

13. Ueberschär and Wette, eds., *"Unternehmen Barbarossa,"* 303–4.

14. Bundesarchiv-Militärarchiv RW 4/v. 577; Ueberschär and Wette, eds., *"Unternehmen Barbarossa,"* 306–8; Nolte, *Der deutsche Überfall,* 100–112.

15. See Peter Longerich, "Der Rußlandkrieg als rassistischer Vernichtungskrieg," in *Der Mensch gegen den Menschen,* ed. Hans-Heinrich Nolte (Hannover, 1992), 78–94.

16. Ueberschär and Wette, eds., *"Unternehmen Barbarossa,"* 343–44.

17. *Der Prozeß gegen die Hauptkriegsverbrecher vor dem Internationalen Militärgerichtshof (IMT)*, Nuremburg, 1949, vol. 32, doc. 3417 PS, report of Kube, 280: "The rear area of the military district has, without feelings on my part, liquidated 10,000 Jews, whose systematic eradication was foreseen by us." For Erren's statement see note 22 below.

18. Hans Mommsen, "Cumulative Radicalisation and Progressive Self-destruction as Structural Determinants of the Nazi Dictatorship," in *Stalinism and Nazism: Dictatorships in Comparison,* ed. Ian Kershaw and Moshe Lewin (Cambridge, 1997).

19. Ian Kershaw, "Working towards the Führer," in Kershaw and Lewin, eds., *Stalinism and Nazism,* 102.

20. This story has been reconstructed in Hans-Heinrich Nolte, "Die Leere in Slonim: Nachwort zu Ljuba I. Abramowitsch," in Ljuba I. Abramowitsch, *Die faschistische Gehenna am Beispiel der Stadt Slonim,* Schriftenreihe der Niedersächsischen Landeszentrale für politische Bildung, vol. 13 (1995), 13–32; see also Hans-Heinrich Nolte, "Zur Zahl der jüdischen Opfer in Slonim, 1941–1943," in *Nationalsozialismus und Region: Festschrift Herbert Obenaus,* ed. Marlis Buchholz, Claus Füllberg-Stolberg, and Hans-Dieter Schmid (Bielefeld, 1996), 79–84.

21. For a collection of sources on the genocide in general see Peter Longerich, ed., *Die Ermordung der europäischen Juden* (Munich, 1989). For the necessary maps see Martin Gilbert, *Endlösung: Die Vertreibung und Vernichtung der Juden* (Rowohlt, 1982). For Russian-language collections of sources see Itschak Arad, *Unichtozhenie evreev SSSR v gody nemetskoj okkupatsii (1941–1944)* (Jerusalem, 1992); R. A. Chernoglasova,

ed., *Tragediia evreev Belorussii v gody nemetskoi okkupatsii (1941–1944)* (Minsk, 1995); V. D. Sverdlov, ed., *Dokumenty obviniaiut: Cholokost—svidetelstva Krasnoi Armii* (Moscow, 1996). The most important collections of articles are Norman Davies and Antony Polansky, eds., *Jews in Eastern Poland and the USSR, 1939–1946* (London, 1991); Lucjan Dobroszycki and Jeffrey S. Gurock, eds., *The Holocaust in the Soviet Union: Studies and Sources on the Destruction of Jews in the Nazi-Occupied Territories of the USSR* (Armonk, N.Y., 1993).

22. Bericht der Gebietskommissars, Zentralstelle Ludwigsburg, *Verschiedenes*, band 25, pp. 127ff.: "The open land was for a period largely cleansed by the Wehrmacht, although only in the villages with fewer than 1,000 inhabitants" (6). Erren goes on to say that the Wehrmacht was not willing to do that anymore, maybe because the command changed, maybe because they needed Jews for labor.

23. The first figure is from Israel Gutmann, ed., *Enzyklopädie des Holocaust* (Berlin, 1993), the second is from Nachum Alpert, *The Destruction of Slonim Jewry* (New York, 1988), 9.

24. Abramowitsch, *Die faschistiche Gehenna*, 6.

25. Akademija Nauk Belaruskai SSR, *Entsiklopediia Belarussii*, vol 5. (Minsk 1976), 155–74. I am indebted to Harald Pinl for this count.

26. Niania Tsirinskii, "Podpole Slonimskogo getto," unpublished paper, Omsk, 1980 (available at the Municipal Museum of Slonim), gives forty-three thousand (2).

27. *Ereignisberichte* (Exemplar des Instituts für Zeitgeschichte, Munich), Meldung No. 32, 24.7.1941, 4–5: "In conjunction with the Order Police, the part of the Commando unit ordered to Slonim carried out a large action against the Jews and other elements loaded with communists, in which about 2,000 people were taken into custody on suspicion of communist intrigues and plundering. Of those, 1,075 persons were liquidated on the same day. By the Commando group alone another 84 persons were liquidated in Slonim."

28. Zentralstelle Ludwigsburg, *Verschiedenes*, band 25, p. 6.

29. Ibid., 21.

30. Kershaw, "Working towards the Führer," 102.

31. Ljuba Abramowitsch reported two such cases when being questioned in the trial against Erren. Landgericht Hamburg, *Protokoll der Zeugenbefragung vom 11. März 1969*, 13–14.

32. Chernoglasova, ed., *Tragediia evreev Belorussii*, 98–99.

33. Arno Lustiger, ed., *The Black Book of Polish Jewry* (New York, 1943; Bodenheim, 1995), 113.

34. Cf. Cholawsky, *Jews of Belorussia*, 122, 127.

35. Liuba Abramovich, "Soprotivlenie evreev nemetskim zakhvatchikam," n.d., unpublished paper in the author's possession, 2. Available in German as "Jüdischer Widerstand gegen den Genozid in Weißrußland," in Bömelburg and Eschment, eds., *"Der Fremde im Dorf,"* 353–66.

36. Tsirinskii, "Podpole," prilozhenie. There also are forty photographs of Jewish partisans (and the non-Jewish leadership of the brigade).

37. For the Soviet side of the following see A. V. Chatskevich and R. R. Kriuchok, *Stanovlenie partisankogo dvizhenija v Belorussi* (Minsk, 1980). The participation of Jews, however, is not adequately recorded in this book. For an overview see Bernd Bonwetsch, "Sowjetische Partisanen," in Gerhard Schulz, ed., *Partisanen und Volkskrieg* (Göttingen, 1985), 92–94.

38. Tsirinskii, "Podpole," 10.

39. G. A. Proniagin, *U samoi granice* (Minsk, 1979).

40. Cf. Cholawsky, *Jews of Belorussia*, 114. According to Cholawsky, Epshtein had been a member of the Belorussian Communist Party. Obviously this man is different from the person of the same name mentioned by Cholawsky on 87–88 and 247–48 (despite the index).

41. Tsirinskii, "Podpole," 16–19.

42. Ibid., 7–14.

43. Cholawsky, *Jews of Belorussia*, 141, gives the figure of one thousand Jews hiding in bunkers at the time of this *Aktion*.

44. Report of the German driver Metzner in Arad, *Unichtozhenie*, 198–201.

45. The *Tätigkeitsbericht* is reproduced in Fritz Baade, et al., eds., *Unsere Ehre heißt Treue: Kriegstagebuch des Komanndostabes Reichsführer SS* (Vienna, 1965), 242: "In the course of this action we cleansed the Jewish ghetto in Slonim. About 4,000 Jews were put in the earth that day."

46. *IMT,* vol. 32, doc. 3418-PS, 280.

47. Tsirinskii, "Podpole," 14–15.

48. A German prisoner of war from an infantry division gave notice in May 1943 that the ghettos of Baranovichi and Slonim had already been liquidated in 1941, but obviously he was not well informed. See Sverdlov, ed., *Dokumenty obviniaiut*, 27–28.

49. Report from Metzner (Arad, *Unichtozhenie*, 198–201), who took part in the shooting.

50. See Yitzak Arad, *The Partisan, from the Valley of Death to Mount Zion* (New York, 1979); Dov Levin, *Fighting Back: Lithuanian Jewry's Armed Resistance to the Nazis* (New York, 1985); Reuben Ainsztein, *Jüdischer Widerstand im deutschbesetzten Osteuropa während des Zweiten Weltkries* (Oldenburg, 1993); Shmuel Spector, "Jewish Resistance in Small Towns in Eastern Poland," in Davies and Polonsky, eds., *Jews in Eastern Poland,* 138–44.

51. One Jewish woman from Kosov who had been brought to Treblinka in March 1942 and succeeded in escaping returned to Kosov and hid there until the town was liberated. See Sverdlov, ed., *Dokumenty obviniaiut,* 103.

52. For pictures see Yitzhak Arad, ed., *The Pictorial History of the Holocaust* (New York, 1990), 336–58 (partisans in general), 365 and 369 (family camps). For close-up maps see Gilbert, *Endlösung,* 101–5, esp. 151–52 (forest of Parczew in Poland).

53. Natsionalnyi Arkhiv Respubliki Belarus (NARB), fond (f.) 3500, opis' (o.) 4, delo (d.) 311, list (l. or ll.) 2. I am indebted to V. D. Seliameneu and Natalia Redkozubova for helping me find my way in this archive.

54. As Niania Tsirinskii wrote in "Podpole," 19.

55. Abramovich, "Soprotivlenie," 13–15. Proniagin was proposed for this title, but opposition arose from various sources, among them his Jewish girlfriend of those days in the woods. See Ella Maksimova, "Zhil li pravednik po pravde," *Izvestiia,* 1 Mar. 1995.

56. Abramowitsch, "Jüdischer Widerstand," 353–66.

57. NARB, f. 3500, o. 4, d. 311, l. 12, is a map of the camp, showing Brigade 51 in the center of the camp near the command staff. The map is dated 30 October 1942 and was signed by Mersliakov.

58. Tsirinskii, "Podpole," 28.

59. NARB, f. 3718, o. 1, d. 5, has a list that provides date of birth, home address, nationality, party affiliation, and other categories. Only one Jew was from Kosov, which probably means that the Jews from Kosov generally comprised part of those staying in the "freed" zone.

60. Ibid.

61. Had Mersliakov known about Deliatitskii's former membership it would not have alleviated the position of these Jews, since persons who had left the Communist Party or had been purged were especially distrusted.

62. Abramovich, "Soprotivlenie," 13–15. Cf. Maksimova, "Zhil li pravednik po pravde."

63. Ainsztein, *Jüdischer Widerstand,* 113–14, 119–32.

64. While for Abramovich the battle for Kosov was to liberate the ghetto, for Guzhkovskii it was a battle against a German garrison. See his final report, NARB, f. 3500, o. 4, d. 311, l. 100, where the liberation of two hundred Jews is noted following the enumeration of enemies killed and booty taken.

65. See Cholawsky, *Jews of Belorussia,* esp. 239–49.

66. The fate of the Jewish Antifascist Committee in Moscow was probably not known in the provinces. See Mikhail Gefter, "Endlösung: Domashnyi proekt," in *Ekho Kholokausta* (Moscow, 1995), 47–55.

67. *IMT,* vol. 33, doc. 3943-PS, 567.

68. NARB, f. 370, o.1, d. 481, ll. 95–101.

69. Ibid., 102–3.

70. "Landbewirtschaftungsgesellschaft Ostland," Minsk, noted on 17 June 1943 that from August 1942 on, 26,077 quintals of grain had been delivered while 41,602 had been "destroyed" by partisans. NARB, f. 370, o. 1, d. 481, l. 30. Probably most of the "destroyed" grain was eaten by partisans.

71. Cf. note 22 and Cholawsky, *Jews of Belorussia.*

72. Cf. Werner Haupt, *Heeresgruppe Mitte* (Dorheim, 1968).

73. Nechama Tec, *Defiance: The Bielski Partisans* (New York, 1993), 196–98.

74. They are not mentioned in Ruth Bettina Birn, *Die höheren SS und Polizeiführer: Hitlers Vertreter im reich und in den besetzten Gebieten* (Düsseldorf, 1986), or Breitmann, *Architekt der 'Endlösung.'*

75. Spector, "Jewish Resistance," 143.

76. Cf. Z. Paznjak, *Kurapaty* (Minsk, 1994). The victims of the NKVD were shot in the back of the head and laid into the mass graves in rows.

77. U. M. Michnjuk, ed., *Njametska-fashystski genacyd na Belorusi* (Minsk, 1995).

3

The Popular Mood in the Unoccupied Soviet Union:
Continuity and Change during the War

Gennadi Bordiugov
Translated by Robert W. Thurston

The adherents of the social system created in the USSR during the 1930s, having retreated within their own country in view of ferocious criticism of Stalinism, have fallen back on the victorious war against Hitler's Germany as their last defensive position. Their logic runs this way: even if Stalin himself did everything wrong, his model of social structure secured the victory over fascism, and by that token alone it was the right structure. But an approach to the issue that strictly follows the historical documents shows something else: the system that, it seems, was created for the conduct of war and that was justified in many people's eyes by the expectation of a coming war unveiled its incapacity in the first weeks and months of the fighting.

The big shots of the Soviet system at the time, having already taken massive repressive actions against the people, strengthened their power as the German invasion began at the price of the submission of the whole country to the secret police. The leadership achieved the alienation of those people capable of thinking for themselves. The illusion arose that a monolithic unity had been created, but this monolith baked in the ovens of Stalinism, as quickly became evident in the fighting, was simply not in a position to conduct the war.

The first clashes with the Germans showed that many people who had been advanced to commanding positions after the purges and repressions of the 1930s were of poor quality, incapable of demonstrating initiative. The extraordinary situation of the early days of the war, both at the front and in the rear, required extraordinary action, not the blind fulfillment of an order no matter how petty. Independent and creative actions were required; blanket orders had no effect and sometimes led to disastrous results. A completely different kind of logic for action was required: the unconditional

Soviet collective farm families leave their village after their homes have caught fire. (Courtesy of the Bilderdienst Süddeutscher Verlag, Munich)

fulfillment of an order but with freedom of choice of the means to carry it out. However, such thinking was absolutely contradictory to the logic beaten into the heads of the new stratum of commanders on the eve of the war. Time was necessary to allow those with some intellectual, cultural, and political potential to rise through the system.

Perhaps it was Stalin himself who was the first to sense this crisis of his brand of socialism. At the end of the war he let out a secret: in 1941 the people had the right to demand the government's resignation, but had not done so.[1] We can say today: yes, but not because the government had done such a good job. The "system" proved to be wrong for the war; it was fit only to strengthen Stalin's personal dictatorship. Fundamental changes were required to overcome the crisis of the first days of the invasion.

The rapidly shifting situation at the front and in the rear did not require giving up the hierarchical, inflexible mode of leadership. On the contrary, under wartime conditions power must be concentrated in a single center. But the problem was how to divide power and functions between the center and local authorities. The type of management that had been created by the end of the 1930s permitted no autonomy of action. Ordinary people were reduced to "little screws" of the mechanism.[2]

On the surface it seemed that all Soviet citizens were for the regime and for comrade Stalin. But that is a myth; reality was vastly different. Not the official, public documents, but others now available to researchers reflect the real feelings of the people. These new sources allow us to reconstruct a more accurate picture of the past in place of the one that Stalinist leaders and other Soviet officials into recent years so ardently desired.

The study of popular attitudes during wartime is extremely complicated. Such attitudes have meaning that one wants very much to understand, but which one should not judge. Although we have our own ideas and notions about World War II, we do not have the right to impose these views of history and life on the wartime generation, which after all operated under extreme pressure from various directions.

There is another, possibly even more serious difficulty in trying to draw a composite picture of people's mentality during the war. Frank accounts of popular attitudes for the years 1941 through 1945 have been saved in unusual and rare sources—namely, the closed channels of party and state information, intended only for the Stalinist elite. In its analysis of popular attitudes, Soviet historiography long relied on exclusively official sources: the central and local press and lectures and speeches from all types of meetings (usually censored in advance). All of these materials had a particular orientation, demonstrating social unity, patriotism, and loyalty to the party and Stalin. In this way, a unified picture of popular attitudes developed. Almost to the very end of the USSR's existence, its leadership considered discussions of diversity in popular wartime perceptions and reactions to be unacceptable. The party hierarchy therefore diligently kept much information on the war secret from all but a limited circle of high officials.

Documents made available in 1991 by the Communist Party Central Committee's Bureau of Propaganda and Agitation, preserved in the former Central Party Archive in Moscow, point toward a picture of widely varying responses, hopes, and criticisms expressed during the war. Who recorded social attitudes from 1941 to 1945? Answering this question identifies the main channels through which information reached the top authorities.

Surveillance of public attitudes mainly occurred in small social groups and was led by party cadres and workers of the regional NKVD-NKGB, the security police. As a rule, on this level, the most pervasive, spontaneous, emotional, and often fluctuating feelings and opinions of simple people were recorded. In such records there is no precise personalization. Instead there are anonymous mass rumors, as well as rejoinders, slips of the tongue, and so on—everything that might be called "the voice of the people."

Reports to higher party echelons by leaders and members of the propaganda groups of the Central Committee (CC), which traveled around the country, were also clear and constant channels of information. The most interesting component in these reports is the voluminous lists of questions asked in very different places, from lectures on factory floors or collective farms to plenary sessions and meetings of active party members. All these questions were categorized according to standard methods and directed to the CC.

On the local level, spontaneous and unconscious moments rarely appeared, in proportion to the small share of anonymity accorded people as they participated in meetings. Yet the questions sometimes illuminate popular attitudes. In their content, these questions are much more valuable and interesting than the texts of lectures, which had to be approved in advance by central authorities.

The next traditional channel of surveillance was opening private correspondence. This process was carried out by the departments of censorship in the NKVD-NKGB.[3] However, in spite of its wide use, this source of information yielded practically no ideological content. The summaries of correspondence prepared by the departments of censorship between 1941 and 1945 are filled with everyday materials as well as coverage of complaints about disastrous conditions, for instance, among workers of evacuated enterprises. This means that after the machinery of repression began to work well during the 1930s, people learned not to trust personal writings for the elaboration of their thoughts and ideological views.

It is possible to use anonymous letters (often signed with fake surnames) as an important source and wide channel of information. These letters were received in enormous quantities by central and regional party committees and by newspapers.

Of the relatively nontraditional channels of surveillance of popular attitudes, the following were most important: selective secret recording of conversations involving representatives of various elites (academic, military, etc.) by NKGB agents;[4] reports to the authorities by security employees circulating among the population; and reports by magazine salespeople about discussions among people in line at kiosks.[5]

What were the main features of the secret information about popular attitudes? Throughout, this information reveals popular reactions to the major events of the war: the retreat of the Red Army, the opening of the second front when the western Allies invaded Normandy in June 1944, and so forth. The regime closely monitored anti-Soviet dispositions; dissatisfaction with the leadership; attitudes toward Germans and Hitler; attitudes toward the dissolution of the Communist International (Comintern, the organization to which all communist parties recognized by the Soviet party belonged) in 1943; perspectives for international revolution; attitudes toward collective farms and the private, commercial trade that was allowed during wartime and was traditionally associated in popular memory with the New Economic Policy of the more liberal 1920s; and views of postwar society and further developments in Soviet relations with the country's allies.

In principle, these subjects are also indicators of popular attitudes before the war. Having directed its attention toward these topics, the regime inadvertently found the weak places in its policy and doctrine. At these points lies the strongest confrontation, however much it was hidden, between society and the state.

Of course, popular thought hardly ended with the problems listed above. During wartime, human consciousness intensifies its consideration of questions about the meaning of existence, life, death, love, fear, aggression, treason, charity, and altruism. However, for the Stalin regime, these were questions about elevated subjects and were, consequently, superfluous and irrelevant.

The sources imply that some people fought for socialism, though perhaps not for Stalin's particular brand of it. Others fought not for socialism but for the homeland. Still other citizens seemed to act from bitterness accumulated in the long prewar years. At least at the start of the invasion the officials, the leaders of the "system," often did not act at all: they found themselves paralyzed in the face of the immense German attack.

When the war began, the Soviet people as a whole did not at once realize how fateful the situation was. As an engineer of the Leningrad Metal Factory, G. Kulagin, put it, "Who do they [the Germans] think they're fooling with, what's going on, have they gone completely out of their minds?! Of course the German workers will support us, and all the other peoples will rise. It can't be any other way!" There was no lack of happy prognoses. "I think," said one of the workers of the Leningrad Metal Factory, "that now our forces will thrash them, so that it will all be over in a week." "Well, in a week, maybe, it won't be over," answered another; "we have to go to Berlin. . . . Three or four weeks will be needed."[6]

This "domestic strategy," the expectation of a quick victory, was the fruit of ignorance of the real relationship of strength between the two sides. In fact the complete confusion of the first hours of the sudden German attack, when Stalin still could not believe in Hitler's "treason" in breaking the Nazi-Soviet Nonaggression Pact of 1939, cost uncounted victims and secured for the invaders their initial successes.

A different mood soon emerged. In October 1941 the enemy was approaching Moscow. In Privolzhsk, a town in the Ivanovo region some 175 miles (265 kilometers) to the northeast of the capital, two to three hundred workers started a strike. The workers were dissatisfied with the methods of mobilization, the construction of defensive positions in the area, and the lack of consumer goods. They voiced their complaints openly. From 15 to 20 October, a critical period in the fighting around Moscow, disorder broke out in Ivanovo, the district capital. Shouts rang out: "Every boss has run away from the town, while we are left alone"; "The People's Commissariat of Light Industry, the NKVD, the *obkom* [provincial party committee] have evacuated their families, while we are still here"; "they didn't let us dismantle and remove the equipment"; "they didn't ask us and started to take down the work benches on a day off"; "they didn't let us take the benches apart [for evacuation]."[7] When local party officials tried to disperse the workers who were spreading these rumors, people shouted, "Don't listen to them, they know nothing, they have been deceiving us for 23 years now!"[8] Such words could not have been spoken before the war.

These incidents occurred in the birthplace of the country's first soviets, which sprang up during the turbulent year 1905, an area where the capacity for critical, sober views of things had not been completely expunged. But negative comments about the course of the war appeared elsewhere as well. The former director of a rural primary school, the party member Koniakhin, who had served in Latvia, appeared in Tula province, south of Moscow. He told collective farmers there that the Red Army was not ready for the war, that Soviet airplanes were sitting at the aerodromes without gasoline, and that not one of them got into the air.[9]

The mood was bad in Archangel province: "Everyone said that we would beat the enemy on his territory. It turned out the other way around. . . . Our government fed the Germans for two years, it would have been better to have saved food for our army and for the people, but now all of us expect hunger."[10] Such conversations occurred not only among rank-and-file peasants and workers; a former partisan of the civil war and a party member, Ia. S. Romanov, announced that, "The Germans are squeezing us badly, while our people don't have the enthusiasm they had during the Civil War, especially among us partisans. We went ourselves and fired people up. The present leaders are incapable of organizing and raising the masses."[11]

Attitudes like these were officially called "defeatism" and "alarmism," but were in fact neither. A worker from the Kaluga region named Balakin declared in July 1941 that he would defend the Soviet land but not those sitting in the Kremlin.[12] That is, he distinguished between the Soviet system as a whole and the current evil and inept leaders in the Kremlin. To him the Soviet system was *nash,* the Russian term that can simply mean "ours" but often connotes a deep division between what is "ours" and what is foreign, with a great deal of affection and loyalty attached to the first category. Balakin hardly considered Stalin and his cronies to be "ours," yet his statement suggests that he would fight hard for what he had come to believe was his Soviet homeland.

At first the regime did not respond to people as human beings but instead tried its usual levers of control. All radio receivers were removed; Moscow was stricken with "spy-mania." Distrusting the soldiers at the front, the leadership restored the institution of "military commissars," whose job was to oversee the regular officers in the army. "Political departments" in the rural machine and tractor stations (which managed and allocated large farm machinery), abolished several years earlier, were also restored. Stalin did not trust the rear either. In prisons and labor camps mass executions took place. Inmates of camps knew that mass executions meant that another city was taken by the Germans or that another army was defeated. Yet soon it became clear that "screw-tightening" in order to intimidate people and to support the unstable system was possible only in peacetime. In wartime, however paradoxical it may seem, repression was the shortest way to a collapse of the system. Overly zealous control, like tightening a screw too much, could break key parts of the political structure and render it unable to respond effectively to emergencies. Serious changes in approaches to the extreme demands of war had to occur, and they soon began. This trend started spontaneously among the people but was quickly co-opted and directed from above.

Stalin participated personally in this change, however forced upon him it was by the situation and however late it came to save millions from death and occupation. In his address to the country on 3 July he touched the people's feelings, ignored hitherto: "Brothers and Sisters!" he began, instead of the usual "Comrades." He pretended, of course, that the situation was improving, saying that "the best divisions of the enemy and the best units of its air force are destroyed."[13] Soviet propaganda took the same line at the time, announcing to the populace that Red Army losses had not been severe. Despite these lies Stalin himself became a necessary, uniting factor when the fatherland was in grave danger. There was no other choice.

Ordinary citizens began singing that "the people's war is going on." After a while the decorations of Suvorov and Kutuzov, great commanders of tsarist Russia, were introduced. The slogan of the socialist mass media, "Workers of

the world, unite!" was replaced by the slogan "Death to German occupiers!"
All these facts meant a collapse, not of the people, but of the system of repression, not of a patriotic idea, but of the official ideology. The command system—with its bureaucratic nature, supremacy of careerism, and ignoring of people's interests—had collapsed.

Stalin had to rely on the people who had taken the place of those removed in the 1930s. Merit in battle became the key criterion for command appointments, in sharp contrast to the recent system of promotion according to political loyalty. The heavy fighting of the summer and fall of 1941 forced the removal of incapable commanders in favor of those with talent and ability.

Contrary to the usual tough repression, some prisoners were released from the camps. Following decrees of 12 July and 24 November 1941, issued by the Presidium of the USSR Supreme Soviet, over 600,000 people were freed from the labor camps; 175,000 of them were mobilized.[14] And they were true champions of the USSR. They coped with their new military tasks, since the liberation of the homeland was their personal concern. As for the former leaders, they did not disappear, of course. They hid, entrenched for the time being. Stalin needed them too, though for a different purpose—as spies to remember the creative, independent individuals who were to be disciplined later on.

The Soviet state began to resemble any other state at war. The regime could only step aside and let the people display all their might. After the fighting the people would have to be put back in their place. In the meantime, an important change had happened in the people's consciousness.

Let us take the Ivanovo region in the center of Russia. The regional newspaper, *Rabochii Krai*, received about six thousand letters in 1942. In one of them, a woman wrote, "I have never thought that I could hate our leaders so much, the leaders who have their party-membership cards in their pockets. They have exemptions from military service that give them the right to hide like mice in holes. But when we defeat the fascists, they will be the first to shout about their merits. They will assert that they are victors. And they will again use the advantages of their position."[15]

What was the direct reason for this woman's anger? It was the fate of her husband. He had an exemption from military service, but volunteered and perished at the front. The war indeed brought grief and privations to people, but it also awakened them. Under such extreme conditions, the people's instinct of self-preservation made them behave differently from before the war: the woman's husband had made a deliberate choice instead of obediently following orders. His wife then dared to severely criticize local *apparatchiki* (party or other bureaucrats) who had hidden from military service, and had signed her name, Zhalkova, on her letter. This name could be a pseudonym based on *zhaloba* (complaint), *zhalkii* (pitiful), or *zhalit'* (to sting). Even if she did use a pseudonym, not necessarily much protection if the police wished to find her, the very sound of the name has a painful ring in Russian and thus added emotional weight to her protest.

People were learning to think independently. Tragic events at the front determined the nature of changes in the minds of many people. The fate of the USSR was a matter of life and death that touched everyone, that produced a degree of freedom and helped people to rise above *klassovaia obida* (class offense). Referring to the way grievances had to be expressed as those of an entire class, this term had been applied to any independent opinion and action before the war and had helped to create a herd mentality. But now people were beginning to think for themselves. A woman who before the war had earned good pay making children's toys quit work and moved to a defense plant, in violation of the labor laws, when the fighting began. She explained, "Our leaders [at the toy enterprise] made a lot of noise. Two weeks of the war went by, but we were still knocking out some kind of idiotic toys. . . . They threatened to take me to court for leaving without permission, but I didn't even dignify them with a glance. Having come to work here, I'm learning how to weld. What kinds of things I'll weld here, I don't know, but I'm sure that these 'toys' will have their effect."[16]

Thus the initial period of the war witnessed a crisis in governing, a huge effort by society as a whole to respond to the invasion, and the abandonment of repressive and punitive socialism spontaneously from below and deliberately from above. When this stage passed, by November 1941, Moscow had been saved. A first strategic offensive against the Germans was organized. But despite the great enthusiasm and self-sacrifice of the Soviet people, it became clear that the war would be long. The battles before Moscow had inflicted heavy losses on the German army, but not on German industry. The Reich used the economic and manpower capacity of occupied countries and, as it turned out, continued to be a powerful military opponent. In the summer of 1942 the situation at the front again grew serious. A Soviet strategic initiative failed. The military measures undertaken were not enough to change the course of the war, and once more an impasse arose.

More profound changes unconnected to military action had to be introduced. Such changes occurred in 1942. Some rights of the people, the defenders of the Fatherland, were stipulated, though never formally or in writing. People recognized as defenders, usually a result of excellent work records, could, for example, make frank comments about production plans in their factories; offer various ideas and initiatives on their own; criticize the factory administration freely and without fear; or go to the front on their own account, without waiting for orders from the military command. In short, they had various opportunities to cut through or circumvent existing regulations.

An army drawn from the whole eligible population was created. Elite guards units, similar to those under the tsar, were restored. The dual command system of regular commanders and political commissars was abolished in 1942. Something great and significant seemed to manifest itself. This trend is evident in the tone of party propaganda and instructions to its own cadres in the summer of 1942: "The party is interested in having people think"; "stop instructing the masses, learn from them"; "the main object of party work is not the [production] plan, but those who fulfill it"; "don't whitewash the danger, don't downplay the difficulties, don't hide the unavoidability of serious deprivations and sacrifices"; "we can't underestimate the strength of the Germans, they are strong and organized."[17]

Some serious steps almost bordering on real reforms were taken, such as a rapprochement with the church and the dissolution of the Comintern. Of course, these moves were far from constituting substantial reform. Reform presupposes a system of action, an overall conception. Such a course is impossible under wartime conditions. Stalin was simply taking the actions necessary at the moment to change the course of the war. For this purpose he leaned on the new people who had come to the fore. Nevertheless, the image of a "monolith" was broken by the war.

In 1943–44 a highly differentiated public atmosphere arose, a real mosaic of moods. During a church ceremony in the village of Nikolo-Aziasi, Penza province, peasants cried out to passersby, "If there weren't any collective farms, you wouldn't see such torment."[18] In the same area the opinion that churches had to be reopened was widespread.[19] A collective farmer from a village in Kuibyshev province said, "I want to live the way I want to." When asked what he had in mind, he replied, "This way, that I don't have all sorts of chairmen and brigadiers above me giving orders. Just let the government give me as much land as I can work."[20] In Rostov province, party lecturers from Moscow were asked: "When will the kolkhozy be divided?" "When will trade in manufactured goods be free?" "When will there be freedom for various political parties?"[21] There was a rumor that not only would other parties be allowed but that free trade would open and even that a new tsar would be elected, while America and Britain "will rule the world after the war."[22] Thus peasants, speaking more freely than they had for many years, indicated their ardent desire to see the end of the collective farms and the reopening of free trade for their produce.

However, workers still indicated interest in some of the standard socialist notions about the future. In Sverdlovsk province rumors and questions asked of party cadres in one factory pointed in this direction: "Will the slogan 'Workers of the world, unite' still be used?" "Well, so what, it's the price of the second front [an invasion of Western Europe by the United States and Britain] that we are giving up the Comintern, so they, of course, are preparing the second front." "Who will lead the world revolution now?"[23] These workers accepted more of the Soviet system as theirs than the peasants did, although some of the workers, like their peer Balakin cited earlier, may well have distinguished between that system and Stalin.

The intelligentsia, the brain of the nation, had been persecuted for years. Many were expelled from the country or to remote places, left to rot in labor camps, shot, and so on. Only a small part of the old intelligentsia survived. But the sprouts of a new one were shooting up vigorously. Of course, the new intelligentsia did not match the old one in the quality of its education; however, the school of war could not but form an independent way of thinking. All these developments had profound implications for the future of the country; they were forerunners or preconditions for later liberalization.

Much of the Soviet intelligentsia had been closely connected with the prewar regime and had become suffused with Stalinism. But this was far from true of the entire intelligentsia. The articles of the Ukrainian writer and film director Aleksandr Dovzhenko differed little from any official Soviet publications during the war. Yet in his "Notes for Myself," published in 1989, he wrote, "The quality of war reflects the quality of the organization of a society, of a nation. All our falsehood, all our dullness . . . all our pseudodemocratism mixed with satrapism—everything turns out badly. . . . But over all this—'We will win!' . . . We had no culture of life before the war, [now] we have no culture of war."[24]

As the war began, Vladimir Vernadskii wrote in his diary,

1) . . . the real power is the C[entral] C[ommittee] and even dictatorship by Stalin. . . . 2) [There is] a state within a state, the power—the real power—of the GPU [the political police, called NKVD after 1934] and its decades-long transformations. *This is a growth, gangrene, which is driving the party in all directions—but without which it cannot get along in real life.* As a result—millions of prisoner-slaves, among whom are . . . the flower of the nation, the flower of the party, who created its victory in the civil war. . . . 4) the removal by the GPU and the party of [the country's] intelligentsia. . . . The party was "stripped of people" [*obezliudilas'*], many from its [leading] staff—this presents a riddle for the future. . . . Simultaneously with this [removal] has been created 1) a tradition of such a pol-

icy, 2) *a lowering of the moral and intellectual level in comparison with the average level . . . of the country.* (emphasis added)

In October 1941 Vernadskii added, "the weakness of our army's leaders is clear to all." In November he found that "the great defeats of our power—are the result of its cultural weakening: *the average level of the communists . . . is lower than the average level of non-party people.* . . . The flower of our nation is comprised of affairists and career-ration seekers" (emphasis added).[25]

Vernadskii commented that the alliance with "the 'Anglo-Saxon states'" was of "huge significance." They are "democracies in which the ideas of freedom of thought, freedom of faith, and forms of great economic changes have been profoundly established. . . . In the global conflict we are a totalitarian state—despite the principles which drove our revolution forward and [which] are the cause of the at[tack] [on us by the Germans]. . . . The near future will bring us much unexpected and basic change in the conditions of our life. *Can we find people for this?*" (emphasis added).[26]

Other citizens began to look at the future more fearlessly and practically. In liberated Khar'kov in 1944 a university professor named Tereshchenko said, "After all that we have lived through, the government must change its policy. In the political life of the country must take place, in fact are already proceeding, serious changes [the agreement with capitalist England and the United States, the disbanding of the Comintern, the division of educational institutions into male and female, the creation of the church committee, private trade, and others]. The changes taking place should go *further, in particular, toward more democratization in the life of the country*" (emphasis added).[27]

An assistant professor, Seligeev, expelled from the Communist Party for disagreeing with its policy, reasoned this way: "In the process of future [postwar] reconstruction there will occur what might be called diffusion: *the best thoughts, the ideas of western culture not only in the sphere of science and technology, but also in the area of morals and politics, in the area of worldview* will unavoidably begin to penetrate to us and will leave their stamp on our entire life" (emphasis added). The "keystone" to this "moral-political, ideological reconstruction," he thought, would be "the refusal to realize any kind of socialist ideas by force of arms" together with "the general penetration" of the ideas he had mentioned in their "best western sense."[28]

What is most striking about these ideas is that they were expressed in 1943, when the Commissariat of State Security was highly active both in liberated towns and behind the front lines. It took considerable bravery for the innovators of new actions and ideas to speak out. Nevertheless their voices were heard;

V. A. Malyshev, the people's commissar of the tank industry, told executives of the Uralmash plant, "I assume that for you now and in the future a legal basis for displaying bravery will be necessary, so to speak."[29]

Other industrial leaders began to think about making self-responsibility possible for all citizens, not to pay wages according to a standard scale but according to what work was worth, and not to shift responsibility to a higher level. These notions contained the threat of weakening the planned and centralized nature of the economy. The director of Moscow's important Stalin Auto Factory, I. A. Likhachev, said, "the time will come when we will forget altogether about [specified] funds [to be used for determining pay and allocating resources in production], and the consumer will deal directly with the producer." Likhachev wanted a type of national economic management that would not limit freedom of movement for the sake of socially important goals, but would "create the basis for the appearance of broad technical and economic initiatives." In 1944 he decisively refused to allow production shops in his plant to do their accounting separately, using the fixed prices and costs assigned from above. Instead Likhachev demanded assignment of work tasks according to the rule that production of each part should at least pay for itself.[30] Likhachev did not suffer for his views, but continued in his place as one of the USSR's most prominent industrial managers until his retirement in the 1950s. His ashes are buried in the Kremlin Wall, the USSR's highest honor for its dead.

Also in 1944 the engineer K. V. Belov wrote a memorandum to his superiors in the Commissariat of Lathe Construction in which he praised American industrial sociology and called for the introduction into the USSR of its principles of "human relations." Before the war Belov and his wife had traveled to the United States to take delivery of industrial equipment ordered there by the Soviet authorities. The Belovs returned impressed by American methods, which could be used to improve the organization of production in Soviet factories. Such methods would create optimum conditions for unfettering the capabilities of Soviet workers, allowing their inventiveness and initiative to flower.

K. V. Belov's superior found that the memorandum's ideas almost smacked of "cosmopolitanism," which in Soviet parlance meant inadequate patriotism, a dangerous charge. The memorandum, according to this superior, "lays out theories of bourgeois scholars concerned with issues of sociology and psychology of human relations which are alien to us."[31] Yet the commissar of the lathe industry, A. I. Efremov, appraised the Belovs' work highly and deemed it worthy of serious attention. Still, the time for that consideration did not arrive quickly.

All the new ideas and innovations were crowned by the work of the econo-mist N. I. Sazonov in his "Introduction to the Theory of Political Economy," presented in 1943 as his doctoral dissertation for the Institute of Economy of the USSR Academy of Sciences. In his opinion, ignoring such economic laws as the circulation of money and goods and the formation and movement of prices by the market had led to major mistakes and had held back the devel-opment of the country in the 1930s. The liquidation of trade by state and co-operative organizations in favor of a ration system in the early 1930s had af-fected the economy negatively. The absence of free trade in towns at prices set by the market brought forth a sharp decline in agricultural production by the peasants. This situation complicated issues of food supply to the cities, which led in turn to a lowering of labor productivity and to great labor turnover.

Sazonov believed that the main cause of the serious financial crisis in the country was that the largest portion of profits made by individual enterprises was not left to them but was taken by the state. Handling most of the income and expenses of the country through the state budget produced a huge increase in its size, which in turn led to the rapid growth of state institutions. This struc-ture bureaucratized the whole financial arrangement of the country and was one of the most serious reasons for the large breakdowns in the economy in the first months of the war.

To fix these problems Sazonov recommended "reestablishing the work of economic exchange on commercial rails." Goods might be sold through a rationing system but according to the prices developed in a free market. He considered it essential to end interference in economic processes through na-tional planning and the system of central funding. Enterprise directors should have the freedom to arrange expenditures for materials, the size of the work force, and pay as they saw fit. Central planning should be limited to the regu-lation of economic processes, record keeping, and prognoses of trends.

Sazonov also called for large foreign investments in the Soviet economy through the sale of stock in enterprises and concessions in various areas of the economy. Stocks could be both sold privately and held by the government, which should always retain a majority interest. The state's monopoly on for-eign trade should be abolished. Sazonov commented that those who might oppose his ideas would do so because they operated from the point of view of "statistical well-being," which had already cost the country dearly in the war with Germany.

The Central Committee reacted by condemning his work as a "seditious attempt" to vilify prewar policy and to argue for the need to return the coun-try to capitalism after the war.[32] For his efforts Sazonov was subjected to party discipline—what, exactly, is not known—and was forbidden to defend his doctoral dissertation, thus depriving him of the USSR's highest academic degree. Nevertheless, the fact that someone of his stature had the initiative to think about the economy in a fundamentally different way than was typical under Stalin, and then to write up his ideas and present them to the party, is indicative of broader trends during the war. Once again, the great pressure of the fighting and its results throughout the country made people question their surroundings profoundly.

Dovzhenko noticed this tendency among more ordinary people. He wrote in January 1944, "I was very astonished at one of my talks with a soldier-driver, a Siberian youth: 'We live badly . . . and you know, every one of us looks forward to some changes and revisions in our life. We all look forward to that. Everyone. It's just that they don't say it.'" Dovzhenko commented, "The people have some sort of massive, huge need for some other, new forms of life on the earth. I hear it everywhere. I don't hear it and I won't hear it among our leaders."[33]

During the war there were two interconnected but heterogeneous active forces, the people and the system. In the first stage of the war, the system was the leading but ineffectual force. It was the people who turned into the real leading force and produced talented commanders from their ranks. It was the people who sacrificed twenty-seven million lives.[34] The people made their contribution to the victory. But while the force of the people brought about victory, the force of the system gripped the victory in its iron vice.

From late 1943, Stalin again began to be idolized in the press and other media. The defeats of 1941–42 were explained as the actions of "panic-mongers," "cowards," and "traitors." The victories of 1943–45 were ascribed to the genius of Stalin. The war still went on, while the renewal of the totalitarian regime was already regarded as an important task of the current moment. It was suddenly realized that ideological work had been neglected. Immediate measures were taken.

In our literature it has been popular to quote a famous toast that Stalin made in May 1945 to the long-suffering Russian people. But few remember that only a month later he belittled these same people by calling them "little screws," substituting a single word in the initial toast.

A tale about the end of the war still circulates among our people. They say that at a rehearsal held before the victory parade of June 1945, Stalin mounted a white horse to ride in the procession. The animal had the impertinence to throw him. This story is just a legend, but it shows more convincingly than truth what the people indeed wished to happen. Did they want to keep the dictator and his system in the saddle? No, they wished a white horse to throw the dictator. They wanted to see Marshal Georgii Zhukov, George the Victorious, the symbol of the people's role in the war and their capabilities, riding the white horse, as he in fact did during the victory parade. Thus the people distinguished between the two forces on the scene, one worthy of their approval and one not, and in their minds placed one on the white horse of victory.

Notes

1. See Adam Ulam, *Stalin: The Man and His Era* (New York, 1973), 614.

2. In a speech in June 1945, Stalin referred to ordinary citizens of the USSR as "little screws" (*vintiki*). *Pravda* (*P*), 27 June 1945.

3. Rossiiskii tsentr khraneniia i izucheniia dokumentov noveishei istorii, formerly the Central Party Archive or Tsentral'nyi partiinyi arkhiv (RTsKhIDNI), fond (f.) 17, opis' (o.) 161, delo (d.) 92, listy (l. or ll.) 73–75; d. 102, ll. 80–87.

4. See for example ibid., o. 125, d. 84, ll. 5–7; d. 310.

5. Ibid., o. 121, d. 426, ll. 124–26.

6. G. Kulagin, *Dnevik i pamiat': o perezhitom v gody blokady* (Leningrad, 1978), 17.

7. RTsKhIDNI, f. 17, o. 88, d. 45, ll. 8, 12–14.

8. Ibid., l. 14.

9. Ibid., f. 17, special opis', inv. N 6329s.

10. Ibid., f. 17, o. 88, d. 31, l. 12.

11. Ibid., d. 31, l. 35.

12. Ibid., l. 12.

13. I. V. Stalin, *O Velikoj Otechestvenoj voine* (Moscow, 1948), 7.

14. RTsKhIDNI, f. 17, o. 125, d. 84, l. 17.

15. Ibid., o. 88, d. 119, ll. 2–3.

16. I. I. Gudov, *Sud'ba rabochego* (Moscow, 1974), 263.

17. *P*, 11 Sept. 1989.

18. RTsKhIDNI, f. 17, o. 125, d. 181, l. 13.

19. Ibid., l. 11.

20. Ibid., o. 121, d. 310, l. 3.

21. Ibid., o. 125, d. 82, ll. 12–24.

22. Ibid., d. 181, l. 5.

23. Ibid., ll. 3–4.

24. *P*, 11 Sept. 1989.

25. *Literaturnaia gazeta*, 16 Mar. 1988.

26. Ibid.

27. RtsKhIDNI, f. 17, o. 125, d. 181, ll. 52–53.

28. Ibid., l. 51.

29. V. Chalmaev, *Malyshev* (Moscow, 1987), 173.

30. *Direktor: I. A. Likhachev v vospominaniiakh sovremennikov,* ed. V. A. Krasilnikov (Moscow, 1971), 68.

31. I. Gudov, *Druz'ia na vsiu zhizn': dumy o materiakh* (Moscow, 1980), 166–67.

32. RTsKhIDNI, f. 17, o. 125, d. 133, ll. 4–5.

33. *P,* 11 Sept. 1989.

34. On the debate about the number of people lost in the war, see John Erickson, "Soviet War Losses: Calculations and Controversies," in *Barbarossa: The Axis and the Allies,* ed. John Erickson and David Dilks (Edinburgh, 1994).

4

The Social and Political Situation in Leningrad in the First Months of the German Invasion: The Social Psychology of the Workers

Andrei R. Dzeniskevich
Translated by Robert W. Thurston

In the literature on the war with fascist Germany, which became for the people of the Soviet Union the "Great Patriotic War," various questions have not been investigated deeply. Among these issues are many that would advance our knowledge of the social processes occurring in the country in the years 1941–45. The subject of this chapter has to do with one of these phenomena, the social psychology of Leningrad's soldiers, militia volunteers, and workers.

In the historiography of the defense of Leningrad it has been traditional to write of a great patriotic upsurge among the city's workers in the first days of the war. This in fact occurred, though it is not the whole story. Reality was much more complicated and multifaceted; it may not be described in simple and convenient terms.

The outbreak of the war was marked not only by a sharp rise in patriotism but also by a series of negative responses: the spread of all sorts of rumors, the surfacing of bitterness among the aggrieved and oppressed, and a wave of justified critical remarks from workers who were agitated and discomfited by the obvious mistakes made by the party and the government in domestic and international policy.

In reports of local events during the first days after the invasion began, the dominant tone is of patriotic meetings and feelings. There is no indication of the negative side. Fortunately for the purposes of understanding people's reactions to the war, this approach to observations of the populace did not last long. It was necessary for the leadership of the city to develop a fuller picture of events. Upon receiving a report of the situation in one part of Leningrad,

A female Soviet parachutist being interrogated after capture by the Germans, September 1941. (Courtesy of the Bilderdienst Süddeutscher Verlag, Munich)

the *raion* (regional) party secretary Efremov sent the following response, dated 23 June 1941: "Comrade Shubin—1) There has to be something on the mood of the population. 2) Are there any negative sides?"[1] Information began to appear in a more evenhanded form, and historians now have the opportunity to learn facts that did not appear in the newspapers of the time.

When the German military machine launched aggression against the Soviet Union, it already possessed considerable experience in the conduct of psychological warfare. In France and other European countries, special propaganda units of the Wehrmacht successfully carried out operations to spread disinformation, with the goal of hampering the enemy's "conduct in certain circumstances."[2] These efforts were the responsibility of "propaganda forces," which were charged with political work among the enemy armies and population, spreading rumors ("propaganda by whisper"), and attempting to create panic.

It was therefore not coincidental that one of the characteristic events of the first months of the war was the appearance of alarming rumors among the Soviet people. The source for many such stories was German intelligence agents specifically sent across the lines for psychological purposes. Two themes are easily distinguished in these rumors: agitation in favor of Hitler and the Germans in general, and alarming stories of various sorts, intended to arouse a lack of confidence in the Soviet authorities as well as fear and panic. The first group of rumors was small and fairly primitive in content. As a rule, they were said to have originated with a woman who had spent time in occupied territory. She had supposedly confirmed that the Germans conducted themselves fully correctly and had even helped her with something, and that the Soviet newspapers lied about them; the Germans were a cultured nation, and so on.[3] Variations on this theme were accompanied by assertions that the German forces were very strong, that they could not be defeated in any case, and that life would be better under German rule. Neither these rumors nor the leaflets dropped by the fascists on the territory of Leningrad had any success among Russians.[4] But the fact that fascist posters appeared in the center of town, and were even pasted on walls, evoked real concern among the populace. Obviously German intelligence knew this and bet on the creation of confusion, fear, and lack of confidence behind Soviet lines. On 26 June someone spread a rumor at the Kirov factory, one of the city's largest and most important, that Soviet sailors had scuttled a ship in the sea channel to the Baltic.[5] In lines for food and other items people spoke of how the Germans had "circular tanks" that spit out shells in all directions.[6] Another rumor, this one about German paratroopers landing in the city dressed as Soviet police, caused much harm. The story led to a number of incidents in which crowds detained real police and even beat them up, resulting in temporary disorganization of the organs of public order.[7]

The Germans went to considerable lengths to slander the Soviet military and civilian leadership. Rumors in several variations mentioned the "treason" of Marshal Semion K. Timoshenko and the "disappearance" of the party leadership from the city of Leningrad.[8] Stories about a disagreement between Stalin and Voroshilov on the fate of Leningrad caused dissatisfaction. Supposedly Stalin intended to burn the city and surrender it as a ruin to the enemy; Voroshilov also wanted to give it up.[9] Anyone who believed such rumors must have considered Leningrad's fate hopeless.

A good deal of discontent arose owing to the usual poor management and poorly thought out and organized measures of the authorities. One of these steps was the evacuation of children from the city toward Novgorod, directly into German bombardment. Soviet authorities had not expected the enemy to appear there nearly so quickly.

I was one of the children. Nine years old at the time, I well remember the sound of the motors of the German planes, the whistles of the bombs, and the bright traces of machine-gun fire in the night sky. We children were quickly returned to Leningrad. Some were later evacuated a second time, to the "deep rear," in other republics and areas of the USSR. Naturally all this caused great distress among worker-mothers, who protested vigorously at the factories.

Officials fought the spread of rumors and panic with mass explanatory efforts and, after a decree appeared on responsibility for spreading false and inflammatory information in wartime, by means of repression. But despite the fact that at the beginning of the war employees of the Commissariat of Internal Affairs (NKVD) handled many cases related to the struggle against rumors, the police did not pay sufficient attention to this issue. A Communist Party official in the Kirov raion informed the municipal committee of the party that rumors were stirring up the district, but that the procuracy (state's attorney's office) had lodged only one charge about their dissemination. Believing that wartime was the moment to carry out not educational work but harsher measures to combat disinformation, the raion official turned to the head of the district NKVD, only to receive the reply that party organizations should struggle with rumors, "but we should punish least of all."[10]

These organs devoted considerably more attention to the appearance of dissatisfaction, a wave of which appeared among the population in the first months of the war. Part of this feeling had been prepared long before but was carefully hidden; only in wartime conditions did it suddenly come to the surface. The workers who felt this way were generally former peasants who had undergone dekulakization and collectivization in the villages in 1929–31. Among so-called hereditary workers, those who had not migrated from the villages but rather came from working-class families, the disgruntled ones had been subjected to decrees and a whole system of repressive measures adopted in 1938–40 in connection with efforts to strengthen discipline in the factories. These measures included severe penalties for being even twenty minutes late and also forbade workers to change jobs without supervisors' permission. However, these statutes were often circumvented.

To a great degree, dissatisfaction was linked to social origin. Among those who cursed collectivization, complaining about "slavery" and hunger among the collective farmers, who gave all their grain to the state but themselves "sat naked" on the farms or had to buy bread in the towns, were a saddler, a carpenter, a worker, and cleaning women, all of whom were former peasants. They connected the failures of the Red Army to the oppressive situation of the peasants on the collectives. The second place in their "anti-Soviet" expressions concerned "forced labor for lateness to work."[11] In these cases, dissatisfaction, as a rule, was voiced in the course of explaining some event. Here is a typical case of such a conversation. A worker at a mechanical shop of the Kirov factory, a party member, approached a harness maker and asked him to sew a set of reins better, as they often broke. The harness maker replied, "There isn't any leather, and where am I supposed to get it? On the collective farms 15 calves are left, and they're dying of hunger. . . . They feed them twigs. . . . Life isn't easy on the collectives."[12] This was not really anti-Soviet agitation, as similar conversations were classified at the time, but only an explanation of the situation from the point of view of an offended victim who had an interest in the question at hand.

Much less frequently found are reasoned imprecations as an expression of outright ill will and hatred for the government, the party as a whole, or Stalin himself. Thus, commenting on the unsuccessful beginning of the war for the Red Army, one worker of the unfinished products mill of the Kirov factory said to another, "Stalin can't lead the government, he's only good for herding sheep!"[13]

From the long-term "cadre" or "hereditary" workers, negative expressions related mostly to the decrees on labor discipline. They offered sharp criticism of labor duties and imprisonment for lateness and absenteeism. For the most part, the critics were people who had personally suffered from administrative and judicial sanctions.[14]

Most of the dissatisfaction and critical remarks, regarded then as anti-Soviet and counterrevolutionary, had to do simply with sound objections, sincerely expressed, arising from natural concern and alarm about the fate of the fatherland and the state. It must be said that such expressions were the great majority among all complaints. In particular, there was completely justified criticism of the party and government and of Stalin personally for the obvious failures of foreign and domestic policy, for the poor preparation for the war, and for other mistakes and shortcomings. Among volunteers for the workers' militia there was often resentment over mistakes in foreign policy, for the regime's "faith" in Hitler, and for the lack of preparation for the fighting. Sometimes disappointment and dissatisfaction appeared during political education or just after it in a more limited circle of acquaintances. Workers asked their assigned political educators, who offered the official line in the factories, why the government, knowing about Hitler's *Mein Kampf* and its clear depiction of his plans to conquer Soviet territory, as well as knowing his attitudes in general toward the USSR, did not come to the necessary and appropriate conclusions. Why was Maxim Litvinov, who maintained a pro-British policy and did not trust fascist Germany, removed as foreign minister in early 1939?[15] The idea that "the German

bulls his way forward," since he stockpiled grain and tobacco supplied by the USSR during the period of Nazi-Soviet economic and political cooperation, appeared in various forms between August 1939 and June 1941.[16] From such considerations followed the conclusion that serious mistakes had occurred in foreign policy. This point of view generally arose during the discussions that characterized political education sessions, in which political agitators and sometimes soldiers "explained that such ideas were mistaken."[17]

Even more painful and difficult was the theme of unpreparedness for the war and for thwarting an attack by fascist Germany. Workers constantly and with great resentment remembered the regime's assurances that it would not give up "one inch" of Soviet land to the enemy, the promises that a war, if it broke out, would be conducted on the territory of the aggressor, and so forth.[18] Frequently the criticism took the form of questions posed by workers at political education sessions and other meetings. For example, during a general gathering at the Red Chemist factory, workers asked, "Were our frontiers fortified? Why did fortification of Leningrad begin so late? Why didn't we answer the bombing of Moscow by bombing Berlin? Why don't we get details at meetings about places seized by the enemy?"[19] The question "Why didn't the government send troops abroad at the right moment?" was frequently asked.[20]

General conclusions about the obvious unpreparedness for war were always closely linked to the particular situation of one's unit of the popular militia. To ask why the Red Army was not prepared for the defense of the state ("the army didn't show any strength!"), when the people had subscribed to loans every year for the development of the armed forces, resounded as a bitter reproach.[21] Some people, having considered that all organs and offices were especially "counterrevolutionary," came to the conclusion that "Stalin made a mistake!"[22]

More often the communists were impugned in general; people accused them of all kinds of disasters and of "squandering state resources" in particular. Sometimes the desire arose to put the blame for the outbreak of the war on the communists: "If you communists weren't around, then this wouldn't have happened!"[23] That is, Hitler attacked the Soviet Union only to destroy the communist state. This notion completely ignored the fact that the Second World War began among countries of the capitalist camp. Sometimes scorn for the regime reached the extreme of threats against the state and especially against Stalin and Molotov,[24] but such cases were extremely rare and were suppressed quickly and mercilessly.

Nevertheless, judging by archival materials, the overwhelming majority of workers maintained loyalty to the party and the Soviet state. Countless meetings testify to this conclusion. They are described in our historical literature, and there is no necessity to examine this theme in detail yet again. The statements made at meetings, the addresses printed in factory and city newspapers, and also the collective letters of workers to the army testify to the significant patriotic upsurge and the understanding of their necessary role in defense among workers in the factories and mills. It is impossible to ignore the high activity of workers in the formation of the popular militia or their statements about their readiness to increase the length of the workday.

Moreover, the movement among workers to collect money and valuables for the defense fund became widespread. As a rule, older workers stepped forward as the initiators of this campaign. On 5 July labor veterans at the Kirov factory turned to their comrades with a call to follow the example of Kuzma Mnin and Prince Dmitrii Pozharskii, two heroes of the early seventeenth century who formed a national army to oppose the invading Poles. Soviet workers should enter the ranks of the army of liberation and donate silver and gold items for the defense of the Motherland, to "recast household utensils into fighting swords."[25] Workers contributed money, bonds, valuables, and one day's pay. There were cases in which retired workers, returning to their enterprises, contributed their pensions to the defense fund for the duration of the war. By 6 August in the Kirov raion alone, fifty-three thousand rubles had been collected. Subscriptions to donate a day's pay were drawn up. On the same day such subscription lists collected in the pay office of the Kirov factory pledged 93,890 rubles from 4,366 workers of the enterprise.[26]

It quickly became clear, however, that the factory offices were not the best place to collect valuables. They had no specialists capable of appraising gems or jewelry made of precious metals and had no possibility of safely storing such items or of delivering them to banks. Sometimes valuables were lost. For instance, in Petrograd raion a samovar donated to the defense fund "stuck to" dishonest hands. A city commission ordered the collection of valuables at enterprises to stop and directed the gathering of funds for defense to the banks. But even after this change people continued to bring money, bracelets, earrings, brooches, silverware, and so forth to their factories. Of course, it was possible to pressure someone to sign away a day's wages for aid to the front. But only a person deeply concerned with the fate of the Motherland and ready to make any sacrifice for its sake would give up gold earrings or a single silver spoon, about which no one else knew.

What was the basis for the massive patriotic sentiment among the majority of workers? What determined their moral and political outlook? There is no single answer to these questions. It is necessary to discuss a complex range of reasons that formed the whole response.

Not the least of the factors was primordial, national patriotism, which in 1812 inspired downtrodden, deprived peasants against the French invaders. Also at work in 1941 was a specific characteristic of all territorial formations, among them the Leningrad army of the popular militia: a desire to act in the direct defense of one's own city, one's enterprise, home, and family. There was, finally, a certain idealization of thought, fairly characteristic in these years for Leningrad workers, especially the cadre and hereditary ones.

Information from party organs about the mood of the laboring population in the factories and the reports of divisional commissars of the popular militia provide a reasonably good opportunity to judge the nature of what workers said at political education sessions, in conversations with political agitators, and among themselves on a series of troubling themes. Among these materials it is common to find expressions of faith from older workers in the invincibility of the global proletarian revolution and the mission of Soviet workers in it. For example, at a political education session of the Vasil'evskii Island division of the popular militia in July 1941, workers asked, "Will we fight with the capitalist world after the destruction of fascist Germany?"[27]

The ideas of world revolution and the opposition of socialism to capitalism are frequently found in letters from militia volunteers to the army newspaper *For the Defense of Leningrad*. It will suffice to discuss one particularly interesting document of this type. Entitled "Address to All Toilers of Foreign Countries of the Entire World," it was written by a "volunteer militiaman," M. M. Gerasimov, of the First Battalion of the First Infantry Regiment of the Popular Militia's Fourth Division. The author indicated his work speciality, the number of his factory and shop, and even his individual work number, as though he were writing a petition to the administration of an enterprise. He clearly considered the matter extremely important and urgent, as he wrote the document through the night of 15–16 July, and at 6 A.M. delivered the text to an officer of the political department of the Leningrad Army of the Popular Militia for publication. At that point Gerasimov obviously believed that Soviet newspapers would print his address.[28]

His work begins with the words, "Dear comrades, brothers and sisters, oppressed by capitalism! We, workers at the bench, go—and old men, and grandfathers—and we ourselves ask our government and have applied to join the ranks of the volunteers, to uproot the arrogant bloodthirsty reptile, to overthrow fascism, to liquidate the exploiters and the overseers of all humanity."[29]

Thus the first paragraph echoes the famous call, "Workers of the world unite!" Completely clear was a second thesis: between capitalism ("exploiters and overseers") and fascism there was no difference—they were one bloc of enemies of the working people. The destruction of fascism was possible only given the liquidation of the whole class of exploiters. The unity of laboring folk against global capital was important: "Dear comrades, brothers and sisters! You well know that we have never been separated from you, that we will not be separated. And you should never be separated from us." The worker Gerasi-mov resolved the problem of various nationalities quite simply: "we have a system in which there is no difference between nationalities . . . all have full rights who are for the liquidation of exploiters." That is, all are equal on con-dition that they stand for united "class" positions—equality in the spirit of the "dictatorship of the proletariat." Within this framework all have the right to work, rest, obtain education, and to the guarantee of equal well-being. "Such is our constitution." In all this there is an astonishing trust and naiveté, yet it is fully sincere. Between the constitution and reality there was no contradic-tion, Gerasimov felt. His naiveté appears again in his depiction of workers' leading role in the state: "Without the worker not one gathering or meeting takes place here, because the working class decides everything."

Gerasimov was fully satisfied with his own situation and was ready to help all toilers to achieve such a happy life: "Dear comrades! We not only run our own affairs, we want to be a big help to you, so that you can run your own states and so that no masters, exploiters, and humiliators will be over you. We want you to be the masters of your state. We believe and feel that in your country there are fine human minds that are being wasted and are not considered as people."[30] An assurance of inevitable victory for the Soviet people, "of the full-blooded great Soviet power," follows. As proof of this prediction Gerasimov lists all the victories of the Soviet Union, beginning with the defeat of the anti-Bolshevik General Iudenich in 1919. The main conclusion is a call to people everywhere to rally to the side of the USSR: "Destroy all your White Guards [*shutskorovtsev*], fascists, and other kinds of enemies of the people of every stripe, rise up, as we did. . . . Strengthen the Communist International! Vic-tory will be ours!"[31]

Judging by the correspondence and the resolutions of political workers, M. M. Gerasimov's address was met with sympathy but evaluated as semilit-erate, while full of real patriotism and proletarian internationalism.[32] How-ever, to publish it even in a local or army newspaper was of course not possi-ble. The government of the USSR sought support and military aid from all the same capitalist countries in which the worker Gerasimov was ready to foment a proletarian revolution. His address was sent to the archives, and the head of the propaganda department, Battalion Commissar M. Pavlov, replied to the author. He wrote to Gerasimov that his address could not be published after Stalin's speech of 3 July.[33] The political officer was not about to take the risk of formulating new positions on the war, which might have brought extreme unpleasantness down upon him. Probably Gerasimov received a fuller expla-nation orally.

In any event, the "Address to All Toilers of All Foreign Countries of the Whole World" contains basic conceptions that made up the worldview of the majority of workers. In part these notions are found in reports on political education sessions, in accounts of meetings and private conversations, in workers' letters to newspaper editors, and so on. Gerasimov's "Address" represents and preserves the basic and typical concepts of the workers' sphere surrounding him. The main lines of his document are the inclination to a clear, simple (even oversimplified) scheme of the world, naiveté, and hence faith in the possibility of world revolution and a recognition that all toilers faced a common foe.

In 1941 this naiveté in thought and conduct was evident among workers in many of their remarks and actions. At times all this had an infantile character. Seven volunteers of the October division of the popular militia were sent on 5 July to one of the warehouses of the military district to get ammunition. Discovering disorder and inefficiency at the warehouse and feeling astonished and extremely upset, they wrote not to just anyone, but immediately to "Comrade Stalin." They reported that warehouse number seventy-five was wooden, that fire prevention and extinguishing equipment were inadequate, and that removal of military supplies was practically uncontrolled, among other problems. Resolutely demanding that order be established at the warehouse, they gave their letter to the department of political propaganda of the division for direct dispatch to Moscow. Their missive, of course, did not leave the division.[34]

A surprising inclination to schematic thinking also appears in the statements of volunteer militia members when their highly emotional and patriotic remarks at meetings are analyzed carefully. For example, an old *Putilovets*,[35] the gunnery master Gon'kov, said that, "In 1918 my father was shot by White bands. Then I was young and could not avenge the death of my father. Now, when the German bandits again attack our Motherland, I have enrolled as a volunteer in the popular militia in order to avenge my father's death."[36]

Thus the father was shot by "White bands," and the son would take revenge upon "German bandits." The extremely emotional and sincere speech did not evoke any bewilderment from the audience. Let us assume that there were "German bandits" on the scene in 1918, in the form of German troops close to the city; no direct link existed between them and the Fascists of 1941. However, this did not bother anyone, as in their minds they had already formed an image of the internal enemy ("enemy of the people," "counter," as in counterrevolutionary) and of the external foe (capitalist, exploiter). Both were essentially class enemies, bandits, and exploiters. There was no difference between White Guards and Fascists. They were enemies, and that was that.

It is especially remarkable how many speakers made no distinction between the fascist aggressors and the enemies of the Civil War period. One Morozov, a participant in the Civil War, said, "Despite my 48 years, I have enrolled as a volunteer in the army of the popular militia and call upon all our youth to beat the fascist scum just as we beat them in the Civil War."[37] It turns out that Morozov had already beaten "fascists" in the years of the Civil War, but no one paid attention to this absurdity. The main thing in the speech, a form of encouragement desperately needed at the moment, was that the fascists had already been beaten, which meant they could be beaten this time too.

References to the Civil War appear constantly in workers' statements. Analogies with the Soviet-Finnish War were significantly rarer, for example, while mention of Russia's wars before 1917 was still less frequent. Workers spoke relatively rarely of the "achievements of socialism" and about their well-being. Almost never did the nationalist theme arise, although it became so widespread toward the end of the war, as in the "victory of Russian arms," the heroism of the "Russian soldier," and so on. More often resounded the themes of tradition, revenge, blood ties, and the cause of the fathers passed on to the sons.

These are the general outlines of the workers' mood and of their social psychology in the first months of the war. Personal concerns combined regularly with social and political issues. Characteristic of this mixture was thinking in ideological terms, patriotic inclinations, and profound anxiety over the future of the city.

It is necessary to give the party organs who carried out ideological work their due. They reacted quickly to the mood of the people. In everyday agitational and propaganda work, secondary theoretical issues yielded to matters that concerned ordinary citizens more. Into the forefront of discussion came the themes of love for the Motherland, civic duty, military traditions, and the unity of all peoples of the Soviet Union in repelling fascist aggression.

Notes

1. Tsentral'nyi Gosudarstvennyi Arkhiv Istoriko-politicheskikh dokumentov g. S. Peterburga (TsGAIPD). Formerly the Leningradskii Partiinyi Arkhiv. Fond (f.) 417, opis' (o.) 17, delo (d.) 42, list (l. or ll.) 4.

2. Iu. Ia. Orlov, *Krakh nemtsko-fashistskoi propagandy v period voiny protiv SSSR* (Moscow, 1985), 122, 129, 135.

3. TsGAIPD, f. 417, o. 17, d. 42, ll. 139, 153, 164; f. 2281, o. 1, d. 18, l. 81.

4. Ibid., f. 2281, o. l, d. 22, l. 149.

5. Ibid., f. 417, o. 17, d. 42, l. 29.

6. Ibid., f. 2281, o. 17, d. 43, l. 14.

7. Ibid., d. 15, l. 8–9.

8. Ibid., d. 23, ll. 49, 56; f. 417, o. 17, d. 42, ll. 57, 77.

9. Ibid., f. 2281, o. 1, d. 21, l. 36; d. 221, l. 31.

10. Ibid., f. 417, o. 17, d. 42, l. 59.

11. Ibid., ll. 50, 90, 106, 201; f. 2281, o. 1, d. 211, l. 15.

12. Ibid., f. 417, o. 17, d. 42, l. 90.

13. Ibid., l. 195.

14. Ibid., l. 108; f. 2281, o. 1, d. 221, l. 50.

15. Ibid., f. 2281, o. 1, d. 92, l. 36.

16. Ibid., d. 18, l. 82; d. 221, l. 61; f. 417, o. 17, d. 42, l. 29.

17. Ibid., f. 2281, o. 1, d. 150, l. 18.

18. Ibid., d. 23, l. 128; d. 212, l. 111.

19. Ibid., f. 417, o. 17, d. 42, l. 156.

20. Ibid., f. 2281, o. 1, d. 221, l. 83.

21. Ibid., d. 212, l. 111.

22. Ibid., d. 23, l. 128.

23. Ibid., f. 417, o. 17, d. 42, l. 164.

24. Ibid., f. 25, o. 12, d. 16, l. 3.

25. Ibid., f. 417, o. 17, d. 42, l. 48.

26. Ibid., l. 220.

27. Ibid., f. 2281, o. 1, d. 92, ll. 40–44.

28. Ibid., d. 126, l. 57.

29. Ibid., d. 66, l. 44.

30. Ibid., l. 45.

31. Ibid.

32. Ibid.

33. Ibid., d. 69, l. 43.

34. Ibid., d. 21, l. 3; d. 17, l. 28.

35. A worker at the Putilov Factory, renamed the Kirov factory in the late 1920s. The *Putilovtsy* were famed for their revolutionary zeal in 1917.

36. TsGAIPD, f. 2281, o. 1, d. 43, l. 2.

37. Ibid.

5

Survival Strategies in Leningrad during the First Year of the Soviet-German War

Richard Bidlack

The essays in this book examine how broad sections of the Soviet population responded to their nation's war against Germany and its allies between 1941 and 1945. They devote attention to three categories of Soviet citizens: military personnel at the front, civilians at the home front, and military and civilian personnel caught behind enemy lines. These groups faced vastly different sets of wartime challenges; hence it is not surprising that their responses varied widely.

This essay deals with an aspect of the response of Leningrad's civilians during the first year of the Soviet-German War by focusing on ways in which they tried to survive the horrific ordeal of being blockaded, bombarded at close range, frozen, and starved. Because the front lines came within three miles of the southern edge of the city, Leningrad became part of both the military front and the home front. The city endured greater hardships than any other part of the Soviet Union (and arguably than any other part of the world) during the war. The siege of Leningrad is one of the greatest epic struggles for survival in history. More Soviet military personnel and civilians died in and around Leningrad (close to two million according to the most recent research) than North Americans have died in all armed conflicts combined from the time of the French and Indian War through the recent NATO campaigns in the Balkans.

The starting point for discussing survivability during the blockade is the recognition that the amount of food available in Leningrad between November 1941 and May 1942 was insufficient to feed the populace. To survive starvation and extreme cold one needed access to a special source of food or warmth, obtained either legally or illegally, that was not available to most other people. At the same time, many *blokadniki* have noted in their memoirs and diaries

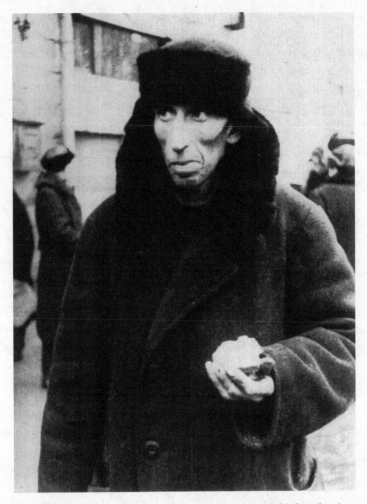

A starving inhabitant of Leningrad during the siege with his bread ration.
(R97250; courtesy of the Bundesarchiv, Koblenz)

that the generosity of others—a relative, friend, or even stranger—enabled
them to survive. Ales Adamovich and Daniil Granin state in their collection
of accounts by siege survivors that "each had a savior,"[1] such as parents who
saved their food rations from work and gave them to their starving children.
The extreme conditions of blockade life, therefore, spawned somewhat paradoxically a keener competition for very scarce resources as well as a strengthened sense of community.

There is no way to determine whether selfishness or self-sacrifice predominated in the hungry city. Moreover, it is difficult at times to distinguish between the two. The person who stole a loaf of bread from a shop was considered to be acting in a selfish way (and might be executed by the authorities if caught); yet often the theft was committed for an unselfish purpose—to save loved ones from starving to death. Soviet historiography on the siege, which commenced under Khrushchev and came to include roughly four hundred monographs, highlighted the unqalified heroism and self-sacrifice of ordinary Leningraders, such as the tens of thousands who volunteered for military service in an auxiliary "people's militia" (*narodnoe opolchenie*). The "darker" side of coping with the siege, such as the proliferation of criminal activity, including even cannibalism, was rarely noted. Soviet historians of the blockade, most of whom were native Leningraders, including many blokadniki, were not engaged in myth making; they simply told only part of the story.

This essay focuses attention on those Leningraders who were determined to survive the ordeals of total war at close range, especially the *golod* (hunger) and *kholod* (cold) of the first winter, and it identifies and describes seven different techniques that they practiced. These techniques were not mutually exclusive; many blokadniki tried more than one. The essay concludes with a discussion of the political dimensions of the struggle to survive.

The First Six Months of Operation Barbarossa

Shortly after coming to power in 1917, the Bolsheviks moved their capital from exposed Petrograd to Moscow. During the 1920s and 1930s Leningrad was relegated to the status of first among provincial cities, but it also became the second largest industrial center in the nation and the home of many advanced and specialized industries, particularly military ones, such as production of artillery guns, tanks, and fighter aircraft. By the start of the Second World War more than six hundred thousand of Leningrad's approximately three million inhabitants were factory workers.[2]

During the first six months of the Soviet-German War, Leningrad's main tasks were to supply the armed forces with personnel, defend the city from attack, produce as much war matériel as possible for use in the Leningrad area and for shipment to other areas, especially Moscow, and evacuate the nonessential population. From the onset of Operation Barbarossa on 22 June through the beginning of the blockade on 8 September, when Finland reestablished the 1939 boundary and sealed off the city to the north and Germany occupied a strip of land to the south of Leningrad between the Gulf of Finland and Lake Ladoga, Leningraders took part in several massive military and industrial mobilization campaigns. Military reservists were called up as soon as the war began. Over two hundred thousand other Leningraders, males and females not subject to the draft, volunteered for military service. Some 130,000 of them were selected for the opolchenie, which fought alongside Red Army divisions trying to stop the German advance between the Luga River defense line and the outskirts of Leningrad. Another fourteen thousand Leningraders were trained as partisans and sent behind enemy lines. In one of the largest mobilization efforts, roughly a half-million civilians were drafted in the summer of 1941 to build defense fortifications near the front. To replace defense plant workers who had gone to the front, tens of thousands of girls, women, teenage boys, and elderly men either volunteered or were drafted for work in city defense plants, most of which increased work shifts to eleven hours at the start of the war. These mobilization campaigns, particularly the building of defense fortifications, slowed the German advance on Leningrad and were therefore an important part of the reason Leningrad became the first European city that Hitler failed to conquer.

The period between the start of the siege and the onset of winter proved to be critical for Leningrad because the mobilization campaigns continued, but food, fuel, and materials diminished rapidly. During this time, and especially after the start of Operation "Typhoon," Germany's all-out offensive for Moscow, on 2 October, Leningrad's main function was to continue to produce as much war matériel as possible and send a large part of it to Moscow. Throughout the autumn, workers in the city's defense plants and in many other facilities that had been converted to production of munitions had to continue logging very long shifts while subsisting on food rations that sank to starvation levels. According to one study, toward the end of November over half of all factory workers under the age of thirty were still achieving at least double their work norms,[3] for which they received less than a pound of bread per day and little else. Even between 8 November and 9 December, when the enemy held the important rail junction at Tikhvin and thereby forced Soviet food convoys to lengthen their circuitous supply route to Leningrad over Lake Ladoga by about eighty miles, Stalin's State Defense Committee (*Gosudarstvennyi Komitet Oborony* or GKO) would not reduce its demands on Leningrad's defense plants. The factories continued to operate at or near full capacity until they literally ground to a halt when city power plants could no longer supply them with electricity.[4] Hence Leningrad was hardly able to prepare for its first winter under siege.

Survival Strategies

Escape the City

In general, Leningraders did not know that their city was directly threatened until 21 August, when *Leningradskaia pravda* published a letter by the city's party leader, A. A. Zhdanov, the front commander, K. E. Voroshilov, and the chairman of the city soviet, P. S. Popkov, stating that Germany might try to take Leningrad. Prior to that time, most probably felt no great urgency to leave the city. Moreover, parents were reluctant to send their children out of the city separately, especially after the first weeks of the war when trainloads of evacuated children had come under fire and had to return to the city. By 29 August, when the last train left Leningrad prior to the start of the siege, only about four hundred thousand Leningraders had been evacuated, leaving about two and a half million people, including four hundred thousand children, trapped within the city.[5]

The number who wanted to leave Leningrad increased after the announcement of 21 August and accelerated rapidly after Germany started bombarding the city on 8 September and starvation set in two months later. During the autumn of 1941, however, most Leningraders had no chance of leaving. The Military Council of the Leningrad Front (*Voennyi Sovet Leningradskogo Fronta* or VSLF) allocated space primarily to military personnel, factory workers, and industrial equipment on the ships and barges that attempted to cross Lake Ladoga, which was patrolled by German fighter aircraft and coastal artillery, and in a fleet of aircraft (including American-built DC-3s) that flew in and out of Leningrad for two weeks in mid-October. No airlift of nonworking people was ever attempted.

As Ladoga began to freeze over in December and January, the famous "ice road" or "road of life" came into being. The lake froze slowly. Up to 22 January, only 36,118 Leningraders are recorded as having traversed frozen Ladoga. In late January temperatures dropped to forty degrees below zero; between 22 January and 15 April an official tally of 554,186 civilians, mainly nonworking dependents, crossed the lake.[6] No one knows exactly how many actually crossed Ladoga, as desperate people tried any means to escape the starving city, including walking on their own. Nor is it known how many died en route. Many refugees started their journey near death, and there was little food, water, or shelter along the way. Awareness of the mass starvation in Leningrad spread throughout the USSR via the emaciated refugees themselves. Corpses of blokadniki were stacked like firewood at various transit stops. As far away as Vologda, located about 350 miles east of Leningrad along a rail line that connected the two cities, a mass burial ground for deceased blokadniki was established; some twenty thousand were interred there by the end of the war.

Many who held elite political or industrial positions or who could establish connections to the elite used those advantages to leave Leningrad, especially before the start of the siege. Secretaries of the ruling city party committee (*gorkom*) as well top governmental leaders in the city soviet were among the first to arrange for their families to be evacuated. Wives and children of at least sixteen of Leningrad's most prominent individuals, including the gorkom secretaries A. A. Kuznetsov and Ia. F. Kapustin, the chairman of the regional (*oblast'*) soviet, N. V. Solov'ev, and the regional party committee (*obkom*) secretaries T. F. Shtykov and M. N. Nikitin, were evacuated to Cheliabinsk in the Urals prior to 10 July.[7] Some without permission to leave naturally resented the early flight of the elite. For example, in August the city prosecutor's office requested that the party investigate a situation at the Voskov munitions plant in the suburban city of Sestroretsk where the director's wife and several women having no connection with the factory were allowed to evacuate, while many workers who were mothers with husbands at the front had to stay at the plant, which was northwest of Leningrad, not far from the Finnish lines. The prosecutor's report indicated that there were serious morale problems at the factory and among the rest of the population of Sestroretsk.[8]

Party archives also include several accounts of factory directors and others who looted state funds and secured transportation in order to leave the city during the first summer of the war. For example, shortly after the start of the blockade, the director of the Red Chemist factory, one Rovinskii, ordered his bookkeeper to fetch him fifty thousand rubles. He then requisitioned a car and might have made good his escape had the bookkeeper not alerted authorities, who arrested Rovinskii.[9]

Once the "road of life" became fully operational in late January, when the mortality rate was nearing its peak, blokadniki used whatever connections they had and bribes they could offer to get on the trucks crossing the lake. The account of Elena Kochina, a young mother who worked as a chemist, seems fairly typical. In late February 1942 she encountered by chance a former colleague who arranged for Elena, her husband, and baby daughter to evacuate over Ladoga with members of the colleague's institute. To secure a seat in the truck that drove them over the lake they had to give the driver two pints of vodka, which by that time had become common black-market currency.[10]

One final and extraordinarily risky way to try to escape the siege ring was to defect to the enemy. Fraternization with the enemy had become such a problem in the army that the VSLF issued a special order on 5 October that mandated execution of all military personnel who either entered into negotiations with the enemy or attempted to cross over to enemy lines and for the arrest and prosecution of their family members as political criminals. A directive issued several days earlier by the command of the Baltic Fleet (the remnants of which were bottled up at Kronstadt Island and Leningrad) called for the immediate execution of families of traitors; however, that directive was declared illegal and canceled the following January.[11] Among civilians, those most inclined to flee to the enemy were the most desperate and hungry. According to the food rationing scheme, teenagers, whose growing bodies demanded a high-caloric diet, were grouped in the "adult dependents" category, which conferred the smallest rations (see table 5.1). Even teens who worked up to eleven hours each day in trade schools and factory training schools were placed in the "dependent" category. They were among the most vulnerable to the effects of prolonged malnutrition. It has been estimated that roughly 190,000 of the 200,000 who attended these schools perished during the blockade.[12] An NKVD report from late November claimed that at least (and probably far more than) 270 students from twelve schools had attempted either successfully or unsuccessfully to reach German lines in October and November. At the same time, teenagers who were employed full time in factories and were receiving the higher "worker" (*rabochii*) food ration were also beginning to try to escape to the enemy.[13]

Securing Factory Employment

A key survival ploy for tens of thousands of Leningraders was to find work in a factory, many of which became largely autonomous survival enclaves at the start of the winter. The industrial workshop provided many benefits. It issued the worker ration, and many workshops began to manufacture household items that were desperately needed. In addition, workers were more likely than others to escape the darkness and cold of most of the rest of the city.[14] Defense plants were given top priority for electrical current while it lasted, and some had their own power generators.

The most important advantage that a factory could provide, even more important than the basic worker ration, was the presence of raw materials that might be edible. Food-processing plants naturally offered the best protection against starvation, though it was strictly illegal to pilfer food, and punishments could be severe. In addition, a number of factories had large quantities of raw materials that contained some edible ingredients, such as industrial casein, dextrine, and albumen. Workers ate the raw materials—the digestible consumed together with the indigestible—apparently without any objection from

Table 5.1. Daily Bread Rations (in Grams) for Leningrad's Civilians, 1941 and 1942

Starting Date	Workers, Engineers, Technicians	Workers in "Hot" Workshops	Office Workers	Adult Dependents	Children under 12
18 July 1941	800	1,000	600	400	400
2 September 1941	600	800	400	300	300
12 September 1941	500	700	300	250	250
1 October 1941	400	600	200	200	200
13 November 1941	300	450	150	150	150
20 November 1941	250	375	125	125	125
25 December 1941	350	500	200	200	200
24 January 1942	400	575	300	250	250
11 February 1942	500	700	400	300	300
22 March 1942	600	700	500	400	400

Source: N. N. Amosov, "Rabochie Leningrada v gody Velikoi Otechestvennoi voiny," doctoral candidate dissertation, Leningrad State University, 1968, 211–13.

Note: Starting on 22 February 1943, workers, engineers, and technicians in defense industries received 700 grams of bread per day.

their bosses. At the Kozitskii radio factory seven tons of glue (which often contained dextrine) and reserves of industrial alcohol were consumed during the winter. Horses were eaten at some factories.[15]

Another food-related benefit of factory employment was that the largest defense plants received access to special food reserves. The GKO wanted to keep these factories open and their workers as healthy as possible, even if they were performing only manual tasks and machine maintenance, in anticipation of the time when regular production could be resumed. On 21 December the VSLF decided to transfer to Leningrad some three hundred tons of emergency food reserves that had been stockpiled on Kronstadt Island ten miles from Leningrad in the Gulf of Finland.[16] Much of this went to defense plants. Furthermore, as soon as the ice on Lake Ladoga was solid enough to support truck traffic the VSLF permitted several major defense plants to send their own trucks across to pick up food parcels.[17] Some factories, such as the press that published Leningradskaia pravda, received food parcels directly from Moscow.[18] Yet another way workers at defense plants obtained extra food was through trips to the front either as members of repair brigades or in "goodwill" delegations. Soldiers, whose rations were about twice as large as worker rations, exchanged food for items the workers made. According to one estimate, approximately a hundred worker delegations went to the front in November and December.[19] Georgii Kulagin, a high-level manager at the Stalin metallurgy factory, noted that he sought to visit the front as often as possible: "There I could eat until full and occasionally pick up a loaf of soldiers' bread. . . . Without this, I would not have survived."[20]

In addition to providing workers with greater access to food, factory workshops became large mutual-support centers where workers pooled their strengths to carry out essential chores. Many workers went over to "barracks conditions," living round-the-clock at their factories. Workers formed brigades to clean living space in workshops, mend torn clothing, repair shoes, and to set up laundries, baths, showers, and warming stations.[21] These brigades, which were mainly comprised of girls and women, also took food to workers too weak to go to the factory, cleaned their apartments, attempted to place orphaned children in homes (or established children's homes in their factories, as a brigade at the Kirov metallurgy works did), and arranged for burial of corpses.[22] Starting in late December, many factory administrations also set up rudimentary clinics, which typically consisted of several rows of beds and a few small stoves and provided hot soup or kasha and perhaps some hot wine, glucose injections, or even a few antibiotics. By the spring of 1942 a total of 109 clinics were reportedly assisting 63,740 Leningraders, primarily factory workers.[23]

Workers often were able to recuperate from hunger and illness at home and thus could avoid going to work while still receiving worker food rations until the start of the next month when they had to renew their ration cards in person. This was in sharp contrast to conditions prevailing the preceding autumn when an unauthorized absence from a defense plant might be construed as the equivalent of desertion from the front lines and could therefore constitute grounds for being shot.[24] During the winter of 1941–42, most Leningraders were seriously ill and thousands perished daily; hence many doctors stopped issuing certificates of illness, and factory administrators ceased requiring ill workers to present certificates upon returning to work. Many factories simply put all those who did not report for work on sick lists until the end of the particular month.[25] In April 1942 only 51 percent of workers (101,002 of 197,466) at 436 factories surveyed were reporting to work.[26]

The benefits of factory employment attracted many Leningraders. On the eve of the war, there had been about 750,000 industrial and nonindustrial workers in Leningrad.[27] By 6 October 1941, after successive waves of army mobilization and opolchenie volunteering and the industrial evacuation had removed at least 200,000 workers from the city, the number of Leningraders officially receiving worker food rations was 831,400.[28] Hence, at least 281,400 began to receive worker rations by autumn (though not all were working in factories). There were several reasons why people went to work in factories in

1941, including having been drafted through a factory recruitment drive or wanting to contribute one's share to defending the nation and the city. However, the higher food rations available at factories also acted as a powerful magnet. The words of Mikhail Pelevin, a fifteen-year-old machine operator, reflect this popular strategy: "It is no secret that . . . boys tried every means possible to get into the factory, because at the factory canteen you could get three bowls of hot yeast soup and a bottle of soya milk in exchange for a ration coupon for 12 and a half grams of groats."[29]

The number of Leningraders receiving worker rations did not decline significantly during the winter, despite the fact that workers were supposed to drop down to the "dependent" category once their factories were shut down. In December approximately 837,000 people received worker rations; in January that figure dropped to 800,000.[30] It is inconceivable during the winter, when the gorkom closed 270 factories and only eighteen of sixty-eight leading industries maintained any semblance of activity,[31] that anywhere near a majority of factory workers were actually working. Many were probably in a situation similar to that in which Elena Skrjabina found herself on 15 January: "Friends found me a position in a sewing shop. This puts me in the first category as far as rationing goes. True, the workshop does very little; there is no light or fuel, but they give out the rations just the same. In this way I get a little more bread, and now every crumb is vital."[32] In most cases it was not until at least the spring of 1942 that the gorkom redistributed workers from closed plants to working ones. The fact that so many people were attracted to and managed to obtain the higher worker ration only placed added pressure on city authorities to cut rations further, because food supply was not increasing.

Of all the survival schemes considered in this essay, factory employment permits the most detailed description of effectiveness. How successful was the factory enclave in saving lives during the winter? To answer this question, one must first establish an approximate mortality figure for the entire civilian population. No one knows exactly how many Leningraders died during the first siege winter, but a reasonable range would be from approximately eight hundred thousand to a million.[33] From these figures it can be estimated that between one-third and two-fifths of Leningrad's civilians who were in the city at the start of the winter died there during the winter. Of those who did not leave the city during the winter, perhaps as many as half perished.[34]

It is not known how many of Leningrad's industrial employees died in the winter. To estimate that figure we have to piece together available data from individual factories. Those records reveal that mortality varied considerably but that most factories fall into one of three categories. At one extreme were those that produced food or used materials that were edible. The most coveted jobs were in bakeries, candy factories, other food-processing plants, cafeterias, buffets, and hospitals. There was fierce competition to get on their payrolls, and the starving begged for food on their premises.[35] These places became excellent havens for their employees, and their starvation rates were very low; at several food plants no one died. Some quality control inspectors were even overweight. Food workers could rationalize their petty pilfering with the argument that they had to continue to live in order to produce food for others. Of the 713 people employed at the start of the winter at the Krupskaia candy factory, none starved to death.[36] Likewise, no one succumbed to starvation at the city's number 4 bakery.[37] At the Baltika bakery, 276 people, mainly women, were employed on the eve of the war. By the beginning of winter, not surprisingly, the work force had grown to 334. Twenty-seven Baltika employees (8 percent) starved to death; all were men, as women in general are able to withstand longer periods of malnutrition because of higher levels of body fat and stronger cardiovascular systems.[38] At another plant, the city's only margarine factory, there were large quantities of linseed, sunflower seeds, and even coconuts during the winter. (On the eve of the war this plant had obtained two thousand tons of coconuts from the Philippines.) Employees lived off the oil-bearing crops, and not one starved to death.[39]

A foreman named Nikolai Sergeev provided a revealing glimpse into the question of who survived and why in his raw-meat workshop at the city's number 2 sausage factory. In an unpublished statement that he dictated in February 1943, he claimed that during the winter only males died; among the victims were new workers who could not stomach eating raw meat (to which the more experienced workers had become accustomed) and older workers whose teeth were either missing or too weak to chew raw meat.[40]

In a second category were factories that did not have extraordinary access to food or edible materials but did not demand much work from their workers who nevertheless continued to receive worker rations. Mortality at such plants was relatively low. City power plants fit into this group. Only one plant generated electricity throughout the siege period; yet in December 1941 the industry as a whole employed more workers than it did in 1940. The starvation rate among workers at power plants was 20 to 25 percent.[41]

No evidence has emerged of a factory that had a starvation rate higher than the city average; however, at some large defense plants rates approached the average range. For example, Kulagin estimates that approximately 35 percent starved to death at the Stalin metal works and records from the Kirov factory reveal a 25 to 34 percent starvation rate.[42] Of the nearly twelve thousand who were employed at the Bolshevik arms plant at the beginning of the year and were not subsequently evacuated, approximately 22 percent died in the winter.[43]

Data on large defense plants reveal a paradox. They had the best food supply and the most developed mutual-support groups; one would expect their mortality rates to be lower. However, three special conditions at major defense plants combined to increase mortality. First, they were special targets for German aircraft and artillery, especially those such as the Kirov works that were located in the city's southern districts. Second, as noted above, on a per capita basis more men than women starved to death, and of all types of industry major defense plants had the highest proportion of male workers. Large concentrations of men had continued to work in defense plants because jobs there often required a high skill level, which men were more likely to possess, and men in defense industries were granted exemptions from military service. Third, in early March 1942 the GKO ordered a number of Leningrad's large defense plants to resume limited operations. The effort required to fulfill the March orders probably finished off many emaciated workers. At the Kirov works over half of all cases of death by starvation reportedly occurred in March and April. Records from the Bolshevik factory show that three-fourths of the deaths of the winter and spring occurred in April.[44] The effect of the survival benefits at large defense plants was therefore partly negated by these three factors. Had these workers not had special privileges, it can be assumed that their mortality rates would have far surpassed the city average.

Making Use of Privilege

As is well known, a prominent development in the USSR during the period of the Second Five-Year Plan was an increasing social stratification as the revolutionary ethos of egalitarianism gave way to newly emerging hierarchies. "Layers" of power and privilege are recognizable in Leningrad during the siege years. As was noted in the section on evacuation, privilege or influence (*blat*) was an important factor in determining who was able to leave Leningrad. Privilege was also commonly used to secure special access to food. The food rationing scheme, which resembled the system employed during the early 1930s, was egalitarian to a point (see table 5.1). According to the system, all people within a ration category received the same amount of food, and the only big difference among civilian categories was the preference given to factory workers (especially in "hot" workshops, such as those that rolled steel), engineers, and technicians. At the same time, important unpublicized privileges existed for various elites. For instance, in factories there were often "closed" cafeterias and a "director's" cafeteria, which provided marginally better food and larger portions to engineers, managers, and directors.[45] At the apex of Leningrad's pyramid of privilege, party headquarters at Smolny, all sorts of food were in abundant supply. Smolny's cafeteria number 12 provided bread, sugar, cutlets, and small pies on a regular basis during the winter. Employees were strictly forbidden to take food out of this cafeteria for fear that its bountiful supply would become widely known.[46]

A deputy commander in charge of food supply for an army division in Leningrad, Vasily Yershov, relates a telling example of the food privileges of the elite. He describes in an unpublished memoir how he was dispatched to the airport to collect foodstuffs that had been left over from a huge shipment flown to the family members and assistants of gorkom secretaries who had been evacuated eastward during the first months of the war. Yershov organized dozens of trucks to retrieve ten tons of rice, about fifteen tons of white flour, over two tons of caviar, approximately five tons of butter, more than two hundred smoked hams, and large quantities of many other products. Some of these foodstuffs were delivered to Smolny.[47] Another source asserts that Zhdanov regularly received sausages and fresh peaches by airplane throughout the siege period.[48]

Communist Party members as a whole were an elite group that benefited significantly from various forms of privileges. During the first half of 1942, 15 percent of all party members in Leningrad starved to death, which was less than half of the city's overall percentage of starvation victims.[49]

Barter

As the winter set in and reserves of consumer goods and food diminished, the purchasing power of the ruble plummeted, and private barter trade became more common. Private transactions remained technically illegal, and peasant food markets had been closed in September 1941 in an attempt to stifle the growing black market; nevertheless, black-market trade was widely condoned, at least on an individual, small-scale basis. Toward the end of 1941 it became common for blokadniki to walk to markets, such as the central Haymarket, and stand with a pair of galoshes or a coat in the hope of exchanging them for a small amount of food. Scenes of street traders flocking to the markets with personal possessions to trade were not unlike the flea markets that sprang up around the metro stations and elsewhere in the early 1990s when inflation (which reached an annual rate of about 2,000 percent in 1992) turned Russian pensioners and even many employed people into paupers. Documented examples of barter exchanges during the winter of 1941–42 show how desperate many were for food (far more desperate, of course, than in the first post-Soviet years). A gold watch bought only three to four turnips, an ordinary fur coat only a half kilogram of bread, and a large Persian rug two chocolate bars.[50] Exchanges between civilians and soldiers were common as soldiers often had excess food (though there were soldiers within the siege area who starved to death) but lacked warm clothing. As noted above, soldiers received higher rations, had access to American lend-lease canned foods, and some ate their horses. The factory "goodwill delegations" are an example of an established forum for barter between workers and soldiers.

Privilege played an important role in barter trade just as it did in the evacuation process and the official food rationing system. Being able to purchase a large amount of food on the black market required valuable trading items, which members of elite groups were more likely to possess.

Gardening and Farming

During the winter, blokadniki became obsessed with the hope of planting vegetable gardens in the coming spring. Preparations began as early as January for what would become a massive growing campaign that city authorities enthusiastically supported. The first plans for planting gardens were published on 11 January in an article in *Leningradskaia pravda*, and five days later the newspaper announced that several factories had been ordered to manufacture various farm tools (even though most workers were in no condition to resume work). The intent of these early efforts appears to have been mainly psychological, to boost morale, which was a vital component of survival.

On 19 March the city soviet announced procedures for the gardening campaign. The soviet set aside over five square miles of parks, squares, and other open areas for gardens, and each family was eligible to receive plots of 0.15 hectare (about 16,000 square feet) and seedlings from departments of the executive committee of the soviet. City leaders admonished every able-bodied person to stake out and plant a garden, though few needed coaxing. During the rest of the year an estimated 276,000 blokadniki planted over seven square miles of cabbage, lettuce, beets, tomatoes, cucumbers, green beans, rutabagas, carrots, radishes, and onions in virtually every patch of available soil.[51]

At the same time, factories and other enterprises organized so-called auxiliary farms (*podsobnye khoziaistva*), which were located on abandoned state and collective farms outside Leningrad but within the siege area. Produce from the farms went to the factory cafeterias, to the city's general food supply, and to the workers who labored on the farms.[52] Not surprisingly, most Leningraders preferred working on their own gardens rather than on the farms, because everything they grew on their own plots was theirs. All previous rent payments for gardens and taxes on their produce were abolished. Moreover, those who worked on the farms had to leave their homes for several weeks at a time.[53] The gardening campaign of 1942 may have been the most popular program ever promoted by Leningrad's leaders during the entire Soviet period. Together with the auxiliary farms, the gardens helped keep alive thousands of blokadniki.

Crime

Theft of food and related crimes were extremely widespread during the siege. Starving teenage pickpockets worked the crowds around food stores during the dark days of winter snatching rations and ration cards; armed bands occasionally looted stores; food workers stole from their place of employment; and thieves broke into vacant flats. During the winter, the police recovered a total of 455 tons of stolen bread, grain, groats, and sugar. For the entire siege period, police confiscated 16,567,939 rubles, 4,781 U.S. dollars, 1,369 gold watches, 11,739 winter coats, 21,989 suits, 10,790 summer coats, and 81,976 women's dresses, among other items, from thieves and black marketeers.[54]

Systematic theft among workers and administrators in bakeries and food stores was common. In late autumn 1941, for example, the director of a food wholesale enterprise, B. P. Baranov, and his assistant were arrested for illegal sales of several thousand kilograms of wheat and soy flour. Around the same time, the director of a food store in the northern part of the city together with his assistant and the store's warehouse manager were arrested for stealing seven hundred kilograms of food. In another example, employees at the Badaev bakery reportedly stole flour on at least ninety-eight occasions during the winter and spring.[55] Numerous other examples are documented in the archives.

Some blokadniki made a moral distinction between theft from a food store or warehouse and from an individual. It was widely (and sometimes correctly) assumed that administrators and salespeople in food shops cheated customers to save food for themselves; hence, theft from shops could be rationalized as a quid pro quo. Moreover, stealing food from the dimly lit shops or from poorly guarded warehouses did not victimize identifiable people. Theft of a day's bread ration from a person on the street, however, might be the final deprivation that turned a starving person into a corpse.[56]

When thieves and other criminals were apprehended, they were generally punished swiftly and severely. The gorkom secretary A. A. Kuznetsov stated in the spring of 1942: "I will tell you plainly that we shot people for stealing a loaf of bread."[57] Those who received the lesser sentence of imprisonment during the first year of the war were in fact practically condemned to death, because mortality rates were extremely high in the city's jails and in penal battalions.

Criminal survival schemes included murder and cannibalism. There were 560 murders among a total of 30,942 crimes reportedly committed in Leningrad in 1942.[58] City police created a large department to deal with cannibalism,[59] and according to recently declassified documents, about fifteen hundred were arrested for that crime (which was officially referred to as "banditism" under article 59–3 of the criminal code) during the siege, including 886 between the beginning of December 1941 and 15 February 1942. Those arrested were typically young, unemployed women, born outside of Leningrad and having no prior convictions, who were simply pursuing any means possible to feed themselves and their children. There were organized bands of cannibals, and a black market in human flesh arose.[60] Cemetery workers occasionally found corpses that had been hacked apart,[61] and there is evidence of cannibalism in at least one city jail.[62] Yershov, the army food-supply officer, describes a cannibal ring of some twenty medical workers, including doctors. He also claims that when he was stationed in front lines near Kolpino, a town south of Leningrad where army units had been cut off from supplies, he learned of a gang of some twenty cannibals who waylaid, killed, and partly consumed the corpses of military couriers.[63] Another source claims that a student and four research assistants from the anatomy department of a Leningrad pediatric clinic ate cadavers.[64]

Work Stoppages and Pleas for an "Open" City

A final category of survival strategy consists of open acts of defiance. Two basic forms of protest emerged in the autumn of 1941, the first of which was refusal to work without receiving additional food. The second was the plea to surrender Leningrad to the enemy in the hope that German forces would feed the city's inhabitants (though Germany had no such plans) or the demand to open a safe corridor through the front lines so that starving civilians could leave the city. The protests were dangerous and were mounted by desperate people who would grasp at any hope of avoiding death by starvation.

Popular dissatisfaction was greatest between the start of the blockade and the onset of winter, a period during which it was uncertain whether the city could be held and food rations were cut repeatedly but workers had to maintain their "storming" work schedules. Party documents reveal many examples of factory workers who demanded more food as a condition for working long shifts. Occasionally, employees refused to go to work without first receiving food. When rations were lowered, large meetings were convened in factory workshops to explain why the cuts were necessary. At these sessions professional agitators had to respond to such taunting questions as, "Where is that ten-year supply of food?" that authorities had claimed existed before the war. Workers would cry out, "If you demand more work, give us more food."[65]

Workers sometimes took collective action. On 15 September, a day when it appeared that German troops might invade the city, thirty-five female workers at the Engels factory refused to work more than eight hours on the night shift. The plant director gave in to their demand and let them leave. A similar situation occurred in another part of that factory three days later.[66]

Workers could be fined and arrested for refusing to work, but not all were deterred by threats of punishment. On 16 November a group of eighteen workers at an unidentified factory left work two hours early, saying, "They feed us poorly; we have no strength for more work; we worked as hard as we could." When told that they would be fined, several responded that they did not care as there was nothing to buy anyway.[67]

While worker dissatisfaction was peaking, party and NKVD informants took note of a rising number of appeals, both secret and public, to make Leningrad an open city. Anonymous letters were sent to the city's leaders, and printed leaflets were circulated demanding the city's surrender. These appeals were issued most frequently in November, when city authorities and their informants encountered on average fifteen such letters and leaflets each day. They were among a daily average of 300 to 350 expressions of sentiment allegedly detected that month that were considered to be "anti-Soviet." Most of these expressions were probably individual comments overheard by informants.[68] However, punishments for anti-Soviet agitation were harsh and included execution. Although the number of work stoppages and calls for surrendering Leningrad increased in October and November, at no point were they sufficiently large, widespread, or coordinated to constitute a serious threat to the city's leadership.

It would appear that the largest public appeal for the surrender of the city took place on 7 November 1941, the twenty-fourth anniversary of the Bolshevik Revolution. In his memoir Yershov describes a procession of several hundred people, mainly children between the ages of ten and fourteen, that proceeded along Stachek Prospect not far from the Kirov works and only about three miles from the front. They called for opening the city so that starving women and children could leave. Many carried printed leaflets with words similar to the following: "Dear fathers and brothers, your children, wives, and mothers are dying from hunger. The authorities decided to destroy us by a most terrible death. You 24 years ago were able to destroy tsarist power, you are able as well to destroy the hated Kremlin and Smolny executioners as long as you have guns!"[69] According to the account, a commissar of an army division named

Kuplivatskii ordered security guards to open fire on the crowd. The guards, however, refused, at which point Kuplivatskii himself fired into the assembled children. A German artillery attack commenced at this moment, and the crowd dispersed. Shortly thereafter, a Major Kalugin and three others were arrested for not carrying out the initial order to open fire, and eventually hundreds of men, women, and children were arrested for participating in the demonstration. The NKVD was particularly interested in determining who had printed the leaflets. Yershov states that some sixty soldiers and officers were shot for supposedly belonging to an underground organization connected with the demonstration.[70]

Conclusion: The Politics of Survival

Leningraders improvised a variety of strategies to survive the hunger and cold of the first winter of the war, and survival rates varied considerably among different groups of people. At one extreme, very few teenagers in trade schools or newborns and infants survived that first winter unless they were evacuated. At the other end of the spectrum, the large majority of workers in food-processing plants or those connected to power or privilege, such as employees at Smolny, managed to endure. The official means for distributing food reflected a policy that was a mixture of egalitarianism and elitism.

If tensions between rulers and ruled were highest in the autumn, the political relationship changed during the bitterly cold starvation winter.[71] When electricity was cut off to most enterprises by mid-December, factories no longer could produce much war matériel. The Leningrad gorkom then began to place a high priority on assisting Leningraders by evacuating about a half-million nonworking people and trying to ensure the survival of those who remained in the city. Only toward the end of the winter did the GKO succeed in resuming production at a select number of war plants. For the first time during the war, and perhaps for the first time since the Bolsheviks had come to power in 1917, the government and ordinary people in Leningrad basically shared a common goal—simple survival—which necessitated cooperation. The limited activity that continued in the city's factories during the winter, often made possible by improvised fuels and makeshift power generators, was geared mainly toward meeting the immediate needs of blokadniki. Political and industrial leaders generally condoned, and in some cases actively promoted, the development of survival stratagems such as turning factory workshops into survival enclaves, engaging in private trade, and planting private vegetable gardens, as long as the schemes were not clearly criminal in nature or politically subversive. In short, Leningraders were permitted a greater measure of personal freedom to help themselves during this time of dire emergency.

Pro-German sentiment and calls for surrendering the city diminished during the winter as blokadniki displayed an extraordinary desire to persevere. Under the pressure of continual bombardment, frigid temperatures, and mass starvation, the city did not collapse into chaos as the German leadership had hoped. Blokadniki continued to follow their leaders' dictates for a combination of reasons, including contempt for the enemy's genocidal siege tactics, fear of what subsequent enemy occupation of Leningrad would mean, a sincere love of their native city (which on rare occasions was even referred to in *Leningradskaia pravda* by its old nickname, *Piter*), a desire to support friends and relatives at the front, and the ongoing hope that the city was on the verge of being liberated, particularly after the successful counteroffensive outside of Moscow. It should also be noted that the onset of a fierce winter naturally dulled any impulse to protest and tended to restrict people's attention to performing vital daily chores, such as fetching drinking water, standing in line for food, and trying to keep warm. In addition, the NKVD helped to maintain order by maintaining a formidable presence in the city throughout the winter. By contrast, a sense of commitment to communist ideology or to Stalin and his government appears to have played little if any role in motivating the populace. Finally, the fact that Leningrad's leaders during the winter actively tried to protect the general population helped ensure residents' loyalty.

Notes

The section titled "Securing Factory Employment" on pp. 90–95 derives mainly from pp. 179–85 of my essay "Rabochie Leningradskikh zavodov v pervyi god voiny," in *Leningradskaia epopeia: Organizatsiia oborory i naselenie goroda,* ed. V. M. Koval'chuk et al., (St. Petersburg, 1995).

In writing this essay, I am deeply indebted to a number of Russian colleagues who have shared their insights, research, and friendship with me over the past several years. In particular, I wish to thank N. A. Lomagin and acknowledge my deep gratitude to V. G. Bortnevskii, whose untimely death a few years ago is a tremendous loss to the field of Soviet history. My research also benefitted from many discussions on the Leningrad blockade with A. R. Dzeniskevich, M. V. Shkarovskii, V. M. Koval'chuk, A. V. Tereshchuk, and I. I. Klimin. T. P. Bondarovskaia and the late I. I. Sazonova, archivists at the former Leningrad Party Archive, now called Tsentral'nyi Gosudarstvennyi Arkhiv Istoriko-Politicheskikh Dokumentov Sankt-Peterburga (the Central State Archive for Historical-Political Documents of St. Petersburg), provided invaluable assistance in locating siege-era documents. A very special note of appreciation goes to M. V. Korchinskaia, a *blokadnitsa* and dear friend, who was my host during research trips to St. Petersburg. Finally, I wish to thank the International Research and Exchanges Board as well as the dean's office and the history department of Washington and Lee University for supporting this research.

1. This is the title of chapter eleven of Ales Adamovich and Daniil Granin, *Blokadnaia kniga* (Moscow, 1982), 137.

2. A. R. Dzeniskevich, *Voennaia piatiletka rabochikh Leningrada, 1941–1945* (Leningrad, 1972), 85; A. R. Dzeniskevich, *Rabochie Leningrada nakanune Velikoi Otechestvennoi voiny, 1938–iiun' 1941 g.* (Leningrad, 1983), 10.

3. L. Arapova, "Trudovaia deiatel'nost' Leningradtsev v period blokady (1941–1943 gg.)," unpublished doctoral candidate dissertation (Moscow State Historical-Archival Institute, 1965), 280.

4. See Richard Bidlack, "Workers at War: Factory Workers and Labor Policy in the Siege of Leningrad," *The Carl Beck Papers in Russian and East European Studies,* no. 902 (Pittsburgh, 1991), 16–20; Richard Bidlack, "Rabochie Leningradskikh zavodov v pervyi god voiny" (Leningrad's factory workers in the first year of the war), in *Leningradskaia epopeia: Organizatsiia oborory i naselenie goroda,* ed. V. M. Koval'chuk et al. (St. Petersburg, 1995), 173–78.

5. Dmitrii V. Pavlov, *Leningrad 1941: The Blockade,* trans. John C. Adams (Chicago, 1965), 46–48.

6. A. V. Karasev, *Leningradtsy v gody blokady, 1941–1943 gg.* (Moscow, 1959), 199–201.

7. Tsentral'nyi Gosudarstvennyi Arkhiv Istoriko-Politicheskikh Dokumentov Sankt-Peterburga (TsGAIPD Spb), fond (f.) 24, opis' (o.) 2v, delo (d.) 5670, list (l. or ll.) 96.

8. Ibid., o. 2b, d. 970, l. 6.

9. Ibid., o. 2v, d. 4819, l. 38. For similar examples, see ibid., d. 5279, l. 44; d. 5366, ll. 116, 181–84.

10. Elena Kochina, *Blockade Diary,* trans. Samuel C. Ramer (Ann Arbor, Mich., 1990), 94–104.

11. Nikita Lomagin, *The Soviet Attempts to Neutralize Disruptive Fascist Propaganda in the Army during the Battle of Leningrad,* trans. Emily Johnson (St. Petersburg, 1993), 13–14; Nikita Lomagin, "Nastroeniia zashchitnikov i naseleniia Leningrada v period oborony goroda, 1941–1942 gg.," in Koval'chuk et al., eds., *Leningradskaia epopeia,* 243.

12. This statistic was included in the documentary film, *Blokada* (St. Petersburg, 1994).

13. TsGAIPD Spb, f. 24, o. 2b, d. 992, ll. 1–16; o. 2v, d. 5211, ll. 5–8; o. 2v, d. 4819, ll. 111–12; o. 2v, d. 5151, l. 139.

14. According to a survey of factories conducted by a group of medical workers headed by a Professor Vigdorchik, about one-third of industrial work space during the winter was illuminated. A. R. Dzeniskevich, *Nakanune i v dni ispytanii: Leningradskie rabochie v 1938–1945 gg.* (Leningrad, 1990), 100.

15. Dzeniskevich, *Nakanune i v dni ispytanii,* 103.

16. A. V. Burov, *Blokada den' za dnem* (Leningrad, 1979), 106.

17. Dzeniskevich, *Voennaia piatiletka*, 76.

18. TsGAIPD SPb, f. 4000, o. 10, d. 319, l. 5

19. N. N. Amosov, "Rabochie Leningrada v gody Velikoi Otechestvennoi voiny," unpublished doctoral candidate dissertation (Leningrad State University, 1968), 269.

20. Georgii Kulagin, *Dnevnik i pamiat': O perezhitom v gody blokady* (Leningrad, 1978), 39.

21. According to the survey of Professor Vigdorchik, 40 percent of active factories had no heat, 40 percent were partly heated, and 20 percent had temperatures close to prewar norms. Dzeniskevich, *Nakanune i v dni ispytanii*, 100.

22. L. A. Shvetsov, "Deiatel'nost' Smol'ninskoi raionnoi partiinoi organizatsii v period blokady goroda Leningrada," unpublished doctoral candidate dissertation (Leningrad State University, 1966), 120; Burov, *Blokada den' za dnem*, 142, 145.

23. Dzeniskevich, *Voennaia piatiletka*, 78; I. A. Vazhentsev, *Vo glave geroicheskogo kollektiva* (Leningrad, 1959), 119–20; Amosov, "Rabochie Leningrada," 244; N. D. Shumilov, *V dni blokady*, 2d ed. (Moscow, 1985), 162; V. G. Zakharov et al., *Ocherki istorii Leningradskoi organizatsii KPSS, 1918–1945* (Leningrad, 1980), 389; V. M. Koval'chuk, ed., *Ocherki istorii Leningrada*, vol. 5 (Leningrad, 1967), 202.

24. When Marshall Zhukov flew to Leningrad in September to organize its defenses he issued to military officers Order No. 0064, which stated that anyone who abandoned his post without written permission would be shot immediately. Dmitri Volkogonov, *Stalin: Triumph and Tragedy*, trans. Harold Shukman (New York, 1991), 466. In one example, a master craftsman named Khlusov at the Kirov factory left work for four days that month to move his family from the village of Alekseevka, which was near the factory and threatened by the German advance, to the safer confines of the "Petrograd Quarter" district. He was fired and "made accountable" (*privlechen k otvetstvennosti*) for his activities, which was a wartime euphemism indicating some form of harsh punishment. TsGAIPD SPb, f. 1012, o. 3, d. 53, l. 14.

25. *Leningradskaia pravda*, 27 Feb. and 26 Mar. 1942.

26. A. R. Dzeniskevich, "Novye dannye o vesne blokadnogo 1942 goda," unpublished manuscript, 1992, 4–5.

27. Amosov, "Rabochie Leningrada," 119.

28. Karasev, *Leningradtsy v gody blokady*, 120.

29. Adamovich and Granin, *Blokadnaia kniga*, 83.

30. D. V. Pavlov, *Leningrad v blokade*, 6th ed. (Leningrad, 1985), 114; S. P. Kniazev et al., *Na zashchite Nevskoi tverdyni* (Leningrad, 1965), 284.

31. Koval'chuk, ed., *Ocherki istorii Leningrada*, 215–16.

32. Elena Skrjabina, *Siege and Survival* (Carbondale, Ill., 1971), 54.

33. V. M. Koval'chuk and G. L. Sobolev have calculated that not less than eight hundred thousand perished in Leningrad during the entire siege and defended that figure in their "Leningradskii 'rekviem' (o zhertvakh naseleniia v Leningrade v gody voiny i blokady)," *Voprosy istorii* 12 (1965), 191–94. Kniazev et al., *Na zashchite Nevskoi tverdy-*

ni, states that no fewer than a million starved to death in Leningrad and its suburbs. (Almost all starvation deaths occurred during the first winter and spring of the siege.) Both of these references are cited in G. L. Sobolev, "Blokada Leningrada v svete perestroiki istoricheskoi nauki (Ob osveshchenii nekotorykh voprosov istorii blokady Leningrada v knigakh D.V. Pavlova)," in *Voprosy istorii i istoriografii Velikoi Otechestvennoi Voiny*, ed. A. P. Kriukovskikh et al. (Leningrad, 1989), 74–75.

Totals of death by starvation and related illnesses for various groups within the siege ring are estimated as follows: medical doctors: 2 percent (61 of 3,000); military personnel (not included in the civilian mortality rates discussed above): 2.5 percent (12,416 of about 500,000); and registered artists: 37 percent (83 of 225). See Iu. S. Tokarev et al., eds., *Deviat'sot geroicheskikh dnei* (Moscow, 1967), 340; Harrison Salisbury, *The 900 Days: The Siege of Leningrad* (New York, 1969), 294, 495, 516.

34. It is generally accepted that there were approximately 2.3 million people in Leningrad at the beginning of January. Kniazev et al., *Na zashchite Nevskoi tverdyni*, 284. Roughly seventy-five thousand had starved to death in November and December (Pavlov's figure of 52,881 starvation victims for December [*Leningrad v blokade*, 165] is regarded by most other researchers to be low), and perhaps thirty thousand were evacuated, which means that about 2.4 million people resided in Leningrad when rations were cut twice in November and starvation began. Approximately 590,000 Leningraders were evacuated during the winter; thus, had there been no deaths or births in the city during the winter, approximately 1,810,000 would have remained at the start of spring. If eight hundred thousand to a million of the 1,810,000 who remained in the city died during the winter, the mortality rate would have been between 44 and 55 percent. But this range is probably too high, because it is not known what percentage of these deaths might have occurred among the evacuees (who are not included in the figure for the city's population at the end of the winter), nor is it known how many people crossed Ladoga during the winter without authorization and may therefore have been counted inadvertently among those who perished. Hence "as many as half" is offered here as an approximation of the portion of the population that perished among those who did not leave the city during the winter.

35. TsGAIPD SPb, f. 4000, o. 10, d. 297, l. 8.

36. M. I. Frolov, "Istoriia konditerskoi im. N. K. Krupskoi," part 1, unpublished manuscript, 35; comments made by Frolov to the author in January 1994.

37. TsGAIPD SPb, f. 4000, o. 10, d. 592, l. 5.

38. Ibid., f. 417, o. 3, d. 444, ll. 47–48.

39. Adamovich and Granin, *Blokadnaia kniga*, 249–52.

40. TsGAIPD SPb, f. 4000, o. 10, d. 628, ll. 3–6.

41. Dzeniskevich, *Voennaia piatiletka*, 106.

42. Kulagin, *Dnevnik i pamiat'*, 221; Tokarev et al., eds., *Deviat'sot geroicheskikh dnei*, 175–76.

43. TsGAIPD SPb, f. 25, o. 13a, d. 46, l. 103.

44. Salisbury, *900 Days*, 507; TsGAIPD SPb, f. 25, o. 13a, d. 46, l. 103. It is likely, how-

ever, that some of those who were reported to have died in March or April actually perished earlier but were not counted until that time.

45. Kulagin notes, however, that the "director's" cafeteria at the Stalin metal works gradually opened its doors to nonmanagerial personnel. Kulagin, *Dnevnik i pamiat'*, 152.

46. Adamovich and Granin, *Blokadnaia kniga*, 332.

47. Vasily Yershov, "Soviet War Preparation in 1941," Bakhmeteff Archive, Research Program on the USSR, Columbia University, 71–72. Despite its English-language title, the manuscript is typed in Russian.

48. *Ogonek*, no. 40 (1985), 14.

49. Koval'chuk, ed., *Ocherki istorii Leningrada*, 202. Comparing the mortality rate of party members to that of the city's general population is complicated by certain demographic factors. On the one hand, party members would be expected to have a relatively low death rate because they were not among the two age groups—infants and teenagers—that had the highest death rates; nor were they generally very old people, who also weakened quickly during the fall and winter. On the other hand, a high percentage of party members were men, who had higher mortality rates than did women.

50. L. S. Rubanov file, Bakhmeteff Archive, Columbia University, general manuscript collection, 12–14, 19.

51. *Biulleten' Leningradskogo soveta deputatov trudiashchikhsia* 5–6 (1942), 13; *Leningradskaia pravda*, 28 Mar., 12 and 15 May 1942; Amosov, "Rabochie Leningrada," 117; Tokarev et al., eds., *Deviat'sot geroicheskikh dnei*, 260–62; Karasev, *Leningradtsy v gody blokady*, 241; *Propaganda i agitatsiia* 9 (1942), 18; Shvetsov, "Deiatel'nost' Smol'ninskoi raionnoi," 220; Adamovich and Granin, *Blokadnaia kniga*, 118.

52. I. G. Meyerovich and Ia. G. Okulov, *Meropriiatiia Leningradskoi partiinoi organizatsii po snabzheniiu trudiashchikhsia v period blokady, 1941–1942 gg.* (Leningrad, 1959), 16; Karasev, *Leningradtsy v gody blokady*, 240, 243; Vazhentsev, *Vo glave geroicheskogo kollektiva*, 118.

53. *Trudovoe zakonodatel'stvo voennogo vremeni* (Moscow, 1943), 76.

54. S. V. Bilenko, *Na bessmennom postu* (Moscow, 1969), 31; M. E. Skriabin and I. K. Savchenko, *Neprimirimost': Stranitsy istorii Leningradskogo ugolovnogo rozyska* (Leningrad, 1988), 171. Both references are cited by I. V. Piterkin, "Leningradskie nozharnye komandy," unpublished doctoral candidate dissertation (Leningrad, 1989).

55. TsGAIPD SPb, f. 24, o. 2b, d. 5168, ll. 17–19, 24; Shvetsov, "Deiatel'nost' Smol'ninskoi raionnoi," 173.

56. Kochina's *Blockade Diary* is a rare first-hand account in which the author acknowledges complicity in the theft of food. She describes how in mid-January her husband stole about twenty pounds of buckwheat and a bar of coconut butter from a factory warehouse to prevent themselves and their infant daughter from starving to death. Kochina, *Blockade Diary*, 78–82.

57. Salisbury, *900 Days*, 450.

58. Arkhiv Upravleniia Federal'noi Sluzhby Bezopastnosti po g. Sankt-Peterbur-gu i Leningradskoi oblasti (former KGB archive), f. 1, o. 1, d. 118; Piterkin, "Lenin-gradskie," 140.

59. See Salisbury, *900 Days,* 452–53, 474–76, 478–81, for eyewitness accounts and rumors of cannibalism.

60. A. R. Dzeniskevich, ed., *Leningrad v osade: Sbornik dokumentov o geroicheskoi oborone Leningrada v gody Velikoi Otechestvennoi voiny, 1941–1944* (St. Petersburg, 1995), 421–22. The figure of fifteen hundred cannibals is cited by N. Iu. Cherepenina, an ar-chivist at the Tsentral'nyi Gosudarstvennyi Arkhiv Sankt-Peterburga (Central State Archive of St. Petersburg) in the television documentary "Russia's War: Blood upon the Snow," vol. 2 (PBS video, 1997).

61. Dzeniskevich, *Leningrad v osade,* 329.

62. In the commemorative newspaper *Kresti,* which was published on the one-hun-dredth anniversary of the founding of the prison bearing that name, S. Voloshin, a siege survivor, described seeing on one occasion fifteen to twenty cannibals eating corpses in broad daylight.

63. Yershov, "Soviet War Preparation in 1941," 40, 67.

64. TsGAIPD SPb, f. 4000, o. 10, d. 903, ll. 41–41a.

65. Ibid., f. 1012, o. 3, d. 53, ll. 27, 114, 153, 163–64.

66. Ibid., f. 24, o. 2v, d. 4819, ll. 1–4.

67. Ibid., d. 4921, l. 1.

68. Lomagin, "Nastroeniia zashchitnikov i naseleniia Leningrada," 224–26.

69. Yershov, "Soviet War Preparation in 1941," 77–78.

70. Ibid. I have not been able to confirm or deny Yershov's unpublished account in Russian archives or elsewhere. Other information from his rich and detailed memoir not relating directly to this demonstration has been verified.

71. For a more complete discussion of political attitudes during this period, see Rich-ard Bidlack, "The Political Mood in Leningrad during the First Year of the Soviet-German War," *Russian Review* 59:1 (Jan. 2000).

6

Muscovites' Moods, 22 June 1941 to May 1942

Mikhail M. Gorinov
Translated by Robert W. Thurston

When life hangs by a thread, human characteristics that are sometimes hard to discern in "normal" times become condensed and appear more sharply. This was the case in Moscow, located at the front for much of the period under study, which was the most tense of the entire war for the city. The popular mood will be explored in connection with three areas: (1) Muscovites' social composition; (2) living conditions, including food supply, heating, bombings, and the repressive actions of the state, as well as nonmaterial factors such as worldview, official information, and information passed informally from person to person; (3) people's remarks and expressions.

It is extremely difficult to discuss the "mood" of a city. Only a few diaries are available, and by and large the sources tend to emphasize dramatic events or statements. If we have fifty negative remarks about the regime, does that indicate widespread disloyalty, or is it a small number? The best way to approach the issue of how Muscovites felt about Stalinism and the war is to try to draw an overall picture of their responses to events, describing what they said and did.

Social and Demographic Dynamics of the City

The population of Moscow on the eve of the war was about 4,215,800. During the first three months of the fighting this figure remained stable, but in September 1941 the population rose to 4,236,200 as refugees arrived from areas seized by the Germans. Then, beginning in October, the population began to decrease, due to mobilization into the Red Army (altogether during the war more than 850,000 people from Moscow entered the armed forces) and evacuation, above all of children, women, and industrial workers, to the east.[1] In

Soviet citizens dig defense trenches on the outskirts of Moscow, fall 1941. (W0506/317; courtesy of the Bundesarchiv, Koblenz)

October the city's population amounted to 3,148,000 people, in November to 2,476,700, in December 2,243,900, and in January 1942, 2,027,818. The last figure was less than half of the total at the beginning of the war. Then in early 1942 some organizations began to return to the city; nonetheless, at the end of that year reevacuation assumed a mass character, and by early 1943 the city's population was 2,743,649.[2] Because of the evacuation of millions of children, the city became considerably more "adult."

Refugees from occupied zones did not make up the shortfall produced by evacuation. As a rule, refugees did not remain in Moscow; their arrival and subsequent departure from the capital were strictly monitored.[3] Close checking for violators of internal passport regulations and for deserters was also instituted. Between October 1941 and July 1942, 10,610 deserters were discovered, while 20,626 persons were detained for living in the city without official permission.[4]

Simultaneously, the portion of women in the population increased, although statistics on this point are not available. However, the bulletin of the staff of the German security police and the Sicherheitsdienst (SD) of 8 May 1942 noted, "Young men are rarely seen in Moscow, as already before Christmas a large mobilization into the army occurred. Many professions have become feminized. Not only is public transportation staffed by women, but also heavy, even the heaviest, male labor is frequently carried out by women."[5]

Another key change in the city's population was that the size of the Moscow Communist Party organization declined by more than 70 percent during 1941, from 173,000 in June to 50,000 in December. Communists entered the active army, comprised the heart of volunteer formations, and led the work of enterprises evacuated to the east.[6] The quality of the party cadres who remained probably also dropped, as the bravest left for the front.

Thus aging, feminization, and a decline in the level of political commitment proceeded rapidly in Moscow after 22 June. The number of socially and politically active residents raised by the communist regime and of the privileged workers of large enterprises gradually fell. The proportion of the most dedicated citizens, members of the party, decreased even more sharply. As the core groups supporting the communist regime gradually eroded, the proportion of people hurt by the state in some way or less fully politically recast under the influence of new ideas and institutions grew. Such types included those who had come to consciousness before the Revolution of 1917; workers of small, local industry, on the whole comprised of former artisans and peasants who had suffered discrimination under the new order; and those distinguished by a low level of social and political activity. Such changes had a major impact on Muscovites' attitudes toward the Stalinist regime.

Material Conditions in Moscow

The death rate reflected the dynamics of life in the city. The birth rate is less representative, as many husbands and virtually all pregnant women left the city. Mortality in Moscow from 1939 through June 1941 was in the range of ten to fifteen per thousand inhabitants. In 1939, 60,531 died in the city; in 1940, 67,520.

The number of deaths climbed significantly in the last three months of 1941. Altogether in that year 50,571 people died in Moscow. The death rate was particularly high in March, April, and May of 1942: twenty-five, thirty-four, and thirty-three persons per thousand respectively. In June 1942 the rate began to drop slowly, and by the end of the year it stood at twenty-four. Thus mortality in the spring of 1942 was twice as high as in the immediate prewar years. Throughout 1942, 82,284 people died, or 27.6 per thousand.

The rise in the death rate was partly due to the aging of the city's population but more to the worsening material conditions and additional stress of the war. Heart disease and problems in the circulatory system as causes of death rose sharply, from 12.6 percent in 1939 to 31.1 percent in 1942. Here too the age factor played a role. Deaths from tuberculosis increased significantly, from 5,517 in 1939 to 9,050 in 1942. However, the fact that the proportion of deaths from infectious diseases fell sharply speaks well of Moscow's doctors.

Food Supply — Until the middle of July 1941 the situation regarding food and consumer goods in Moscow was not marked by particular problems; the prewar system of trade continued to function. After 17 July a rationing system was introduced in the city for essential food items and manufactured goods.[7] Simultaneously "commercial" trade, that is, at market prices, was introduced in ninety-seven stores.[8]

At first the new system of supply functioned tolerably well, although some cheating occurred regarding ration coupons and food distribution. However, the quality of service declined. The physician A. G. Dreitser of the municipal emergency medical service noted in his diary on 8 August, "Food is more difficult to get. Ice cream is still sold everywhere. Elegant Moscow cafes have been transformed into oldtime taverns: tablecloths have disappeared, tin spoons have appeared, the waitresses have become ruder."[9]

People widely remembered the problems of the food supply in the years of the First World War and especially during the Civil War. Citizens now rushed to withdraw their savings from the banks to buy foodstuffs. However, the French military attaché in the capital reported to the Vichy government, "The population of Moscow remains very calm, but long lines are forming at the savings banks, at bakeries, and for kerosene."[10]

As the front drew nearer, the food situation naturally worsened. From mid-October 1941 we can follow its development daily, thanks to the diary of the journalist N. K. Verzhbitskii, who scrupulously noted "the trifles of everyday life": the supply situation, prices at the markets, and so on.[11] On 17 October he wrote, "in the vegetable stores there are only potatoes (for which there are lines) and lettuce (no lines). There is still vinegar. The newspapers still talk about a great supply of vegetables for Moscow." 18 October: "Stood in line for bread from 4 A.M. Got it at 9." 22 October: "I have numbers written on my palms, on my wrists, on the backs of my hands: 31, 62, 341, 5004. . . . These are my places in various lines. If you look around, you see that everyone has similar 'signs of the Antichrist.'" November 2: "Sales [in stores] at market prices have been ended everywhere." November 7: "A huge line for potatoes, kerosene, bread." Some food was available at the peasant markets, but at astronomical prices. One collective farmer offered a frozen turkey for 320 rubles—"an average month's pay for a worker."[12]

Speaking on 6 December to a meeting of the Moscow party committee, A. S. Shcherbakov, the head of the committee, remarked that in October and November supervision of food trade and distribution was "extremely weak." Stores wasted food, mainly bread, and sold it "without ration coupons, by subscription, by lists, and so forth." There was no "serious accounting for ration coupons or any kind of elementary accounting at all." Lines for food "can be explained only to a small degree by interruptions" in its delivery. More important was poor supervision of the trade and storage facilities by local government and party organizations. There were enough potatoes to meet established sales norms for several months, yet lines to purchase them appeared.[13]

Improvements in distribution did occur, in particular with the assignment of consumers to certain stores. V. P. Pronin, the chairman of the city soviet (council) and in effect its mayor, later claimed, "This permitted [us] to liquidate lines and raised the level of responsibility of retail employees."[14] In December the supply situation was tolerable. Yet Verzhbitskii noted a checkered story. On 17 December commercial sales reopened at the Eliseev grocery, perhaps Moscow's most famous store. "A kilogram of meat is 80 rubles, a kilo of sugar 50 rubles. A kilo of butter is 120 rubles." On 31 December he wrote, "2 bottles of wine have been given out to each Muscovite. But many did not receive the alloted amount of meat and butter in December." In January the picture worsened in connection with curtailing of food deliveries to the city. On 6 January Verzhbitskii found no sales in the city at market prices.[15]

Meanwhile, rations were cut sharply. Verzhbitskii wrote on 16 January: "The bread norm for workers has been lowered to 600 grams, for employees—to 500. Children and invalids receive 400." Some relatively expensive food was still available, however; 24 January: "In restaurants trading at commercial prices, it is possible to get a meal for 4–5 rubles (meat soup, roast fish with potatoes). People stand in line for 3–4 hours." 11 February: "A kilogram of radishes from the collective farmers—25 rubles!" By this time the government often could not honor the population's ration coupons. "Employees, invalids, and children have still not received meat for the second ten days of January. Kerosene is still being given out for coupon number 1 of January. Potatoes are still not released for the second half of January. The situation is becoming extremely hard." This picture continued through March: "For the whole month we received 800 grams of salt and 400 grams of fish. That's all! . . . Good potatoes from the kolkhozniks cost 50 rubles a kilo . . . frozen ones are 20–25 rubles— that is, slime." Customers traded goods for potatoes: a pair of boots for eight kilograms, a saw for five, and so on.[16]

A note from Shcherbakov and Pronin to the Council of Ministers of the

USSR about the food supply for the city, dated 2 April 1942, confirms Verzh-bitskii's observations. "In the month of March the population of the city of Moscow received full rations only for flour and sugar. Meat products were given out for February coupons [as follows]: to workers 1,500 grams of a norm of 2,200; employees 700 of 1,200; invalids 200 of 600; children 200 of 600. Fats were insufficiently released for February coupons: workers [lacked] 100 grams, employees 100 grams. Fish and fish products were not given out for February coupons." As of 1 April the city's grain reserve amounted to one day's supply. Moscow teetered on the edge of starvation.

In this connection the municipal party committee and the executive committee of the city soviet asked the Council of Ministers to take essential measures: "Require the Commissariat of Communications to provide trains with flour, grain, meal, freight cars with meat, sugar, and fish and to send them to Moscow under the rules of military shipments." The local bodies also asked the government to release meat and butter for the city from the state reserves and to create stations in the countryside dedicated to gathering food for Moscow, to be staffed by representatives of the Defense Committee of the USSR, the central coordinating organ for the war effort.[17]

These steps were taken and soon produced positive results. Verzhbitskii wrote on 27 April: "A great supply of food in the stores. They have given out salmon, red caviar, and suet. The March lateness [in covering rations] has been eliminated." Although he reported that the sugar ration was reduced in May, he could also say that "in general, supplies have noticeably improved."[18]

Heating — An extremely difficult situation also developed in Moscow in the winter of 1941–42 regarding fuel. In their report to N. A. Voznesenskii of 26 May 1942, Pronin and Shcherbakov noted, "Because of the acute shortage of fuel in Moscow in the winter of 1942 there were serious interruptions in the work of industrial enterprises and in heating for housing, hospitals, baths, and laundries. Because of the lack of coal and firewood, hundreds of industrial enterprises stood idle for months; 2,400 major apartment buildings were not heated for three months."[19]

Oksana Sobchuk, a schoolgirl who was thirteen or fourteen at the time, somehow kept herself, her two-year-old brother, their cat, and their goldfish alive without heat through a Moscow winter after her mother had to enter a hospital. Each day when Oksana left for school, she would tuck her brother into bed, arrange cushions for the cat, and place a blanket over the fish tank. They cooked nothing, but ate bread side by side on a couch until spring.[20]

Bombing — The Moscow regional antiaircraft defense logged attacks on the capital by 7,146 German airplanes in the first six months of the war; 229 aircraft broke through to the city. But data from the Local Antiaircraft Defense, responsible for coping with the consequences of attacks, show that seven hundred German planes appeared over the city in the same period. The difference in the figures can be explained by the different orientations of the two organizations as well as by the difficulty in counting enemy planes, which carried out their flights mostly at night.

The first attack took place during the night of 21–22 July. For the whole war, air-raid alarms sounded in Moscow 141 times. Breakthroughs by German aviation to the city occurred only in 1941–42. During air attacks 7,708 people were casualties, of whom 2,196 died. While putting out fires and conducting rescue work, 476 soldiers and commanders of the Local Antiaircraft Defense were casualties.[21]

In the first five months of the war alone, 402 apartment buildings were destroyed.[22] The intensity of bombing attacks is indicated by statistics on the number of people who sought shelter in the metro (subway) system (see table 6.1). During October and November, when the Germans were at the gates of the city, there were five or six raids every twenty-four hours.[23] As the Germans were thrown back from Moscow in 1942, the number of air attacks fell sharply.

Muscovites quickly became accustomed to bombings. As A. G. Dreitser, a physician, remembered, on

> 8 August 1941 the air-raid sirens sounded. The populace quickly and deftly put out the lights. . . . At 11 in the evening a call to the Sokol metro station. Down below people lie in four rows, mostly women and children. They lie in careful order. Each family has its area. They spread out newspapers, then blankets and pillows. Children sleep, adults amuse themselves in various ways. They drink tea, even with jam. They visit each other. They talk quietly. They play dominoes. There are several pairs of chess players, surrounded by "fans." Many read books, knit, darn stockings, repair linens—in a word, they were set up well and for a long time. Places are permanent, "subscribed." Along both sides of the tunnel stand trains, where on the seats small children sleep.[24]

Gradually overcoming their fear, Muscovites learned to work under the blows of the bombs without descending into the shelters. N. A. Astrov, a tank designer and engineer, witnessed this development: "They bombed the city, but the designers and the copyists did not leave work. They halted for a while, burying their noses in the drawing boards. If the bombs fell close by, the girl

Table 6.1. Muscovites Taking Shelter in Metro
Stations from Bombing, 1941

	Maximum in a 24-Hour Period	Totals
July (8 days)	350,000	2,900,000
August (8 days)	370,000	2,800,000
September	220,000	1,400,000
October	220,000	2,100,000
November	270,000	2,700,000
December	80,000	400,000

Source: "Spravka o rabote Moskovskogo metropolitena v voennykh usloviiakh," MV, 460.

copyists cried from fear, the tears landing on the inked tracings, making black pools. It was necessary to change the tracings and start to copy again. No one left work."[25]

Repressive Policy of the Government

One of the factors that acted most strongly on the mood of Muscovites and on their opportunities to express themselves was repression by the state. The Stalinist punitive-repressive system was one of the most effective in world history. It did not lose its qualities in the war years.

In the first hours of the war, the police adopted a plan for active measures regarding security in the city and the surrounding area. The document called for arrests for signs of "terrorism, diversions, wrecking, German, Italian, Japanese, or other espionage, bacteriological diversions, Trotskyites, former members of anti-Soviet political parties, antiwar sectarians, and various antisoviet elements." One thousand seventy-seven persons were designated for arrest as a preventive measure. In addition, 230 ordinary criminals were to be removed from the area. These measures were prepared or taken in the space of several hours.[26]

The "competent organs" monitored the appearance of "anti-Soviet, counterrevolutionary, or defeatist" sentiments extremely carefully. People whose "incorrect" conversations were reported were usually arrested. A certain halt to this procedure occurred, apparently, only in the critical days of mid-October 1941. Verzhbitskii noted in his diary for 18 October, "Conversations are heard which 3 days ago would have led to a tribunal."[27]

Obviously this "weakening" did not last long. On 20 October martial law was declared in Moscow and the surrounding regions. One of the points in the decree of the State Defense Committee read: "Violators of order will be quickly brought to answer before the court of the Military tribunal, and provocateurs, spies, and other enemy agents attempting to undermine order will be shot on the spot."[28]

This military tribunal was organized under an order of the Moscow Military District of 23 October 1941 on the basis of the Moscow city court and people's courts in the city. The tribunal began to function on 27 October, at the peak of danger from the Germans and in the midst of attendant panic. By 1 December, 3,528 cases had been heard in the tribunal, resulting in 3,338 convictions. Sixty-nine received the death sentence and 213 received ten-year sentences of confinement. Unfortunately, specific figures on the number convicted for anti-Soviet agitation or other "political" crimes are not available, but it would appear that most offenses were for violations of rules on masking lights, labor regulations, and other less serious matters. Only fourteen people were convicted of spreading false rumors by early December.[29]

Data are available on the work of the tribunal for the first quarter of 1942. Of 727 people brought to the court for counterrevolutionary agitation, 695 were convicted, while 15 were acquitted and 17 cases were ended because the accused were deemed incompetent. Of those convicted, 201 were sentenced to shooting; 494 received various terms of deprivation of liberty, including 325 who got ten years.

What was considered "counterrevolutionary agitation" in the first quarter of 1942? According to the document, these cases involved

> a) praise of fascism and Hitler and simultaneous expression of slanderous thoughts on measures of the Soviet government; b) praise of the fascist army and simultaneous expression of a defeatist mood regarding the Red Army; c) slanderous expressions in regard to the leader of the peoples [Stalin] and the leaders of the party and the state; d) expression of evil slanders about the measures of the Soviet authority on collectivization of agriculture, on raising labor discipline in production; e) slanderous expressions about the difficult conditions of labor and the low material situation of laboring people in the Soviet Union.[30]

If we bear in mind how difficult the circumstances at the front were for the Soviet Union at the time, how collectivization of the peasantry had been carried out, and what the standard of living was, then an objective assessment of the situation might bring severe punishment, even shooting. The reader must decide whether such harsh sanctions were justified in the conditions of a prefrontal city.

Here are data from a report of the administration of the commandant of the city of Moscow on the implementation of martial law for the period from 20 October 1941 through July 1942: 830,060 people were detained altogether; 13 were shot on the spot for anti-Soviet agitation; 906 were charged with spreading treasonous rumors; 887 were sentenced to death for all types of crimes; and 44,168 were deprived of liberty for various lengths of time.[31]

These draconian measures helped ensure that during the war there were no massive antistate or collaborationist efforts in Moscow, even in October 1941. No sabotage has been uncovered.

The Dynamics of Nonmaterial Factors

The most important factors of this type that influenced Muscovites' outlook were (1) worldview and attitude toward Soviet power; (2) official information, including Soviet propaganda, German propaganda, and stories of witnesses from both sides of the front regarding the conduct of Soviet authorities and the situation in the occupied regions and at the scene of fighting; (3) unofficial information such as letters and messages on the fate of relatives and loved ones at the front, in evacuation, and so forth.

Worldview

The successful formation of divisions of the popular militia and other volunteer units, the active participation of the populace in building defensive perimeters, and other measures indicate that most Muscovites complied with the regime. Of course the relationship between patriotic and personal behavioral impulses, particularly fear of punishment, varied in the motivation of individuals and social groups. The mobilizational program of the authorities was accepted, although with some grinding of teeth. If widespread antistate feelings had existed among the population, then when enemy troops stood literally at the gates of the capital the popular mood would have erupted into massive anticommunist discontent despite all the power of the punitive-repressive machine. However, the situation of Petrograd during the Revolution of 1917, on which the Germans evidently counted, was not repeated in Moscow in 1941.

Official Information

Sources speak of the public's sense of an information "famine." The writer Konstantin Simonov described Stalin's speech of 3 July 1941 as "at the edge of the huge gap between the official communications of the newspapers and the actual immense territory already seized by the Germans."[32] N. K. Verzhbitskii wrote in his diary on 16 October 1941, "A lively old man on the street asked, 'Why didn't anyone speak on the radio. . . . Just let them say something. . . . Miraculous, good, no matter. . . . But we are completely in a fog, and each one thinks for himself.'"[33]

People tried to make up for the deficit of trustworthy information by repeating unsubstantiated tales, for example on the "arrest" of the defense commissar, S. K. Timoshenko (which did not occur), or on the "treason" of the army command staff at the beginning of July. Purely fantastic rumors making the rounds in Moscow also bear on this point, for instance that the first German flights over Moscow were led by the Soviet Arctic explorer S. A. Levanevskii, who disappeared without a trace on a flight across the North Pole in 1937.[34]

Soviet Propaganda

As the chapter in this volume by Aileen G. Rambow shows, during the war this area underwent significant changes, especially the gradual replacement of the old accent on communist doctrine and the class struggle by a focus on national traditions and patriotism.

The quality of Soviet propaganda gradually improved. In the early period of the war, in view of the catastrophic situation at the front, propaganda was in a difficult position: reality was too bitter in contrast to the prewar model of conflict ("little blood, [fought] on foreign territory"). In the summer of 1941 the population's skeptical attitude toward official information appeared frequently, along with bewilderment at its lack of concreteness or its falsehood. As N. A. Astrov remembered, "The first alarming, not completely concrete communications of Sovinformburo appeared. . . . And soon after a series of reports that 'at the front nothing of great importance has happened,' Sovinformburo said that our forces had left the city of Minsk. That happened on 29 June, such a short time after the beginning of the war that it seemed unbelievable and crazy."[35] The special reports of the Commissariat of State Security for Moscow and Moscow oblast' on the populace's reaction to Stalin's speech of 3 July noted dubious remarks. "The situation at the front is more serious than Stalin said. . . . Here, as always, we with our usual efficiency are rushing to the showy side. [But] the USSR is on the eve of decisive events," wrote an editor of the Exercise and Tourism publishing house.[36] The municipal Communist Party committee reported on 9 July 1941, "At factory number 32 (October raion), the skilled worker Kalinin said, 'Our [leaders] only babble, but they give up cities. If everyone wrote the truth, it would be better.'"[37]

The quality of propaganda went up according to the improvement of affairs at the front; it became possible to write the truth. The physician E. Sakharova illustrated this point:

> 6 January 1942 . . . Our newspapers have become very interesting, you read them with the gripping desire to take in everything that's there. . . . Today there was a very interesting radio speech by [the British foreign minister Sir Anthony] Eden about his trip to the USSR, which even had a touch of poetry about it. The Americans are noting our victories and adding that they should not be complacent about them but should also take an active role [in helping us], that our front, of course, is the main one and the most difficult.[38]

As the fighting approached, the quantity of unofficial information that confirmed official accounts grew, for example the stories of refugees, among whom were relatives from around Moscow.[39] As this happened and as the regime inside the capital became more severe, the influence of German propaganda spread through radio, posters, and agitators dropped. In the first period of the war, until October and November, tones of approval of German radio transmissions and fliers were fairly frequent. The gist of German propaganda was that "we are fighting not with the Russian people but with the Jews and the communists."[40] Such expressions later became increasingly rare.

Changes in Morale and Mood in the City

After Molotov's radio address, delivered at noon on the day of the attack, meetings took place at Moscow enterprises in which "workers, employees, and ITR spoke with agitation of the bald, robbing activity of German fascism and swore to the party, the government, and to Comrade Stalin personally that they would apply all their efforts to achieve victory," according to a typical phrase from party reports of the gatherings.[41]

In the first day or two of the war the sources do not indicate major problems with the appearance of newly mobilized soldiers for duty, and thousands of Muscovites applied for voluntary enlistment in the army. A report on mobilization prepared by State Security and the Commissariat of Internal Affairs for the assistant commissar, V. S. Abakumov, on 24 June found that army induction was "proceeding in an organized manner in the regions of the city of Moscow and in Moscow oblast'."[42] In twenty-nine regions, 3,519 men had already requested immediate enlistment. Many memoirs emphasize a patriotic upsurge from the first days of the war that was not extinguished during its duration.[43] But the real picture was more multifaceted.

In some district military committees, the call-up evoked "negative expressions."[44] Several men, for example a senior engineer from the Hammer and

Sickle factory, even spoke against the induction at the mobilization points. Other men carried out "defeatist agitation," and several arrests occurred.[45]

A special summary report of 26 June on mobilization by the administration of the NKGB and NKVD for Moscow and the oblast' to B. Z. Kobulov, the assistant head of state security for the USSR, was far from wholly positive. The document started not with a declaration of success but with a reference to "scattered difficulties." If on 24 June two instances of refusal to serve in the army were noted, on 26 June "cases of lack of discipline and refusal of service" were reported in "a certain portion" of the inductees. Several men had injured themselves to avoid the draft; one had committed suicide. In October raion only 814 of 1,800 men had appeared as scheduled for mobilization on 24 June. Perhaps this can be explained wholly or partly by poor work among the district military officials. The document says nothing about such problems, although later in the text it reports inefficiency in several other districts, for instance long lines of inductees and tardiness in dispatching units once they had formed, as a result of which the oblast' and city military authorities did not secure the appearance of 1,772 draftees. The document makes no mention of volunteers, but it does speak of increased cases of "hooligan and criminal" actions. For 21 to 22 June only seven cases of hooliganism were registered, but twenty-three were noted on 23 June, among which were three incidents involving knives.[46] It is possible that this increase was a result of drunkenness, a typical accompaniment to induction into the army.[47]

Party organizations and organs of internal affairs and state security that followed the reactions of the population at the beginning of the war found overwhelmingly patriotic expressions. But there were also conversations of a different sort. Information passed by the police organs to A. S. Shcherbakov on 23 June mentions a series of "negative" comments by Muscovites on the first day of the war. "It's good that the war has begun," said one Makarova, a female factory worker. "Life in the USSR has become unbearable. Forced labor and hunger bother everyone, there should be an end to all this." Spund, a former member of the old oppositionist Socialist Revolutionary Party, said, "this war was begun by our government with the goal of diverting the attention of the broad masses from the dissatisfaction that has overtaken the people due to the existing dictatorship." Other comments were less than positive but not necessarily disloyal: "We do not have a strong, solid rear [behind the front lines], people are embittered, and there will be conflicts inside the country that will complicate the course of events. The war will be difficult and bloody," said Lokshina, another female worker.[48]

Defeatist remarks also surfaced. N. A. Astrov noted that the "level of alarm" had risen. "The retreat was similar to flight and showed that we didn't know how to fight, we had nothing to fight with. . . . Then, in the first months, the mood among us all was terrible, particularly because it was necessary to hide this feeling."[49]

A police report to Shcherbakov of 3 July on popular response to Stalin's radio address noted a sharp polarization of mood. The largest quantity of remarks cited in the report indicated that among part of Moscow's citizenry the speech evoked a "new flood of patriotism, energy, and the will to fight." But another group took Stalin's call to create militia forces and a partisan movement as a gesture of despair recognizing the destruction of the Red Army, a response that strengthened defeatist feelings. No other negative responses were noted.[50]

Konstantin Simonov, recalling the gamut of feelings produced in him by Stalin's speech—the gap between official communications and the actual successes of the Germans, the abandonment of the illusion of a quick encircling counterattack by Soviet troops—noted, "most important . . . I felt that this was a speech hiding nothing, concealing nothing, relating the truth to the end, and telling it the only way it could be told in such circumstances. That made me glad. It seemed that to tell such bitter truth in such painful circumstances meant to bear witness to one's strength. . . . It pleased me and touched my heart to hear the address 'My friends!' This had not been heard in our speeches for a long time."[51]

Thus the harsh, truthful speech by Stalin shook up the population and redirected its attention from internal problems to external ones: the struggle with aggression. It focused the expectations of society on the war.

In the party reports for July through September 1941 published by R. G. Grigor'ev, the overwhelming majority of recorded remarks by citizens concern purely military subjects: the situation at the front, poor food for the soldiers of the active army, treason among the commanding staff as a reason for the defeats of soviet forces, the "arrest" of Timoshenko, and so on. Among social and political topics, antikolkhoz expressions were frequent, as in hopes that the Germans would abolish the kolkhoz system. Often the idea appeared, with reference to German sources, that ordinary people had nothing to fear from the occupation, that only Jews and communists would suffer (once this was said with sympathy for the "outcasts"). In fact, the anti-Semitic aspect prevailed over the anticommunist one; part of the population accused the Jews of avoiding military service and work. Hopes for an improvement of the material situation with the coming of the Germans were expressed.

The social situation of those voicing negative thoughts varied considerably, from ordinary workers and a truck driver to a printer, the instructor of a department of social insurance, and the assistant head of a department of the central committee of unions of political-educational institutions.[52] In any event, a significant portion of the populace, dissatisfied with its political and social position, looked unfavorably on Soviet power.

The sources leave the impression that often in the first days of the war Muscovites expressed anti-Soviet thoughts frankly, though the expectation of anticommunist outbreaks was muffled. The catastrophe at the front, about which the populace guessed, and the harshness of the security organs' actions clearly had an impact on the consolidation of strength on the part of those dissatisfied with the communist regime and on the transference of their hopes for its defeat from forces within to the German army. Given the early military defeats, this response was probably optimal for the state authorities: an internal front did not arise.

But we are not yet in a position to make general conclusions about Muscovites' loyalty or antipathy to the regime. A host of other, changing factors affected feelings.

The Period of the German Attack on Moscow (October–November)

The bulletin of the German security police staff and the SD of 8 May 1942 noted, "In the critical October days of 1941 the population showed a keen anti–Soviet regime attitude because of the incompetence of Soviet authorities, who saved themselves, leaving the populace to the whim of fate."[53] Is this appraisal fair? During the night of 15 October, after the city's people heard the GKO's order "On evacuation of the capital of the USSR, Moscow," a hurried exodus began of a series of organizations and institutions (the government, the administration of the General Staff, military academies, people's commissariats, embassies, factories, and so on) to the interior of the country. The biggest factories, electrical stations, bridges, and the metro were mined. Sale to workers and employees of flour and grain above the norm of one pood (16.27 kilograms) and giving out more than a month's pay in advance were prohibited. Due to the massive flight of leaders of enterprises and organizations, the halting of the metro, and the absence of information, the measures taken by the authorities produced doubt, dissatisfaction, upset, and confusion among part of the population.[54]

Documents of this period give the impression that ordinary people often displayed more heroism than the leadership at the lower and middle levels, especially during the days of "panic" in the autumn. That many Soviet officials and administrators abandoned the population may be explained to a great extent by the weakening of Moscow party organizations in the first months of the war. During 16–18 October, incomplete data show, "of 438 enterprises, institutions, and organizations, 779 leading employees fled. . . . The flight of some heads of enterprises and institutions was accompanied by major thefts of valuable materials and the appropriation of property. . . 1,484,000 rubles in cash, valuables and property worth 1,051,000 rubles. Hundreds of light automobiles and trucks were removed."[55]

The old secret policeman B. Ia. Chmelev remarked,

> The only road that still linked Moscow with other cities of the country was the one to Riazan'. All the others were either cut off by the Germans or were being strafed. Stores were already being looted, above all jewelry ones, and our groups were already apprehending the scoundrels. I remember that we sent to a tribunal one such thief, who had tried to take away two suitcases full of gold and diamonds in a child's pram. . . . Two full suitcases! . . . Doubt appeared among people that Moscow would be able to hold out, and the people fled from the city. Everyone was dressed any which way. They picked up any kind of small suitcases, briefcases, bags, and stuffed in any kind of old junk. The people walked in a wave along the Riazan' highway. The departure from Moscow began. . . . That lasted three days, no more—from the 16th until the 20th of October.[56]

G. V. Reshetin remembered that his factory was ordered to be ready for evacuation on 14 October, but on that day the administrators had already gone. Workers angrily demanded their pay. Finally they received some money and were told that they could follow the bosses to Tashkent on their own. Reshetin detailed a disturbing scene of departure from the city.

> On 16 October Enthusiasts' Highway was full of fleeing people. Noise, cries, racket. People moved to the east, in the direction of Gorky. . . . The Il'ych Gates. There begins the Enthusiasts' Highway. Around the square swirled posters and pieces of paper, trash, it smelled of burning. People here and there are stopping automobiles heading for the highway. They pull out the riders, beat them, throw their things around, strewing them about the ground. Voices cry out, 'Beat the Jews.' . . . I never would have believed such a story if I had not seen it myself. We had Jews at school, but I don't remember any open, clear examples of anti-Semitism. There were some quips, not malicious, more jokes than anything, nothing more. That's why these wild reprisals against the Jews, and not only against them, on 16 October 1941 at the Il'ych Gates shook me up so much.[57]

. N. K. Verzhbitskii noted on 17 October that workers were bitter toward the absent bosses and party members. No one knew who was responsible for the order to close the factories and pay off the workers.

Who is the author of all this mess, this general flight, this confusion in our minds?
. . . The hysteria above reached down to the masses. They began to remember and
count up all the insults, oppression, injustices, pressure, bureaucratic machinations of officialdom, contempt and self-puffery of party members, draconian
orders, deprivations, systematic deception of the masses, the newspapers' bray-
ing self-congratulations. . . . It is terrible to hear. People speak from the heart. Can
a city really hold out when it's in such a mood?

Verzhbitskii also described chaos and violence on "the shameful Highway of
the Enthusiasts."[58]

A further report on the situation came from the head of the NKVD administration for the city of Moscow and Moscow oblast', M. I. Zhuravlev, who
wrote that on "16 and 17 October 1941 in a series of industrial enterprises of
Moscow and Moscow oblast' one part of the workers exhibited anarchistic
tendencies." How was this "anarchism" expressed? Workers demanded the pay
they were owed, did not permit the departure from Moscow of directing employees, got drunk, looted property (mainly alcohol), and tried to break equipment. Altogether thirty-nine "incidents" were counted. Of them only four, and
only by a strained interpretation, can be considered political:

1. On 17 October, after getting drunk the day before with two friends, the
   fitter Nekrasov of the Moscow motorcycle factory "together with these
   same persons conducted at the garage of the factory counterrevolutionary agitation of a pogrom character, calling on the workers to destroy the
   Jews."
2. "At factory number 8 (Mytishchinskii raion) about 1,000 workers tried
   to enter the courtyard. Some people then carried out sharp counterrevolutionary agitation and demanded that the factory be cleared of mines."
3. "On 16 October at factory number 58, after no pay was given out, workers walked about in a crowd, demanding money. Some workers cried,
   'Beat the communists' and others."
4. "On 17 October in Bronnitskii raion at the villages of Nikulino and Tor-
   opovo in some houses of kolkhozniki at two o'clock white flags were hung
   out."[59]

These were the four of thirty-nine cases that might be termed political, and
two of these were in Moscow oblast', not in the city.

Thus it is hardly correct to politicize the tragic events of mid-October 1941
or to speak, as did the Germans, of "the appearance of an anti-Soviet mood
in the population." There was no uprising against the regime. The unrest of
the masses was produced essentially by the wholesale desertion by the middle

level leadership, as a rule members of the Communist Party, who abandoned their collectives and enterprises. The *narod* was not the original source of panic. As Verzhbitskii correctly remarked, the hysteria was passed to the masses "from above"; in this way the "flight from Moscow" was initiated by the leaders of the factories, having suggested by their own efforts that workers evacuate to the east. In fact, the basic manifestations of "hysteria" (panic?) were not anti-Soviet uprisings but (1) suppression of the desertion of the leadership and (2) the mass exodus from Moscow, which illustrated the desire of the overwhelming portion of Muscovites not to remain under the occupiers.

Other, more positive behavior also appeared in those days. L. Kolodnyi remembered that, "Moscow looked different from its [usual] self, people streamed into the center, along the main streets, and headed for the Kremlin: the outskirts were empty of inhabitants."[60] That is, part of the population left under the threat of occupation, but part, concentrated in the center of the city, prepared to fight to the end.

Muscovites' mood was judged correctly in the Kremlin, it seems. According to the testimony of the commissar of the aviation industry, A. I. Shakhurin, who called to see Stalin on 16 October, the *vozhd'* expected the worst. Having heard about the situation in the city, he ordered the end of the extreme measures—evacuation and mining of enterprises—taken the night before.[61] Wasn't it the brave conduct of ordinary Muscovites, in contrast to a significant part of the leadership, that was the decisive factor that changed the course of events? Wasn't this conduct the final argument that persuaded Stalin that it was possible to hold Moscow? This change in thinking explains the difference between the order of the GKO of 15 October and the one issued four days later, which entailed martial law and shooting provocateurs on the spot.

The German source of May 1942 noted that soon Soviet propaganda again succeeded "in bringing under its complete control the mood of the population. In general, thoughts about the fall of Moscow were no longer permitted."[62] K. R. Sinilov, the commandant of the Kremlin, believed, "From the 19th [of October 1941] the city lived more or less a normal life." There was widespread popular support and participation in monitoring letters, conversations, any signaling, and in apprehending "all violators of public order." Without this participation, he commented, "probably we would not have succeeded in maintaining such order." A wide range of citizens wrote to him with ideas on how to manage the city.[63]

The change in popular mood was strengthened—it went from doubt and defeatism to firmness and confidence in victory, bolstered by the historic parade on Red Square on 7 November 1941 and the speeches of I. V. Stalin on 6 and 7 November. Considerable testimony exists on the mobilizing and inspiring effect of the parade on the population.[64] For example, Sinilov recalled that before the parade some of the letters he received "had an air of lack of confidence, and in some there was a palpable feeling that we could hardly hold Moscow. In some there were even indications—true, such letters were very few—that it was not right to put children and old people in danger; wouldn't it be possible in general not to withhold Moscow [from the enemy], not to put up resistance." After the parade such letters came no longer; the people became "completely different," full of confidence.[65]

Stalin's speeches had a dramatic effect. Moscow's military censors checked 2,626,507 items of correspondence, all of the mail posted, between 1 and 15 November; 3,214 were confiscated, and part of the text was blackened out in 30,532 other pieces. The correspondence on the whole evinced "positive sentiments." In 75 percent of the documents there was a particular rise in mood produced by Stalin's words. There were also negative remarks connected with difficulties in finding work, getting food, or evacuation. In both incoming and outgoing mail there were anti-Semitic remarks by civilians and Red Army soldiers, as the population was upset by the perceived massive flight of Jews from Moscow.[66] But political dissatisfaction and defeatist attitudes were absent from the letters.

More or less the same picture obtained for the review of correspondence between 15 November and 1 December. Of 2,505,786 pieces of mail, 3,698 were confiscated, and some part of the text was censored in 26,276. Again, citizens expressed generally positive attitudes. In mail from soldiers on active duty were some negative comments connected with food and lack of warm clothing. Some "anti-Soviet" expressions also occurred, such as doubt in the victory of the Red Army, or the belief that from "the German nothing bad will happen. He does not do anything [bad] to anyone." All such correspondence was confiscated. Some analogous remarks came from the civilian population; these had to do with the difficult food supply. Many letters from Moscow related trouble finding work.[67] Thus the correspondence contained complaints of a purely everyday nature. It is possible that the localization of "negative expressions" almost exclusively in the sphere of everyday social life is partially explained by the "feminization" of the city; women, as a rule, were less politicized than men.

The testimony of an independent witness is curious. The French military attaché to Turkey, Duval, prepared a report in December 1941 to the French General Staff. He relied on materials from the French trade attaché in Moscow, Brias. Referring to the mobilization of Muscovites into the army, construction of defensive barriers, and evacuation to the east, Duval remarked,

> In the city two to three million people remain, who will be armed according to military necessity. The food supply is strictly limited to the minimum necessary, but it operates in an orderly way through the coupon system. Everyone receives a ration of black bread, sausage, cabbage, and tea. Meat, butter, eggs, tobacco—these are rarities. The general mobilization of the population of Moscow was carried out brilliantly thanks to the firm but capable and careful measures ordered by Stalin and Beria. Pronin, chair of the Moscow Soviet, was a great help to them. The administrative apparatus functioned without a hitch. However, the population over the age of 20 is accustomed to discipline under the Soviet regime. In the city there are no disorders, despite the air attacks and the absence of police (*militsiia*), who were suddenly mobilized and for the most part sent to the front during the panic of 15–18 October. A new military police was created. Women's batallions, sent to the labor front, have a military bearing. In military detachments, which constantly move about the city, there are also women, whose number reaches about 10 percent.[68]

The Period of the Soviet Counterattack (December–May)

On 5 and 6 December the Red Army's counterattack began before Moscow. How did the population react to it? An extremely interesting source is the communications of leading party groups prepared for "special work" behind the lines. In the fall of 1941, in connection with the threat that the enemy would seize Moscow, many party and Komsomol organizations began to prepare for illegal work under the German occupiers. After the Soviet counterattack the "special work" groups were preserved; their tasks now included following the mood of Muscovites. In these organizations' crude reports entire conversations are recorded as well as discussions of speeches. The compilers of the reports took down information in the most informal circumstances: lines, public baths, and so on.

In December the general tone of the reports reflects the joy of Muscovites and their growing confidence in victory. The population on the whole greeted with understanding the government's decision to set up a lottery with money and goods as prizes. A fifty-year-old housewife said, "All this money [in profits from the lottery] will go to the Red Army. I welcome this lottery and will be the first to sign up. My sister experienced on her own back and saw how the fascists took everything down to thread, they even took blankets away from nursing infants in front of everybody—so it's really possible to sacrifice something in order to destroy these scoundrels."[69]

Together with similar positive remarks, the reports indicate that Muscovites were practically in despair over the food situation. Obviously the threat of famine again promoted anti-Soviet statements, which had been dampened for a time. On 24 December a woman wearing a Red Army uniform said,

> I'm sick of fighting. I carry an automatic weapon, and I always have a bullet ready for myself. It's bad to be taken prisoner by the Germans, and if you run away from the front, they shut you up in the Stalin camps, you'll be a foresaken person. To end up in the Stalin camps, that's like being in German ones. It would be better to put a bullet in your forehead. Sometimes you think: and what are we fighting for, what have millions of young lives gone for? You think and you don't know. I am a party member. . . . I feel that all the weight of this damned war lies on the shoulders of the working class alone. Do you think that it doesn't affect the army when in Moscow they only talk and are well fed?[70]

Here was a mix of feelings that may have occurred to even the most dedicated citizen at times, along with the soldier's traditional scorn in any nation for those who "only talked" behind the lines.

In a report to Beria on the popular reaction to the defeat of Hitler's forces around Moscow on 30 December 1941, M. I. Zhuravlev affirmed that the successful "actions of the Red Army have strengthened even more the confidence in the city of Moscow and Moscow oblast' in the inevitable destruction of the fascist hordes." Yet a good many remarks were recorded with the theme that "it's too early to be happy about [our] successes."[71]

In the following months the food supply approached disaster. The winter witnessed a growth in antipeasant expressions among the city's citizens. Thus December's calm doubts about the future had given way by spring to a confiscatory mentality, a communist-egalitarian ethos toward the peasants. At the markets urban dwellers referred to "speculators' prices" and cursed the kolkhozniki as "fleecers."[72]

The food issue held first place by a wide margin among "negative communications" exised by the military censorship in March and April 1942. The second most important concern was light, water, and fuel; third was the exchange of manufactured goods for food; fourth was housing. "Anti-Soviet manifestations" did not figure prominently in the letters; perhaps the populace in general avoided such "delicate questions" in correspondence. Altogether in March the military censors of the Second Special Department of the NKVD checked 8,489,275 pieces of mail departing from Moscow; 142,382 (1.87 percent) contained negative remarks; 14,119 were confiscated. In April the total examined was up by almost two million; 1.08 percent featured negative comments, and 11,475 letters were confiscated.[73] Thus the number of items with negative expressions fell by 42.5 percent from March to April. This trend was probably connected with improvement in the food supply.

In general the sources give the impression that in April and May, as a result of successes at the front, a decline in attacks by enemy aviation, and the overcoming of the food and fuel crisis, life in Moscow stabilized and moved into a more or less normal pattern. A bulletin of the staff of the German security police and the SD of 8 May 1942 stated, "Life in Moscow in its external appearance does not differ much from the prewar situation."[74]

The general stabilization was reflected in Muscovites' state of mind. According to the data of the special work groups, the city's residents found their situation fully satisfactory and were prepared to bear further deprivations in the future in order to achieve victory over the enemy. Anti-Soviet phenomena had practically ended, though some resentment toward collective farmers and their pricing practices lingered among workers.[75]

❖ ❖ ❖

As the German invasion began, Muscovites displayed a wide range of reactions. In the first day or two, at least externally citizens expressed patriotic altruism, shown in the quick course of mobilization, the number of volunteers for the army, and statements at meetings. Later, however, such conduct often yielded to more individualistic behavior; some of the men who were called up tried to avoid service, and people demonstrated a widespread desire to save themselves from material deprivation (buying up large quantities of food, withdrawing savings). The stunning catastrophe at the beginning of the war also had an effect. There were scattered defeatist or anticommunist remarks and expectations of anti-Soviet outbreaks.

From July to September the mood in the city polarized, and the spectrum of feelings narrowed as citizens concentrated their attention almost exclusively on military affairs. Society divided into three parts: patriots who decided to remain until death; the "swamp" in the middle that became a breeding ground for any kind of rumors; and the defeatists, hoping for the overthrow of Bolshevism by the Germans. The political enemies of the regime did not consolidate but tied the realization of their expectations to a victory by the Wehrmacht.

The evacuation of Moscow in mid-October showed the predominance of altruistic, patriotic feelings among ordinary Muscovites and the tendency to egotistical and panicked behavior among the lower and middle ranks of the party-state leadership. The tragic events of that period also illustrate the relatively insignificant spread of defeatist and anticommunist attitudes among Muscovites.

From November into the first half of December, these last sentiments practically disappeared; negative emotions among Muscovites shifted from the military-strategic sphere to the social and everyday plane as people became more upset over the food situation.

In the second half of December and into March 1942, strong dissatisfaction with the nearly catastrophic situation in daily life reigned among the negatively inclined part of the populace. Against this background, thoughts evincing a lack of confidence in victory and expressions with an anti-Soviet coloration reemerged, although less frequently than before. The reader might try living on five hundred grams (nearly one pound, two ounces) of bread and little else for several days; see if the world does not seem much darker all around. But most important in Moscow was the progress of the war; pessimism and fear naturally undermined faith in the goverment and Stalin, while the prospect of victory compensated greatly for an empty stomach.

April and May 1942 brought improvement of the popular mood. Muscovites regarded the food situation as bearable; people expressed their readiness to sacrifice for the sake of victory, and the number of negative remarks dropped considerably.

Women in a Moscow factory prepare submachine guns for shipment, fall 1941. (1984/1126/319; courtesy of the Bundesarchiv, Koblenz)

A grid plotting the impact of material and nonmaterial conditions of life in Moscow for the period in question would show that intangible factors played a greater role in determining outlook than did tangible ones. Credible information about the course of the war proved more important than the lack of food, light, or heat. True, war news greatly affected tangible matters: citizens' personal, familial, and social fate in victory or in defeat. People put their faith above all in unofficial information. The greatest interest was in reports of the occupiers' conduct.

Considering the overall story of how Muscovites spoke and acted in the first year of the war, it becomes clear that the majority was loyal. Certainly some were disgruntled to the extent of wishing for a German victory, but these seem to have been relatively few. When Muscovites fled the city, it was to the east, away from the enemy. No evidence of sabotage has emerged, and no anti-Soviet uprisings occurred. Those who remained, even in the darkest days, typically displayed great courage and determination to fight for their homes.

Heroism, anti-Semitism, cowardice, flight, determination to fight to the bitter end, crude self-interest, and wonderful self-sacrifice: all these reactions characterized the Muscovites in 1941 and 1942. Above all, they dug in and persevered.

Notes

1. O. K. Matveev, "Chislennost naseleniia Moskvy v gody Velikoi Otechestvennoi voiny. (Po materialam TsGAORSS g. Moskvy)," *Otechestvennaia istoriia* 3 (1992), 155.

2. Ibid.

3. *Moskva voennaia, 1941–1945: Memuary i arkhivnye dokumenty* (Moscow, 1995), 359 (hereafter *MV*).

4. Ibid., 548, 552–53.

5. Ibid., 211.

6. *Moskovskaia gorodskaia organizatsiia KPSS, 1917–1988: Tsifry, dokumenty, materialy* (Moscow, 1989), 19.

7. "Rasporiazhenie otdela torgovli Mosgorispolkoma o vvedenii v g. Moskve kartochek na nekotorye prodovolstvennye i promyshlennye tovary," *MV*, 507–11, 729.

8. "Rasporiazhenie otdela torgovli Mosgorispolkoma ob organizatsii kommercheskoi torgovli v g. Moskve," *MV*, 506–7.

9. Nauchnyi Arkhiv Instituta Rossiiskoi Istorii RAN (NAIRI RAN), fond (f.) 2, razdel 8, opis' (o.) 6, delo (d.) 2, list (l. or ll.) 3.

10. "Shifrotelegramma voennogo attashe Frantsii v SSSR v Voennoe Ministerstvo Frantsii (Vishi) o napadenii gitlerovskikh voisk na SSSR," *MV*, 43.

11. In July Verzhbitskii left Moscow as a volunteer for the front; however, because he

was severely nearsighted he was demobilized into the reserves in the fall. For the rest of the war he remained in Moscow and kept a diary.

12. "Iz dnevnikovykh zapisei zhurnalista N. K. Verzhbitskogo," *MV,* 477, 480–81, 486, 491–92.

13. "Iz doklada pervogo sekretaria MK i MGK VKP(v) A. S. Shcherbakova na plenume MGK VKP(b)—Ob obespechenii naseleniia goroda produktami pitaniia, elektroenergiei, avto-i zheleznodorozhnym transportom," *MV,* 520–21, 523–24.

14. *Moskva voennaia: Sbornik vospominanii* (Moscow, 1995), 13. This source is not to be confused with *MV.*

15. "Iz dnevnikovykh zapisei zhurnalista N. K. Verzhbitskogo," *MV,* 496, 498.

16. Ibid., 499–502.

17. "Zapiska pervogo sekretaria MK i MGK VKP(b) A. S. Shcherbakova i predsedatelia Mosgorispolkoma V. P. Pronina zamestiteliam predsedatelia SNK SSSR N. A. Voznesenskomu i A. I. Mikoianu o sostoianii snabzheniia naseleniia g. Moskvy prodovol'stvennymi tovarami," *MV,* 527.

18. "Iz dnevnikovykh zapisei zhurnalista N. K. Verzhbitskogo," *MV,* 504.

19. "Dokladnaia zapiska predsedatelia Mosgorispolkoma V. P. Pronina i pervogo sekretaria MK i MGK VKP (b) A. S. Shcherbakova zam. predsedatelia SNK SSSR N. A. Voznesenskomu o srochnom zavoze v Moskvu topliva dlia promyshlennosti, elektrostantsii, zhilykh domov, bol'nits, gospitalei, ban' i prachechnykh," *MV,* 533–34.

20. "Doklad pedagoga MGPI O. V. Filippovoi 'Uchashchiesia stolitsy v pervye mesiatsy voiny po ikh pis'mam i vospominaniiam'," *MV,* 625–26.

21. *"Moskve—vozdushnaia trevoga!" Mestnaia PVO v gody voiny* (Moscow, 1991), 4–5, 397–401.

22. "Dokladnaia zapiska nachal'nika UNKVD g. Moskvy i MO M. I. Zhuravleva Narkomu Vnutrennikh Del SSSR L. P. Beriia, pervomu sekretariu MK i MGK VKP(b) A. S. Shcherbakovu, predsedateliu ispolkoma Mossoveta V. P. Proninu ob ushcherbe, nanesennom Moskve i progorodu vrazheskoi avaitsiei," *MV,* 427–29.

23. "Spravka o rabote Moskovskogo metropolitena v voennykh usloviiakh, podgotovlennaia nachal'nikom sluzhby MPVO A. Solov'evym dlia komissii po istorii Velikoi Otechestvennoi Voiny AN SSSR," *MV,* 460.

24. NAIRI RAN, f. 2, razdel 8, o. 6, d. 2, l. 3.

25. "Iz vospominanii konstruktora-tankostroitelia N. A. Astrova o sozdanii tanka T-60," *MV,* 384.

26. "Plan agenturno-operativnykh meropriiatii UNKGB i UNKVD g. Moskvy i Moskovskoi oblasti po obespecheniiu gosbezopasnosti g. Moskvy i oblasti v sviazi s napadeniem gitlerovskoi Germanii na SSSR," *MV,* 36–39, 43–44.

27. "Iz dnevnikovykh zapisei zhurnalista N. K. Verzhbitskogo," *MV,* 478.

28. "Postanovlenie GKO 'O vvedenii v g. Moskve osadnogo polozheniia'," *MV,* 125.

29. "Iz doklada voennogo tribunala Moskovskogo voennogo okruga v MGK VKP(b) po itogam sudebnoi praktiki za period s 27 oktiabria po 1 dekabria 1941 g.," *MV,* 545–48.

30. Tsentral'nyi Arkhiv Obshchestvennykh Dvizhenii g. Moskvy, f. 3, o. 52, d. 138, ll. 21–23, 26–27.

31. "Spravka upravleniia komendanta g. Moskvy," *MV*, 550–52.

32. K. M. Simonov, *Raznye dni voiny: Dnevnik pisatelia*, vol. 1 (Moscow, 1977), 65.

33. "Iz dnevnikovykh zapisei zhurnalista N. K. Verzhbitskogo," *MV*, 475.

34. "Moskva voennaia. 1941 god. (Novye istochniki iz sekretnykh arkhivnykh fondov)" ("Mv"), comp. R. G. Grigor'ev, *Istoriia SSSR* 6 (1991), 112, 118, 122.

35. "Iz vospominanii konstruktora-tankostroitelia N. A. Astrova o sozdanii tanka T-60," *MV*, 381–82.

36. "Spetssvodka UNKGB g. Moskvy i Moskovskoi oblasti pervomu sekretariiu MK i MGK VKP(b) A. S. Shcherbakovu o reagirovanii naseleniia na vystuplenie I. V. Stalina," *MV*, 69.

37. "Mv," 116.

38. "Iz dnevnika Moskovskogo vracha E. Sakharovoi," *MV*, 671.

39. Refugees' accounts may be found, for example, in *MV*, 499, 219, 587–88, 382.

40. "Mv," 111, 113, 115–16, 120.

41. "Informatsiia instruktora Leninskogo raikoma partii S. Vaginoi v MGK VKP(v) o reagirovanii trudiashchikhsia stolitsy na vystuplenie po radio V. M. Molotova," *MV*, 42.

42. "Informatsiia zam. narkoma vnutrennikh del SSSR St. Maioru Gosbezopasnosti V. S. Abakumovu," *MV*, 53.

43. See for example "Iz vospominanii predsedatelia ispolkoma Mossoveta V. P. Pronina," *MV*, 46.

44. "Informatsiia zam. narkoma vnutrennikh del SSSR St. Maioru Gosbezopasnosti V. S. Abakumovu," *MV*, 53.

45. Ibid.

46. "Iz spetssvodki upravlenii NKGB i KNVD g. Moskvy i Moskovskoi oblasti Zam. Narkoma Gosbezopasnosti SSSR B. Z. Kobulovu o khode mobilizatsii po Moskve i oblasti," *MV*, 55. Marked "completely secret."

47. "Iz spetssvodki . . . o khode mobilizatsii," *MV*, 55; "Mv," 107–9.

48. "Iz informatsii upravlenii NKGB i NKVD g. Moskvy i Moskovskoi oblasti o reagirovanii naseleniia na napadenie gitlerovskoi Germanii na SSSR": "Informatsiia pervomu sekretariiu MK i MGK VKP(b) A. S. Shcherbakovu," *MV*, 49–50.

49. "Iz vospominanii konstruktora-tankostroitelia N. A. Astrova o sozdanii tanka T-60," *MV*, 382.

50. "Spetssvodka UNKGB . . . o reagirovanii naseleniia na vystuplenie I. V. Stalina," *MV*, 67–69.

51. Simonov, *Raznye dni*, 66.

52. "Mv," 113, 116–19.

53. "Iz biulletenia shtaba politsii," *MV*, 211.

54. L. Kolodnyi, *Khozhdenie v Moskvu* (Moscow, 1990), 130–62; *MV*, 106–23, 249–50, 475–83, 563.

55. "Spravka Upravleniia komendanta g. Moskvy o vypolnenii voennymi komendaturami postanovleniia GKO 'O vvedenii osadnogo polozheniia v Moskve'," *MV*, 550; "Dokladnaia zapiska nachal'nika UNKVD g. Moskvy i Moskovskoi oblasti M. I. Zhuravleva Narkomu Vnutrennikh Del L. P. Beriia o rezul'tatakh rassledovaniia prichin vyvoda iz stroia radiostantsii NKMF SSSR," *MV*, 121.

56. "Zapis' besedy s rabotnikami UNKVD g. Moskvy i MO B. Ia. Chmelevym i P. F. Borisenkovym," *MV*, 250.

57. "Iz vospominanii khudozhestvennogo redaktora G. V. Reshetina," *MV*, 111–12.

58. "Iz dnevnikovykh zapisei zhurnalista N. K. Verzhbitskogo," *MV*, 475–78.

59. "Spravka Nachal'nika UNKVD g. Moskvy i Moskovskoi oblasti M. I. Zhuravleva o reagirovanii naseleniia na priblizhenie vraga k stolitse," *MV*, 116–19.

60. Kolodnyi, *Khozhdenie v Moskvu*, 141.

61. "Iz vospominanii Narkoma Aviatsionnoi Promyshlennosti A. I. Shakhurina," *MV*, 109, 111.

62. "Iz biulletenia shtaba politsii," *MV*, 211.

63. "Iz zapisi besedy s Komendantom g. Moskvy General-Maiorom K. P. Sinilovym i Podpolkovnikom Grebenshchikovym," *MV*, 150.

64. *MV*, 129, 158.

65. "Iz zapisi besedy s Komendantom g. Moskvy," *MV*, 149, 152.

66. "Obzor korrespondentsii, obrabotannoi voennoi tsenzuroi g. Moskvy i Moskovskoi oblasti s 1 po 15 noiabria 1941 g.," *MV*, 158–60.

67. "Obzor korrespondentsii, obrabotannoi voennoi tsenzuroi g. Moskvy i Moskovskoi oblasti s 15 noiabria po 1 dekabria 1941 g.," *MV*, 165–69.

68. "Iz doneseniia voennogo attashe Frantsii v Turtsii Polkovnika Diuvalia v Genshtab Vooruzhennykh Sil Frantsii ob organizatsii oborony Moskvy," *MV*, 184–85.

69. "Spravki rukovoditelei grupp po spetsrabote v raionakh goroda o nastroenii naseleniia posle razgroma nemtsev pod Moskvoi," *MV*, 200–201.

70. "[Report of] Rukovoditel' gruppy 'Kliment'," *MV*, 203.

71. "Dolkadnaia zapiska Nachal'nika UNKVD g. Moskvy," *MV*, 206–8.

72. "Iz dnevnikovykh zapisei zhurnalista N. K. Verzhbitskogo," *MV*, 502.

73. "Svodka obrabotannoi voennoi tsenzuroi NKVD SSSR korrespondentsii grazhdan za mart-aprel' 1942 g.," *MV*, 210.

74. "Iz biulletenia shtaba politsii bezopasnosti i SD—o polozhenii v Moskve v kontse 1941–nachale 1942 g.," *MV*, 211.

75. "Spravka rukovoditelia gruppy 'Klavdiia' po spetsrabote v raionakh goroda o nastroeniiakh moskvichei," *MV*, 218–19; "Iz soobshcheniia rukoviditelia spetsgruppy 'Kliment' o nastroeniiakh moskvichei posle voennoii zimy 1941–1942 gg.," *MV*, 222.

Part 2

Culture and Intellectuals during the War

7

War as a "Breathing Space": Soviet Intellectuals and the "Great Patriotic War"

Bernd Bonwetsch

Eight of us were gathered around Ben Levich's dinner table all talking at once. So many complaints were being raised by Ben's relatives about the vexations of life in Moscow today that I deliberately changed the subject by asking them what had been the best period in Russian history. Conversation came to a halt. . . . "The best time of our lives," [Ben] said finally, "was the war."

His answer surprised me, and evidently the others as well. Ben grinned shyly, obviously pleased to have caught us off guard. Given the enormous devastation and suffering that all Soviet people associate with World War II, the immediate astonishment was understandable. Moreover, this was a company of sceptics, reluctant to echo or endorse any cliché of Soviet propaganda, especially one so constantly invoked as the Soviet victory in World War II.

"The war," Ben repeated quietly. "Because at that time we all felt closer to our government than at any other time in our lives. It was not their country then, but our country. It was not they who wanted this or that to be done, but we who wanted to do it. It was not their war, but our war. It was our country we were defending, our war effort."

This is a quotation from Hedrick Smith's book about his experience in the Soviet Union as correspondent for the *New York Times* in the early seventies.[1] Ben, at whose apartment the conversation took place, was a Jewish scientist who had gotten on well under the Soviet system until he applied to emigrate to Israel in 1972. He had participated in the war as a trained chemist, which means he was then already old enough to compare and to make his own judgment. He illustrated his point by recalling an episode from the war:

Hanged Soviet partisans. The executions were carried out in public and the hanged left behind for a while as a warning to the population not to support partisans. (Courtesy of the Bilderdienst Süddeutscher Verlag, Munich)

"I remember I was in Kazan in my room sleeping . . . and in the middle of the night, someone from the *cheka* [secret police] came and woke me up, and I was not afraid. Think of it! He knocked on my door in the middle of the night and woke me up and I was not afraid. If some *chekist* had done that in the thirties, I would have been terrified. If it had happened after the war, just before Stalin died, it would have been just as frightening. . . . If someone did that now, I would be very worried, even though the situation has changed. But then, during the war, I was absolutely unafraid. It was a unique time in our history."[2]

The others taking part in the conversation concurred with this opinion. And it seems that this view could be considered representative of a considerable part of the "front generation" (*frontovoe pokolenie*), the male population of the Soviet Union born between 1890 and 1923 and serving already in the army at the outbreak of the war or called to arms during it. This outlook may even characterize the entire war generation, men and women alike, whether serving in the army or at the home front—at least if they did not belong to those sections of the population that underwent wholesale repression toward the end of the war.[3]

To understand such feelings one has to take into consideration what preceded and what followed the war, as Ben suggested. Before the fighting came the "revolution from above" that forcibly transformed Soviet society within a short span of time. "Forcibly" here has a double meaning. First, in a structural sense, within the two five-year plans that began in 1928 the Soviet Union changed from being a predominantly peasant society based on a small-scale subsistence economy to an industrial society, however backward, with a developed division of labor.

In a more direct sense "forcibly" means that the process of social transformation was accomplished to a very large extent by use of physical force. This applies most of all to the peasants. They faced a virtual war with the regime under the name of collectivization and "liquidation of the *kulaks* [the supposedly wealthier peasants] as a class," or class war. During collectivization about four hundred thousand so-called kulak households, up to two million people, were deported to the Soviet East in 1930–31 alone. The famine of 1932–33, caused by the harsh grain procurement policies adopted as part of the class war in the countryside, cost several million peasants their lives.[4] It would be difficult to say what caused more harm to society, the merciless brutality against the peasants as the larger part of society or the fact that society as a whole was induced to believe that no catastrophe occurred at all. Although there was hunger in the cities and starvation in the countryside, the newspapers did not mention these facts; people accepted this situation as normal. Although important, this was only one expression of the fact that people were losing or had already lost the ability of spontaneously extending their sympathy to suffering compatriots. They were induced to abandon their own judgment and become dependent on the authorities' word alone. Within a few years this led to the division of consciousness as a mass phenomenon, as a characteristic of Soviet society as a whole.[5]

The use of force in pursuit of the state's aims cost, according to recent demographic calculations, 6.6 million premature deaths between 1927 and 1936 alone,[6] with millions of people living in prisons, labor camps or colonies, and "special settlements" of the NKVD. Figures for these fatalities and incarcerations have now been made public, above all by Viktor Zemskov.[7] Soviet society became accustomed to these costs of development. Everyone, including the intelligentsia, who by education and position in society were called upon to make their own judgment, took such social damage as normal. They accepted the treatment of large segments of the population as "class enemies" without any civil rights as proper, as they did the treatment of the kolkhoz peasants as second-class citizens. They took legal terror as normal, for instance the application of the infamous law for the protection of public property of 1932, popularly called "the law on ears of grain," because it provided severe punishment for stealing a few ears of grain or corn cobs. Mere pilfering of food was to be punished by at least ten years of hard labor up to capital punishment, even if the convicts were minors no more than twelve years of age.[8] For the "intelligenty" who, as judges, prosecutors, or in whatever capacity, executed or legitimized this policy, all this appeared to be normal. Even in the memoirs published since perestroika this treatment of large segments of the population is rarely mentioned as something having to do with Stalinism.

Only in 1937 and 1938, when the hunt for "enemies of the people" hit the elite of Soviet society—party and state officials, the officer corps, and the intelligentsia—did the feeling of fear and terror spread among them, although even then many tried hard to see nothing wrong and unnatural in the mass arrests. Of course, nobody could know that only innocent people were arrested, that, according to figures given at the June plenum of the Central Committee in 1957, 680,000 people were shot as "counterrevolutionaries"[9] in 1937–38, and that hundreds of thousands of alleged counterrevolutionaries filled labor camps and "special settlements" of the NKVD.[10]

To understand what was going on in the Soviet Union during the *Ezhovshchina* (so named after Nikolai Ezhov, the chief of the NKVD, or secret police, from September 1936 to November 1938) would have demanded too much from those who underwent it. One of those who fell into the machinery of the Ezhovshchina, Alexander Weissberg-Cybulski, aptly termed it a "witches' Sabbath"—but only long after the fact. His as well as uncounted other memoirs give ample proof of the fact that nobody could find an explanation at the time because all were looking for a logical foundation for events.[11] Even those who ordered and carried out the persecutions had by no means a clear understanding of what they really did. They probably believed they were arresting real enemies.[12]

But however people believed or tried to believe, by rationalizing, what they were being told, and however they lived a normal life, at least outwardly, their mind and psychic condition did not remain unaffected.[13] Society in general, and the administrative, economic, and cultural elite in particular, who executed official policies and had to explain to themselves and to others what was going on, could not preserve an innocent and straightforward relationship to reality. Although good arguments have been advanced to deny it, particularly the presence of fear in people's consciousness,[14] there are also many indications of the fact that society and above all officials and intelligentsia members were deeply affected, in the sense that they could no longer trust their own observation, their own human feelings, or their spontaneous emotions.

Outwardly this society lived normally, but it had lost the criteria for normality. Only this could induce a high-ranking officer like Marshal Zhukov to state in his memoirs that in 1937–38 the training of troops in general went normally while at the same time he deplored the "terrible loss of discipline" among the soldiers because of the mass arrests among officers. The latter no longer felt able to enforce discipline among their troops.[15] Even more intriguing, Zhukov deplores the effect of the arrests on himself and other comrades:

> There arose an awful situation in the country. No one trusted the other, people started to be afraid of each other and avoided meeting and talking to each other; if conversations were unavoidable one tried to talk in the presence of third persons as witnesses. There spread an unheard-of epidemic of slander. They often slandered absolutely honorable people, sometimes even their best friends. All this was done in order to avoid being suspected of disloyalty oneself. And this awful atmosphere continued to get more tense.[16]

And in a different context Zhukov reports that despite the fact that the arrests went on around them, the "basic core of the military and political command staff" of his division "worked exactly and with the application of all their strength."[17] Again Zhukov tries to show that people did not allow themselves to be diverted from their normal duties. But what he also demonstrates is that people did not see any alternative to business as usual, although perhaps they worked harder than usual to show their loyalty. But of course nothing was normal here. People just did not know what else they could do in a world where comrades' ordinary trust in each other had been replaced by distrust, where denunciations were considered to be the honorable duty of every citizen, "valued higher than independence, faithfulness to convictions and comrades, and simple honesty."[18]

Numerous other memoirs confirm that people, because of fear, lived split lives: one personal, natural, and normal, and another official life that made "honest, affectionate, good people in an instant into 'levers' of the state apparatus."[19] People in fact fled reality by behaving "normally." They knew something was going on that they could not understand and dared not examine. They respected invisible barriers, made questions that everybody was interested in taboo, lost the ability for independent judgment and orientation in reality, and replaced this with a fixation on the state as the absolute and only authority. These were alarming characteristics of an "unhealthy division of mass consciousness and mass behaviour" in the Soviet Union, as L. A. Gordon and E. V. Klopov have called it, or of the "social and political pathology" that had its grip on Soviet society on the eve of the war, in Moshe Lewin's words.[20]

On 22 June 1941 war came as a total surprise to this disturbed society. The "pathology" prevented people from expecting the war so soon or preparing properly for it.[21] Even the military on the border had been induced not to trust their professional judgment and to omit almost everything that under normal conditions would have been routine precautions. Nevertheless, Soviet society rose to defend the country against the invader. Except for the newly annexed territories there was, according to all evidence, not the slightest hesitation on any part of Soviet society to serve the country in any position. The authorities were flooded by volunteers who wanted to serve at the front, even from the labor camps.[22] There was no work collective that did not solemnly make pledges for overfulfillment of production targets.[23] Although people did all this more or less ritually, particularly at the very beginning of the war, as had become usual during the thirties, such behavior was by no means lip service for the cause. The people of the Soviet Union really did accomplish miracles under material conditions much worse than before the war.[24] Red Army soldiers fought at least as stubbornly as soldiers of other countries. As the last chapter of this volume shows, the capture of huge masses of Soviet soldiers by the invaders was evidently due to the speed of the German advance and inadequate strategies and tactics on the Soviet side, not to anticommunist feelings among the troops, as historians like Joachim Hoffmann tend to believe.[25]

But just as striking as this firm behavior of soldiers and citizens in defense of their country is the fact that the Soviet leadership did not expect this outcome. Judging by measures taken and statements made during the first part of the war, the Soviet government expected an internal war to become as serious as the one against the Wehrmacht. Persons and groups considered to be unreliable were deported or, when the Germans advanced too quickly, even liquidated on the spot. Labor camp inmates, of course, belonged to this group; 750,000 of them were evacuated to the East during the first months of the war. For many of them this meant marching thousands of kilometers.[26]

Ethnic Germans living in the USSR also belonged to this category of unreliable persons, and even a Jew born in Germany was considered suspicious.[27] Therefore 950,000 Germans living in the European part of the Soviet Union were deported to the East from July 1941 onward, when the Volga Republic, where 450,000 of them lived, was dissolved.[28] The men of working age and even women without children formed part of the "labor army" of the NKVD, a wartime forced-labor organization that built industrial plants, mainly in the Urals. Stalin's first public speech on 3 July 1941 called for vigilance against spies, deserters, saboteurs, and so-called panic-mongers. After this, spy-mania took on "gigantic proportions," while the security organs were busily recruiting new informants and arresting "enemies."[29] Mistrust in the loyalty of the population became visible in measures of all kinds. For example, private radio receivers had to be delivered to the authorities (they were returned at the end of the war), and private telephone lines were disconnected. Spreading "rumors" was to be punished with at least two to five years in prison. Of course, at a time when official news tried to conceal the truth, sensational rumors spread; yet even guesses about the real situation at the front were considered to be rumors.[30] At the same time, party control over public life intensified considerably. "Party organizers" were installed in all war plants, while political departments, a device from the time of collectivization, were reintroduced in the countryside, as were political commissars in the Red Army on 16 July 1941. For counterespionage purposes, "special sections" of the NKVD were reintroduced one day later. Their main task was to prevent treason and desertion; for this purpose armed units of the NKVD were placed at their disposal. At the same time, heavily armed "holding detachments" (*zagraditel'nye otriady*) were installed behind the front lines to prevent retreat, flight, or desertion of single soldiers or whole units.[31] To fall into the hands of the Germans as a prisoner of war, ominously called "surrendering into captivity" (*zdacha v plen*), was declared treason on 16 August 1941. The decree provided for harsh measures against family members of captured soldiers.[32] When the Red Army drove the German invaders back from Moscow in December 1941, the Soviet leadership had no more urgent concern than to decree, on 4 January 1942, that a hundred thousand of the NKVD's internal troops should be stationed in the cities of the territory liberated from German forces in order to cleanse them of enemy agents, traitors, and other anti-Soviet elements.[33]

All this was accompanied by a continuation of what could be called everyday terror conducted under Soviet law. True, at the beginning of the war certain categories of prisoners and labor camp inmates were freed, 420,000 of them directly for service at the front, and by the end of the war almost a million prisoners in all had been released for this purpose.[34] But at the same time millions of people came into conflict with the law and were prosecuted. It was only now that the "ears of grain" law of 1932 and the law prohibiting lateness and unauthorized leave from the workplace, adopted in 1940, came fully into play. For slight violations of labor discipline and for food pilfering and other minor offenses, civil and military courts sentenced no less than 4.5 million people, two-thirds of them to imprisonment, from July 1941 to December 1942.[35] Those not put into jail or labor camps were often sentenced to corrective labor without imprisonment. Nevertheless, they worked under the supervision of the bureaus of corrective work of the GULAG, the NKVD department in charge of corrective labor camps. In December 1944 the number of people sentenced for such offenses reached 770,000; of these, 570,000 had violated the decree of 1940 against absenteeism.[36] These figures are almost unimaginable, especially taking into consideration the fact that during most of this period the German occupiers ruled about one-third of the prewar Soviet population.[37]

Many more features made the war years look on the surface like those before June 1941, but this would be an entirely wrong impression. There was one decisive difference: as the war began, the hunt for "enemies of the people" stopped almost from one day to the next. Some imprisoned "enemies" who were important for the war effort were set free, like the aviation designer Andrei N. Tupolev, the people's commissar of munitions, Boris Vannikov, or the former chief of staff marshal Kyril Meretskov, among many others. New arrests and executions still took place, particularly among generals, but on a minor scale compared to before the war.[38] The victims of the search for "enemies of the people," mainly members of the functional and cultural elite, profited most from this change.[39]

The question of why this change happened and who was responsible for it is not easy to answer; only plausible guesses may be offered. One of the reasons may be that the leadership realized, after its initial panicked reaction, that people were defending their country and taking part in the war effort quite spontaneously, not for fear of punishment. Stalin and his circle may also have realized that the enemy was outside, not inside the country as they had feared. In a sense the German attack and almost irresistible advance seemed to have produced a healthy result, freeing the regime at least temporarily from its conviction that it could mold reality to its will and that reality actually corresponded to its will. As long as the depiction of reality had been an internal Soviet affair, the state had possessed the power, and used it, to enforce belief in these notions. It was some sort of a game, and everybody obeyed the peculiar rules set by the regime.

Thus, for instance, the regime could declare collectivization to be a great success; there was no one to deny it. Those who tried were taken care of by the "organs," as the political police were called. Fiction had replaced reality; nobody dared to declare that the emperor was naked. The Germans were the first to do it, unfortunately in their own brutal way. They did not obey the

Stalinist rules of the game, and for the first time since the late twenties the regime had to face reality as it was and no longer according to ideological stereotypes and wishful thinking.

This shock to the regime also had profound consequences for the population, particularly for those who had to orient themselves in reality and to explain it to others: writers, journalists, agitators, engineers, officers, officials, and members of the intelligentsia in general. Now their professional abilities were urgently needed, and therefore they were allowed again, to a certain degree at least, to trust their own observations and their own judgment.

Several participants in the war have written about the psychic relief that the fighting brought to them, despite all the hardships it produced. Boris Pasternak depicts this mood in his novel *Doctor Zhivago*. He imagines a conversation between two Red Army officers, both members of the intelligentsia. One of them says about "successful" collectivization,

> "I think that collectivisation was both a mistake and a failure, and because that couldn't be admitted, every means of intimidation had to be used to make people forget how to think and judge for themselves, to force them to see what wasn't there, and to maintain the contrary of what their eyes told them. Hence the unexampled harshness of the Yezhov terror, and the promulgation of a constitution which was never intended to be applied, and the holding of elections not based on the principle of a free vote.
>
> "And when the war broke out, its real horrors, its real dangers, its menace of real death, were a blessing compared with the inhuman power of the lie, a relief because it broke the spell of the dead letter.
>
> "It was not only felt by men in your position, in concentration camps, but by everyone without exception, at home and at the front, and they all took a deep breath and flung themselves into the furnace of this deadly, liberating struggle with real joy, with rapture."[40]

Dmitrii Shostakovich aimed different words at the same problem when he wrote in his *Testimony* that the war helped him to tell the truth in his music and to be able to cry when he felt like it:

> The war brought incredible suffering and misery. Life became very, very difficult. There was immense, endless grief, there were endless tears. But before the war it was even more difficult, because everybody was alone with his sorrow. Already before the war there was probably no family in Leningrad without losses. . . . Everybody had to cry for someone. But one had to cry silently, under the bedspread. Nobody must notice it. Everybody was afraid of everyone. Grief choked, strangled us . . . then came the war. The secret, isolated grief became everyone's grief. One was allowed to talk about it, one could cry openly, openly mourn for

the dead. People needed no longer be afraid of their tears. . . . Not only I got the chance, thanks to the war, to express myself. Everyone perceived it like that.[41]

Yevgenii Yevtushenko bears witness to this same feeling when he states in his memoirs that before the war Soviet people had to live a "split life," but that the war, "hard as it is to admit . . . lightened the Russians' spiritual burden, for they no longer needed to be insincere. And this was one of the chief causes of our victory."[42]

But there was more to the feeling that war brought relief. For example, cultural life was freer from ideological tutelage than at any time since the twenties. The Russian Orthodox Church experienced a revival nobody would have predicted. Writers, composers, and artists who had fallen into disgrace before the war could again publish, compose, and appear in public. The situation improved greatly for the study of history; of biology, where genetics got a respite from the attacks of the 1930s; and of other sciences.[43] Some people even dared enter into political conversations or make political remarks in letters, which nobody would have dreamt of a few years earlier.[44] Of course, only relative freedom came to the Soviet Union. But for people who had accustomed themselves to living with a small suitcase packed for all events, as Veniamin Kaverin and many others have related, this relative freedom, this chance to "breathe more easily" (Shostakovich) in spite of all hardships, gave hope for an "easier life" after the war.[45] The physicist Sergei Frish recalls that, during the war, most important for him and his friends was not the conviction that victory would be won and reconstruction of the country accomplished but the belief that the mistakes of the prewar years would be admitted. "We had the impression," he wrote later, that "everyone had understood that the country could not live under the conditions of unlimited centralized power, bureaucratism, and mistrust in the people. All that was bound to be changed. It could not be otherwise. We all were of a very optimistic mood."[46]

But this conviction turned out to be a deception. The breathing space for intellectual life remained limited, even during the war. The Stalinist repressive state, fearful of autonomous thought and action, lurked behind the scene. The Agitation and Propaganda Administration of the Communist Party's Central Committee (CC) allowed more cultural freedom than before, but kept it under tight control nonetheless. Toward the end of the war it warned certain people, summoned them to the CC for criticism of "bad [grubye] political mistakes," and saw to it that news of these incidents spread among the intellectuals. The Ukrainian script-writer and movie producer, Aleksandr Dovzhenko, for instance, was severely reprimanded because of the "anti-Leninist" content of two of his movies and was excluded from several committees. In February 1944 the chief censor of the Ukraine forbade any printing of Dovzhenko's writings without his personal consent, the theoretical party journal *Bolshevik* singled him out for ostracism in the May-June edition, and the Politbureau candidate and CC Secretary A. S. Shcherbakov criticized him several times in public. Dovzhenko himself summarized his predicament in his diary: "You have slain me; more than that, you have trampled me down, humiliated and declared me dead [while] alive."[47]

Like Dovzhenko, Mikhail Zoshchenko and several other writers had their problems with the party and the security organs.[48] Zoshchenko wrote letters to Stalin, Shcherbakov, and other party functionaries, but in vain. He was spared for the moment, but a harsh fate awaited him.[49]

Toward the end of the war and for some time after, the cultural elite as a whole did not suffer more severe measures; their criticism of censoral interference in their work, something unthinkable before the war, was even a sign of continuing internal relaxation. But the Stalinist state demonstrated that with returning self-confidence its head reverted more and more to prewar customs. Victory did not induce Stalin to be generous but, on the contrary, to rely again on old methods. For instance, as territory occupied by the Germans was regained, the state took revenge against those its own officials had left behind. NKVD troops, entrusted with keeping order and security behind the front, followed the advancing Red Army. In 1943 alone they temporarily arrested almost a million people in order to investigate their trustworthiness. Eighty thousand of the arrested were "unmasked [as] agents, traitors, myrmidons, deserters, marauders and other criminal elements."[50]

But not only those who were individually "unmasked" underwent criminal persecution, justified or not; the entire population in the liberated territory suffered discrimination. To have lived under German occupation was considered to be at least a personal failure, if not an expression of the intention to collaborate with the Germans. For decades after the war Soviet citizens in every personal questionnaire had to confess their "guilt" on this point—that is, to state where they spent the war years. The security organs hunted for collaborators, and the suspicion of having collaborated was easily expressed and only with difficulties disproved, if at all. Even Leonid Brezhnev, then the first party secretary of the Zaporozh'e district, points in his memoirs to the difficulties in defending honest people against wholesale accusations of this kind.[51] In these circumstances the GULAG filled once more. In 1944–45 the number of labor camp inmates, which at the end of 1943 had reached its lowest figure since 1935, swelled by half a million people.[52] The population of "special settlements" of the NKVD increased even more, since not only individuals but entire peoples, for example the Crimean Tatars, were deported because of alleged collaboration. Thus almost nine hundred thousand people were removed from the Northern Caucasus and the Crimea in 1943–44. These and other deportations from the Ukraine, Belorussia, and the Baltics caused the population of the "special settlements," after a sharp decline at the beginning of the war, to increase again to 2.2 million, an unprecedented figure.[53]

All these mass repressions were supplemented by accusations and persecutions against several million repatriates, whether prisoners of war, forced laborers removed to the west by the Germans, or displaced persons.[54] Only a small portion were actual collaborators, among them Vlasovites (members of General Vlasov's Russian Army of Liberation, which donned German uniforms and fought for the Reich), members of police units set up by the Germans, and local administrators under the occupiers. But everyone who had been under German occupation or control underwent arbitrary treatment, beginning with the "filtration" process behind the advancing Soviet front, at the demarcation line in Europe between the Soviet and western zones of occupation, or in Soviet ports, where the western Allies handed over Soviet citizens who had wound up in their custody at the end of the war. These unfounded mass repressive measures profoundly affected Soviet society and were by no means kept secret. But it seems that this extensive reappearance of Stalinist terror escaped the attention of the Soviet intellectual elite, or once again they suppressed the perception of this side of Soviet reality. This conclusion is supported by the testimony of Ilia Ehrenburg, who wrote in his memoirs that he learned of the treatment of repatriates delivered by Allied ships to Odessa and asked himself, as did others, if the events of 1937 could be repeated. He rejected the idea in view of the changes that had occurred with the victory over fascism and in view of the sacrifices and achievements of the Soviet people. But he conceded when he did so that he took wish for reality.[55]

This wish had been nourished by the relaxation in relations between state and society, with results such as the revival of the church, to name one of the most striking examples still to be seen in public. At the end of the war this partial liberalization that had particularly affected the position of intellectuals gave way to a harder line. The same was true of mass repressions. But the Soviet intellectual elite closed their eyes before this renewal of Stalinism in order to "extend their own breathing space," as Nadezhda Mandelshtam suggests.[56] They wanted to keep the peace that, ironically enough, war had given them. In August 1946 the new cultural restrictions, termed the *Zhdanovshchina*, after Stalin's lieutenant Andrei Zhdanov, began to eliminate all the little freedoms that intellectuals had gained during the war. Anna Akhmatova confessed her deep depression to her friend Nadezhda Mandelshtam: "One almost cannot bear the thought that the best time of our life was the war, when incredibly many people lost their lives, when we suffered from hunger, and when one's own son was in a labor camp."[57]

Only then did Ilia Ehrenburg change his mind and concede that the terror of the thirties could repeat itself, since the campaigns against prominent and less prominent members of the Soviet cultural elite reminded him of those years.[58] It was not the mass repression that arose again toward the end of the war but the Zhdanovshchina that forced Soviet intellectuals to open their eyes once more to Stalinist reality. Only now it turned out for them that the hope to extend their "breathing space" beyond the war had been an illusion.

Notes

1. H. Smith, *The Russians* (London, 1976), 369–70.

2. Ibid., 370.

3. E. S. Seniavskaia *1941–1945: Frontovoe pokolenie* (Moscow, 1995), 157–69; E. S. Seniavskaia, *Psikhologiia voiny v XX veke: Istoricheskii opyt Rossii* (Moskva, 1999), 171–90; B. Bonwetsch, "Der 'Große Vaterländische Krieg': Geschichtsbewußtsein und Geschichtswissenschaft in der Sowjetunion," in *Geschichtsdidaktik* 10 (1985), 427–34.

4. S. Merl, *Bauern unter Stalin: Die Formierung des sowjetischen Kolchossystems, 1930–1941* (Berlin, 1990), 98–99; S. Merl, "Wieviel Opfer kostete die 'Liquidierung des Kulakentums als Klasse'?" *Geschichte und Gesellschaft* 141 (1988), 534–40; *Sud'by sovetskogo krest'ianstva* (Moscow, 1996), 361; V. N. Zemskov, "Kulatskaia ssylka v 30-e gody," *Sotsiologicheskie Issledovaniia* no. 10 (1990), 3–21.

5. L. A. Gordon and E. V. Klopov, *Chto eto bylo? Razmyshleniia o predposylkakh i itogakh togo, chto sluchilos' s nami v 30–40-e gody* (Moscow, 1989), 221–42. Gordon and Klopov refer to a "division of mass consciousness, mass behaviour and culture."

6. V. V. Tsaplin, "Statistika zhertv stalinizma v 30–3 gody," *Voprosy Istorii* no. 4 (1989), 175–81.

7. V. N. Zemskov, "Zakliuchennye, spetsposelentsy, ssyl'noposelentsy, ssyl'nye i vyslannye (Statistiko-geograficheskii aspekt)," *Istoriia SSSR* no. 5 (1991), 151–65.

8. R. Medvedev, *Let History Judge: The Origins and Consequences of Stalinism*, 2d ed. (London, 1989), 349; G. T. Rittersporn, *Stalinist Simplifications and Soviet Complications: Social Tensions and Political Conflicts in the USSR, 1933–1953* (New York, 1991), 149, 246–50.

9. *Kommunist* no. 8 (1990), cited in O. V. Khlevniuk, *1937-i: Stalin, NKVD i sovetskoe obshchestvo* (Moscow, 1992), 156. This contradicts figures quoted by Zemskov, "Zakli-

uchennye," 153, according to which 642,980 people in all were sentenced to death for "counterrevolutionary crimes" between 1921 and 1954. G. A. Kumanev, "V ogne tia-zhelykh ispytanii (iiun' 1941—noiabr' 1942 g.)," *Istoriia SSSR* no. 2 (1991), 6, quotes archival sources according to which there were 353,074 executions in 1937 alone. Exact figures are obviously not yet available, if they ever will be.

10. Exact figures given by Zemskov, "Zakliuchennye," 152. A résumé and evaluation of statistical data on Soviet labor camp inmates is given in E. Bacon, "Glasnost' and the Gulag: New Information on Soviet Forced Labor around World War II," *Soviet Studies* 44 (1992), 1069–86; J. Keep, "Recent Writing on Stalin's Gulag: An Overview," *Crime, Histoire, et Sociétés* 1 (1997), 91–112. See also J. O. Pohl, *The Stalinist Penal System: A Statistical History of Soviet Repression and Terror, 1930–1953* (Jefferson, N.C., 1997); E. Bacon, *The Gulag at War: Stalin's Forced Labor System in the Light of the Archives* (London, 1994).

11. A. Weissberg-Cybulski, *Hexensabbat: Die Gedankenpolizei—Die große Tschistka* (Frankfurt am Main, 1951). The English edition is entitled *Conspiracy of Silence*, trans. E. Fitzgerald (London, 1952); the title of the American edition is *The Accused*, trans. E. Fitzgerald (New York, 1951).

12. G. T. Rittersporn, "The Omnipresent Conspiracy: On Soviet Imagery of Politics and Social Relations in the 1930s," in *Stalinism: Its Nature and Aftermath*, ed. N. Lampert and G. T. Rittersporn (London, 1992), 101–20.

13. See B. Bonwetsch, "Der Stalinismus in der Sowjetunion der dreißiger Jahre: Zur Deformation einer Gesellschaft," in *Jahrbuch für Historische Kommunismusforschung* 1 (1993), 11–36.

14. R. Thurston, *Life and Terror in Stalin's Russia* (New Haven, Conn., 1996).

15. G. K. Zhukov, *Vospominaniia*, 10th ed., vol. 1 (Moscow, 1990), 220; K. M. Simonov, *Glazami cheloveka moego pokoleniia* (Moscow, 1988), 348–49.

16. Zhukov, *Vospominaniia*, 220.

17. Ibid., 224.

18. Gordon and Klopov, *Chto eto bylo*, 231. For the psychological results of the arrests on the Red Army's officer corps see B. Bonwetsch, "The Purge of the Military and the Red Army's Operational Capability during the 'Great Patriotic War,'" in *From Peace to War: Germany, Soviet Russia, and the World, 1939–1941*, ed. B. Wegner (Providence, R.I., 1997), 395–414; B. Bonwetsch, "Stalin, the Red Army, and the 'Great Patriotic War,'" in *Stalinism and Nazism: Dictatorships in Comparison*, ed. I Kershaw and M. Lewin (Cambridge, 1997), 185–207.

19. V. Kaverin, *Epilog: Memuary* (Moscow, 1989), 64.

20. Gordon and Klopov, *Chto eto bylo*, 231; M. Lewin, *The Making of the Soviet System* (London, 1985), 284.

21. Stalin's role in the assessment of German war plans and in preparing for an eventual German attack has often been described. Among the memoirs see Zhukov, *Vospominaniia*, chap. 9. From the war literature see J. Erickson, *Stalin's War with Germany*, vol. 1, *The Road to Stalingrad* (London, 1975).

22. P. Afanas'ev, "Da, eto bylo . . . ," in *Zaveshchanie (Ural'skie memuary)* (Sverdlovsk, 1989), 42.

23. See for example the countless pledges for support of the government and for fulfilling raised production targets in *Chuvashskaia ASSR v period Velikoi Otechestvennoj voiny: Sbornik dokumentov i materialov* (Cheboksary, 1975).

24. B. Bonwetsch, "Der Große Vaterländische Krieg," in *Handbuch der Geschichte Rußlands,* vol. 3, ed. G. Schramm (Stuttgart, 1992), 909–1008; J. Barber and M. Harrison, *The Soviet Home Front, 1941–1945* (London, 1991).

25. J. Hoffmann, *Die Geschichte der Wlassow-Armee* (Freiburg, 1984).

26. "GULAG v gody Velikoi Otechestvennoi voiny," *Voenno-Istoricheskii Zhurnal* no. 4 (1991), 19. The overall figure of labor camp and colonies inmates at the beginning of the war was 2.3 million. For the treatment of prisoners see also S. Shved, "Vospominaniia," in *Zaveshchanie,* 125; Bacon, *Gulag at War,* 89–90.

27. W. Admoni, "Krieg und Blockade," in *Blockade: Leningrad 1941–1944* (Reinbek, 1992), 167.

28. V. V. Zemskov, "Spetsposelentsy (po dokumentam NKVD-MVD SSSR)," *Sotsiologicheskie Issledovaniia* no. 11 (1990), 8. See also B. Pinkus, "The Deportation of the German Minority in the Soviet Union, 1941–1945," in *From Peace to War: Germany, Soviet Russia, and the World, 1939–1941,* ed. B. Wegner (Providence, R.I., 1997), 449–62.

29. D. Lichatschow, "Wie wir am Leben blieben," in *Blockade,* 22, 29–30; S. Rosenberg, *A Soviet Odyssey* (Harmondsworth, 1991), 95; Kaverin, *Epilog,* 231–43; A. V. Kol'tsov, "Leningradskie uchrezhdeniia Akademii nauk v gody Velikoi Otechestvennoi voiny," in *Leningradskaia nauka v gody Velikoi Otechestvennoi voiny* (St. Petersburg, 1995), 19.

30. "GKO postanovliaet . . . ," *Voenno-Istoricheskii Zhurnal* no. 3 (1992), 17; S. E. Frish, *Skvoz' prizmu vremeni: Vospominaniia* (Moscow, 1992), 275–77; "Das Blockade-Tagebuch von Georgi Zim," in *Blockade,* 60. See also Barber and Harrison, *Soviet Home Front,* 65–6.

31. "GKO postanovliaet," 20.

32. Stalin's order no. 270 may be found in B. Bonwetsch, "Die Geschichte des Krieges ist noch nicht geschrieben," *Osteuropa* 39 (1989), 1034–37.

33. G. S. Beloborodov, "Brali vraga 'ezhovymi rukavitsami,'" *Voenno-Istoricheskii Zhurnal* no. 9 (1993), 9–12.

34. "GULAG v gody," 20; Bacon, *Gulag at War,* 103.

35. "GULAG v gody," 23.

36. V. N. Zemskov, "GULAG (Istoriko-sotsiologicheskii aspekt)," *Sotsiologicheskie Issledovania* no. 6 (1991), 19.

37. Stalin himself, in his famous order no. 227 ("Not a step back!") of 28 July 1942, spoke of seventy million people in occupied territory. *Voenno-Istoricheskii Zhurnal* no. 8 (1988), 73–80. The same figure, without a source, is given by Kumanev, "V ogne," 16. Differerent figures have also been offered, ranging from fifty-five to eighty million.

38. L. E. Reshin, V. S. Stepanov, "Sud'by general'skie," *Voenno-Istoricheskii Zhurnal*

no. 11 (1992), 24–27; A. Vaksberg, "Taina oktiabria 1941-go," in *Vozhd', khoziain, diktator* (Moscow, 1990), 384–89.

39. Of course there were prisoners of all strata of Soviet society in the camps. But "counterrevolutionaries," the number of whom was raised by several hundreds of thousands in 1937–38, were apparently mostly members of the Soviet elite. See Barber and Harrison, *Soviet Home Front*, 110–11.

40. B. Pasternak, *Doctor Zhivago* (London, 1958), 453.

41. S. Volkov, ed., *Testimony: The Memoirs of Dmitri Shostakovich*, trans. Antonina Bouis (New York, 1979), 135.

42. Y. Yevtushenko, *A Precocious Autobiography* (New York, 1963), 23.

43. C. E. Black, "History and Politics in the Soviet Union," in *Rewriting Russian History*, ed. C. E. Black (New York, 1962), 25; D. Joravsky, *The Lysenko Affair* (Cambridge, Mass., 1970); Zh. Medvedev, *The Rise and Fall of T. D. Lysenko* (New York, 1969); M. Pokrovskii, *Delo akademika Vavilova* (Moscow, 1991).

44. J. Orlow, *Ein russisches Leben* (Munich, 1992), 106–11; A. Solzhenitsyn, *Der Archipel GULAG*, vol. 1 (Bern, 1974), 136–37.

45. Kaverin, *Epilog*, 64–65, 130; S. Volkov, ed., *Testimony*, 272; Rosenberg, *Soviet Odyssey*, 84; I. Ehrenburg, *Menschen, Jahre, Leben*, vol. 3 (Munich, 1965), 135.

46. Frish, *Skvoz' prizmu*, 303.

47. D. Babichenko, "Aleksandr Dovzhenko: 'Ia protiven vam i chem-to opasen,'" *Istochnik* no. 0 (1993), 122–27, quotation on 123.

48. R. Usikova, I. Shevchuk, "Po agenturnym dannym . . . ," *Rodina* no. 1 (1992), 92–96; D. L. Babichenko, *Pisateli i tsenzory: Sovetskaia literatura 1940-ch godov pod politicheskim kontrolem TsK* (Moscow, 1994), 82–102.

49. Kaverin, *Epilog*, 65–70, 476–79; M. Zoshchenko, "Budu stoiat' na svoikh pozitsiiakh," *Istoricheskii Arkhiv* no. 1 (1992), 132–43; Babichenko, *Pisateli*, 72–81.

50. Cited from a report by Beria to Stalin in D. Volkogonov, *Triumf i tragediia: Politicheskii portret I. V. Stalina*, vol. 2, bk. 1 (Moscow, 1989), 260.

51. L. I. Brezhnev, *Vozrozhdenie* (Moscow, 1978), 21–22. Writers have treated this subject in novels: L. Tschukowskaja, *Untertauchen* (Zurich, 1978); V. Nekrassow, *Ein Mann kehrt zurück* (Berlin, 1957).

52. Zemskov, "Zakliuchennye," 152; Bacon, *Gulag at War*, 24.

53. N. F. Bugai, "40–50-e gody: Posledstviia deportatsii narodov," *Istoriia SSSR* no. 1 (1992) 128, 138–39; Zemskov, "Spetsposelentsy," 8–9; Bacon, *Gulag at War*, 30, 118–19; V. Tolz, "New Information about the Deportation of Ethnic Groups in the USSR during World War 2," in *World War 2 and the Soviet People*, ed. J. Garrard and C. Garrard (New York, 1993), 161–79.

54. V. N. Zemskov, "K voprosu o repatriatsii sovetskikh grazhdan 1944–1951 gody," *Istoriia SSSR* no. 4 (1990), 26–41; B. Bonwetsch, "Die sowjetischen Kriegsgefangenen zwischen Stalin und Hitler," *Zeitschrift für Geschichtswissenschaft* no. 41 (1993), 135–42; B. Bonwetsch, "Sowjetische Zwangsarbeiter vor und nach 1945: Ein doppelter Leidensweg," *Jahrbücher für Geschichte Osteuropas* no. 41 (1993), 532–46; P. Polian,

Zhertvy dvukh diktatur: Ostarbajtery i voennoplennye v Tret'em Reikhe i ikh repatri-atsiia (Moscow, 1996).

55. Ehrenburg, *Menschen, Jahre, Leben,* 224–25, 233–34.

56. N. Mandelstam, *Generation ohne Tränen* (Frankfurt am Main, 1975), 215.

57. Ibid.

58. Ehrenburg, *Menschen, Jahre, Leben,* 268.

8

The Siege of Leningrad:
Wartime Literature and Ideological Change

Aileen G. Rambow

The blockade of Leningrad during World War II put the population of the Soviet Union's second largest city in an extremely exposed frontline position for two and a half years. The German army surrounded Leningrad by 8 September 1941, cutting it off from the rest of the country, and kept the city under siege until 27 January 1944, with the intention of destroying the city and its population. About a million Leningraders died from starvation and shells. This immense suffering must always be borne in mind when discussing people's attitudes and the more abstract topic of literature.[1]

The subject of this chapter is literature written during the siege of Leningrad, mostly in the city or at the Leningrad front. Some of it was printed in books or pamphlets, some in newspapers, and some read over the radio. In a city under siege for nearly three years that was systematically being starved by the besieging German army, it is impossible to assess the role literature actually played for the population. Nonetheless one can gain valuable insights into the situation in the city from an investigation of the role literature was supposed to play, the ideas, feelings, and ideology it was supposed to transport.[2]

This chapter concentrates on a cross-section of poetry from the years 1941 through 1945, a concise and representative body of work that can serve as a basic framework for the analysis of themes. Since the approach is mainly thematic, biographical data on single authors will be left aside. Special attention will be given to the themes of patriotism and nationalism, loyalty to Leningrad as opposed to Stalin, and to shifts in policy that are visible in the literature.

War Literature

Soviet war literature was shaped by the doctrine of socialist realism and by the cult of Stalin.[3] But the retreat of the Red Army during the first months of the

Leningrad during the winter of 1941–42. A group of women look for new accommodations after the buildings they lived in were bombed. (Courtesy of the Bilderdienst Süddeutscher Verlag, Munich)

war and the tremendous effort demanded of the entire population for the defense of the country forced the regime to compromise in the realm of ideology. Hence a limited area of freedom appeared for literary expression. To allow literature to reach the people some new themes were accepted. Generally during the war a new interpretation was given of prerevolutionary Russian history and the role of the Russian Orthodox Church. In Vera Dunham's words, "Stalin's wartime rule . . . introduced some permissive elements into a basically draconic practice."[4]

Blockade Literature

In Leningrad this permissive area was increased by the extraordinary situation of the city during the siege, especially during the first year, and by its isolation from Moscow. After the war this limited literary freedom was abruptly cut off, and it seems that the city of Leningrad was punished for its victory, its pride, and its myths in the arrests and executions of the "Leningrad Affair."

Since the city was dying during the blockade, little energy was left for cultural activity. The literature produced in this period is short and largely goal-oriented, intended for army or factory newspapers, for posters and wall newspapers, for small books and brochures, and for the radio. During the first winter of 1941–42, for some Leningraders the only functioning medium was the radio, for which most homes had outlets and which was also broadcast via loudspeakers in the streets. *Leningradskaia Pravda* was published throughout the blockade, but because of the extreme conditions it could not always be distributed in all areas of the city.[5]

The writers, already organized in a union, were delegated to certain areas of activity; for instance Ol'ga Berggol'ts worked for the radio. Others were attached to the navy or parts of the army. Writers were required to visit the troops to strengthen the liaison between soldiers and and civilians and to boost the mood at the front lines. This propaganda activity on the part of the writers had its parallel in the literature itself, which often had the characteristics of appeal. The population of the city was called upon to volunteer for the front and for construction of fortifications. There were also appeals to the population to persevere, to resist, and to remain vigilant. The city was often compared to the front with the purpose of showing that mere survival within the city was as important as frontline fighting.

Themes and Patriotisms

At the beginning of the war there was an emphasis on internationalism as well as a new kind "subjectivity." As will be shown, these tendencies all appeal to groups formerly neglected or to personal feelings of individuals and hence can be viewed generally as similar to "local patriotism." "Objectivity" in the Stalinist context refers to the state, the Soviet Union as a whole, and ultimately to Stalin himself, and is therefore directly opposed to local and, in this case, Leningrad patriotism.

Even though the themes of Leningrad blockade literature vary over the course of the war years, an analysis of a sample of one hundred poems published in the city under siege shows a definite emphasis on the theme of Leningrad. This is what makes blockade writings different from the rest of Soviet war literature.

Generally the literary themes can be related to three different patriotisms: local Leningrad patriotism, Russian patriotism (or nationalism), and socialist or Soviet patriotism. The chronological development within these areas can help to identify ideological change during the blockade. Sometimes themes can point to several patriotisms at the same time, while many poems are not clear and contain mixtures of patriotisms, but even here certain tendencies emerge. The theme or themes of a poem undergo a "mythification" by the ritual use of words and thus take on the function of pointing to a certain patriotism.

"Soviet patriotism" includes themes that refer to the term as defined by

Erwin Oberländer, embracing the community of the peoples of the Soviet Union, but also all other references to socialism and the socialist fatherland, to Lenin, and to the revolution. In this area there are overlaps with issues specific to Leningrad/Petrograd. The latter name was used for the city from 1914 to 1924; it suggested revolutionary zeal and leadership in the country, since Petrograd was the capital and site of major revolutionary developments in 1917.[6]

"Russian patriotism" refers to elements of Russian history and glorifications of "the people" and the "motherland." These themes are generally prevalent in Soviet war literature, but they appear in blockade literature in combination with local patriotism, especially since Aleksandr Nevskii, a thirteenth-century Russian hero, and Peter the Great, for example, can easily be combined with local pride. At the beginning of the war Stalin had particularly recommended historical figures for emulation: "Let yourselves be inspired in this war by the brave image of our great ancestors—Aleksandr Nevskii, Dimitrii Donskoi, Kuz'ma Minin, Dimitrii Pozharskii, Aleksandr Suvorov, Mikhail Kutuzov! May you be led by the victorious banner of the great Lenin!"[7]

The term "Leningrad patriotism" contains the themes of "Petersburg," "Petrograd," "Leningrad," "blockade," and "city and country," that is, all direct descriptions of the blockade and all allusions to the city in its previous historical metamorphoses. These subdivisions and mixtures with other patriotisms are the main subject of this chapter.

Chronological analysis of the one hundred poems shows that in 1941 and 1944–45 the thematic emphasis was on pure Leningrad descriptions; in 1941 quite a few works presented a mixture of Leningrad with Russian patriotism. In 1942 and especially in 1943 there were relatively few poems with pure Leningrad descriptions. A mixture of the themes of Leningrad and the blockade prevailed for the years 1942 and 1944–45 but was entirely missing for 1943. There are blockade poems for 1943, but the emphasis in that year was clearly not on the city, but more on the general situation along the Soviet-German front, visible in the increased number of unspecific front poems. Even though each year from 1942 through 1945 did produce literature on the blockade, 1942 was the high point for city-specific themes and hence for Leningrad patriotism.

City Myths and Themes of the Leningrad Blockade Literature

Central to the content of the three areas of patriotism is the use of myth. I will discuss this in detail only for Leningrad themes. Myths are stories that relate to creation, be it the universe, certain customs, or, in this case, a city. They may relate to other historical events, or may explain natural phenomena. Mythic thinking involves a kind of ubiquitous causality that draws connections from pure proximity of events and objects in time and space, as well as the concept of a mythic time, a glorified and distant past.

As language, a system of signs, myth is nonetheless perceived to be true, since it is based on ritual and the repetition of gestures or formulas. This aspect is important for understanding blockade literature. Lynn Hunt makes a similar observation in her study of the rhetoric of the French Revolution: "the symbolic sources of unity included the constant repetition of key words and principles." Hunt links the use of "ritual words" and "ritual oaths," which also play an important role in blockade literature, to what she calls a "mythic present."[8]

New texts can be seen as myths, provided they are widely accepted and repeated. Claude Lévi-Strauss emphasizes the proximity of myth and ideology, as does Roland Barthes in his study of bourgeois myths.[9] The literature of the blockade drew on the myths of Petersburg, Petrograd, and Leningrad and began to create its own myth of the siege.

Petersburg

Nikolai P. Antsiferov and Ottore Lo Gatto write about "The Myth of Petersburg" and analyze its sources in legends and literature and the ways in which it differs from "historical facts." Antsiferov links different kinds of myths to different ideologies, for instance the myth of Peter the Great as antichrist to the thinking of the Old Believers, the religious schismatics of the seventeenth century and later.[10]

Both authors cite Pushkin's "Bronze Horseman" as central to the Petersburg myth, and indeed virtually everyone writing about the city refers to this famous poem. Images, phrases, and words from Pushkin's poem have been repeated over and over and have been inserted into different contexts with clearer messages than the inscrutable original. The ideological employment of myth for propaganda purposes uses extracts from the literature that can be reduced to unambiguous meaning. It is only one side of the myth that is of importance during the blockade, the notion that Petersburg stands for enlightenment, culture, the arts and sciences, and the quest for knowledge, rationality, and humanity.

During the blockade the city's cultural heritage was something to be proud of and to cling to, giving hope for the future, as in the poem by Vera Inber, "Daytime Concert," where she invokes the lives of Chaikovskii, Pushkin, Glinka, Gogol', and Blok as a worthy cause for Soviet tanks and cannon.[11] Inber also contrasts the culture and beauty of Petersburg with the barbarism of the attacking Germans, who burn libraries and destroy palaces and gardens. "The parks and gardens of Leningrad" is one of the standard expressions for the city that is frequently repeated. It includes the parks of the tsarist palaces around Leningrad that the Germans destroyed.[12] Culture and humanism are expressed in these blockade poems by reference to Pushkin and things connected with him, like "Tsarskoe Selo," with its palace and the statue of the milkmaid, as well as other cultural institutions like the Hermitage Museum, or other palaces like Peterhof. Even the statue of Samson in the fountain arrangement of Peterhof becomes symbolic of the strength of Leningrad.[13] All of this refers to the cultural heritage of tsarist times and has nothing to do with the socialist realist art of the Soviet Union. It is also specific to this city in a way that is unique among Soviet war literature.

A definite declaration of Petersburg patriotism is voiced in Ol'ga Berggol'ts's poem "Arrival in Pushkin," at the end of which she quotes Pushkin directly: "Our home is—Tsarskoe Selo." For "home" she uses the word "fatherland." This is certainly an expression of local patriotism, even if it refers more to an ideal than to a specific locality, since the town, the palaces, and the park had been devastated by the Germans when they were forced out. Again the culture connected with that locality gives the author something to cling to.[14]

Petrograd

Allusions to revolutionary Petrograd and the defense of the city during the civil war tend more to imitate authors of that time, for instance with broken lines in the style of the poet Vladimir Mayakovsky. In Ol'ga Berggol'ts's "February Diary," a reference to the people of revolutionary Petrograd falls out of her usually classicist structure:

> [The people] went with immortal
>   outcry
>   in their hearts:
> "We will die, but Red Piter
>   we won't yield!"[15]

The mythical periods of the foundation of the city and of the revolution are connected by the construction of parallels: the "city of Peter" is compared to the "city of Lenin." The poem "Leningrad" by Nikolai Tikhonov, for instance, begins with the lines "Built by Peter's will / Filled with meaning by Lenin's light."[16] A poem by Vadim Shefner personifies the entire city, but along with the houses, streets, canals, and trees, hurrying to the defense of the city are the bronze horseman on his "proud horse" and Lenin's armored car (*bronevik*) from in front of the Finland station. This overwhelming movement to the front refers to the *narodnoe opolchenie* (people's militia), but is expanded to include steel and stone as well. Here Lenin is not so much the founder of the Soviet Union and the legitimation for Stalin's power, but rather a local hero, along with Peter the Great.[17]

Another parallel consists in the comparison of the defense of Petrograd during the Civil War with the defense of Leningrad against the Germans decades later. A good example is Tikhonov's poem "1919–1941," which links the revolutionary patriotism of the Civil War period to the local Leningrad patriotism of World War II.[18]

Leningrad

Leningrad as a theme is partly mixed with Soviet patriotism, because usually it refers to the development of the city during the thirties, when the author's personal memories of his or her youth in the peaceful city necessarily include the Komsomol. So in this area the subjective perspective is muted, even when the theme is love for one's home town for purely personal reasons. A typical expression of this is the easy combination of Komsomol and first love, as in Olga Berggol'ts's poem "To My Sister," where the author recalls a happy childhood in Leningrad. It is definitely a Leningrad poem, but the young pioneers and with them the Soviet state are present. This concession to the Stalinist state is minimal, though, and in most of the blockade literature of 1942 it is absent altogether.[19] There are reminiscences of prewar Leningrad that exclude all allusions to the Soviet state, that feature "first love" without the Komsomol, as in Shefner's poem "On Petrograd Side" (1942).

Blockade

In addition to the themes of Petersburg, Petrograd, and Leningrad, the theme of the blockade is central to local patriotism. In the literature it leads to the construction of the blockade myth, which feeds on the parallel with the defense of Petrograd during the Civil War. By making a historical comparison, the author sets the frame for blockade literature and also indicates optimism, implying that the enemies of 1941 will be overcome as were those of 1919.

In many poems written during the siege there is already a conscious construction of the future blockade legend. It is mostly visible in a phenomenon I would call "anticipated reminiscence." Especially in the poetry of Ol'ga Berggol'ts there are many images of future peace and of the future remembrance of the heroic days of the blockade, as in this example from her poem "February Diary":

And you, my friend, even in days of peace,
As the height of life you will remember
The house on Red Commanders Avenue,
Where the fire barely glowed and a draft blew from the window.[20]

The poet considered it one of her duties as a writer not only to encourage people during the blockade, but also to ensure that future generations would remember. The construction of future vistas of peace and happiness is a mythical function of socialist realist literature in general, but here it is the idea of looking back from that mythical future that creates the blockade legend.[21]

This is a way of softening the horrors of blockade reality and of giving hope to readers or listeners. Detailed descriptions of the situation were not possible for emotional as well as political reasons. The impossibility of description is mentioned frequently, as in a letter written by the author Vsevolod Vishnevskii to Ilia Ehrenburg on 27 February 1942: "I see and have seen much . . . it is impossible to talk about."[22] Clearly there is a sense of living through something that cannot be put into words.[23]

Authors could only allude to hunger, suffering, and death, so single words took on immense meaning, understandable only to those who experienced the siege. This is what is meant by "myth" in this context: the ritual repetition of certain words or phrases that allude to something more general and more horrible. Some of these words are "night," "cold," "dark," and references to the sound of bombs. "Hunger" is rarely spelled out; it is more often indicated by the preciousness of bread, as in a poem by Tikhonov where bread is compared to gold. Bread takes on mythic and even religious dimensions in this context, where words and images acquire a new reality. The squeaking of a sled on snow is equivalent to death, since that is how corpses were transported in the frozen city. Similarly, "streetcar" means death when it is stopped and frozen, hope when it is running. The searchlights combing the sky for German airplanes are equivalent to security and hope.

The most detailed description of the effects of hunger is to be found in Inber's "Pulkovskii Meridian," where she describes the faces of suffering Leningraders. Toward the beginning of the poem are two stanzas in which the poet fantasizes about bread; she describes its taste and smell and the way it feels when it is fresh.[24] But it was especially important to express the will to live, to resist. This stance made Ol'ga Berggol'ts famous. To the very limit of ideological constraint, in her poetry she expressed the subjective view of a woman caught in the blockade. It was effective because it appealed to other women in a personal way. The "culture" theme symbolizes this will to live and shows that a "life worth living" continued throughout the blockade. The horrible situation called for emphasis of the beautiful and the elevated, and there are indeed religious elements in the literature. "The muse" is a central myth of blockade literature, the idea that art and literature not only continued throughout the siege ("the muses were not silent"), but sustained the population. For the writers themselves this was certainly true; for the rest of the population there is no way of knowing.

City and Country

There is also a certain amount of literature that emphasizes the connection between Leningrad and the rest of the country. There are allusions to Petersburg as Russia's son, in accordance with the tradition that Peter the Great's military capital is male and Russia and Moscow are female. It is fitting that Berggol'ts should address her "sister" in Moscow, assuring her that Leningrad will resist the invader. "Mashenka, sister mine in Moscow, / The Leningraders speak to you," is how the poem begins. Toward the end she writes: "Steadfast and fearless is Leningrad. / He does not tremble, does not submit."[25] In a poem by Aleksandr Prokof'ev, "I Am Your Guard," this relation is quite obvious, especially in the line "Your city, your soldier, your fighting son," where the city of Leningrad speaks to the rest of the country and promises to protect it. This personification of the city is partly explainable by the city-myth, and it increases the identification of the Leningrad citizens with their hometown.

An interesting variation is expressed with the image, "key to the heart of Russia."[26] In the Soviet Union there existed the opinion that the defense of the rear and of Moscow itself would be endangered if Leningrad fell. The city was important strategically, but also symbolically. Petersburg stands for Russia's rise to the status of a European power. On an economic level the city is a "key to Russia" with its harbor, on a cultural level as an interface between East and West, on a political level as the capital and especially as the cradle of the revolution. From its very beginning Petersburg combined opening toward the West with military defense against it; even this paradox of purposes is contained in the image of the "key to Russia." According to the emphasis on these various myths and their connection with more general Soviet themes or topics from Russian history, one can discern varying patriotisms: Soviet patriotism, Russian patriotism, or local Leningrad patriotism.

The chronological changes in the literature of the blockade show a certain emphasis on Soviet themes in 1943. For that year there is even a poem by Saianov that includes a vision of Stalin in Leningrad, which seems like a final destruction of Leningrad patriotism.[27] But in 1944 and 1945 there are some melancholy poems of lingering subjectivity that seem to suggest sadness about the past horrors and a determination to continue to believe in the local Leningrad victory. Berggol'ts was later to be criticized for adhering too long to the theme of the Leningrad blockade, which indeed became the main subject of her writings.[28]

Ideology

Ideological Constraints — Since Leningrad was considered frontline territory, it was subject to military censorship that extended to everything from private correspondence to radio broadcasts. Stories that were to be published were checked for ideological content as a matter of course. For example in May 1942 the author Vsevolod Vishnevskii received a letter from the editor of the army newspaper *Red Star,* David Ortenberg, thanking him for the story he sent in, but criticizing the ending. The story is about the Civil War of 1918–20, and in the end the heroes are taken prisoner by the enemy. "Our newspaper follows the line that our fighters cannot give themselves up to the Germans as prisoners *under any circumstances,*"[29] Ortenberg writes. He asks Vishnevskii to change the ending of the story accordingly. In August 1941 Stalin had decreed that any member of the Red Army who surrenders to the enemy under whatever circumstances would be considered a deserter.

Ideological Changes — The emphasis of the censorship changed during the course of the blockade. A good example is the poem by Ol'ga Berggol'ts, "February Diary," which was broadcast at the beginning of 1942, the worst period of the blockade, and then again half a year later in June 1942. Since radio was at times the only functioning medium in the city, the messages it conveyed were all the more important. The typewritten versions that the poet handed in to the radio committee are identical, but for the broadcast in June handwritten changes were made on the page. One stanza was crossed out entirely:

> When we get through to Berlin on the day of revenge,
> And German women bring out their children,
> And will crawl, howling for forgiveness,
> We shall not forgive, not pity them.[30]

This change was in accordance with the policy of turning away from the indiscriminate hatred so common in the first year of the war. It was in 1942 that Stalin made his famous differentiation between Hitler and the German people.[31] Another line that appears three times throughout the original version of the poem by Berggol'ts has been changed each time, so that instead of "In this dirt, darkness, hunger, sorrow," it now reads first "In today's bondage and sorrow," then "In the enemy's ring, in hunger, in sorrow," and then "In today's suffering and sorrows."[32] One cannot say that the lines have been softened or are any more positive, but they are nobler, more abstract, and the dirt has been removed. This may seem like a small change, but in historical context this one word, "dirt," transports a large part of the horror of daily life under siege—without food, heating, water, or drainage systems, and with people dying all around.

Change outside the Sphere of Literature

In 1943–44 organizational changes were introduced in the Leningrad writers' union. Self-criticism and criticism of colleagues' ideological mistakes started in the union, always a sign of ideological changes and approaching purges. The editors of the literary magazines *Zvezda* and *Leningrad* were criticized in 1944, a premonition of the harsher criticism that was to come.[33] The closure of the magazines effected in 1946, along with Zhdanov's attack on the writers Mikhail Zoshchenko and Anna Akhmatova, can be seen as the culmination of this development, or possibly as a drastic step in the direction of the "Leningrad Affair" of 1949, when large parts of the Leningrad intelligentsia and of the Leningrad party organization were purged.

Ideological changes that took place during the siege of Leningrad were linked to changes that took place in the entire country, however in Leningrad they were to have special consequences. After the battle of Stalingrad it became obvious that the Red Army would be able to force the Germans to retreat, and the central authorites in Moscow could begin reinstating control. In Leningrad the changes took place at different levels: at the party level, in industry, and in the area of propaganda, agitation, and culture. In all of these areas after the first winter of the war in 1941–42, increased discipline, control, and centralization began to appear, though generally these trends did not become well established until 1943.

The newspaper *Leningradskaia Pravda* was subject to direct party control all along. Already in 1942 it was reprimanded for "serious political mistakes," its editor, Solotukhin, was attacked, and the secretary of the Urban Committee for Propaganda, Shumilov, was informed that he "controlled insufficiently the work of the editing-collective of *Leningradskaia Pravda.*" The controversy concerned the way in which an editorial of 8 February presented the tasks of the war.[34]

In August 1942 the Department of Propaganda and Agitation of the *gorkom*

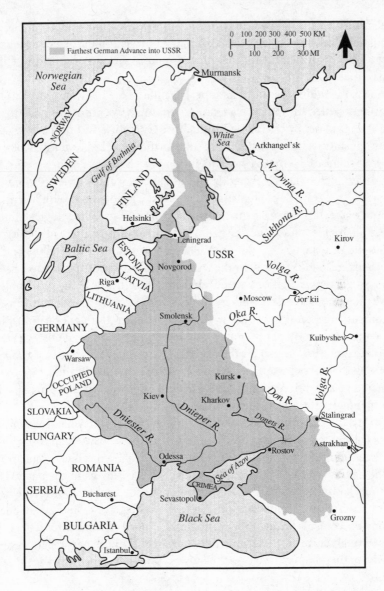

(the city committee of the party) addressed the more than fifty war correspondents who were stationed in Leningrad for various newspapers. According to party opinion the war correspondents had taken on too much importance. They should be controlled more effectively, because the editors-in-chief and their staffs often did not even know how to locate their own correspondents.

The party made the following recommendation for war reporting: "babble less about hate and show more of its material manifestation in the newspaper. It is necessary to dispense with the standard and to seek an original presentation of materials."[35]

In 1943 the undifferentiated hate-propaganda of the first war years was increasingly criticized, and even a famous writer like Ilya Ehrenburg had to revise his hard line. By criticizing the quality of literature and propaganda the party reinstated its control. Right after the German attack allowances had been made in this area, as long as the outcome enhanced defense readiness, but after the leadership had recovered from the shock it wanted to exert more influence on the content of literary and journalistic production. With increased control of single journalists the party could press for more ideological differentiation. In this context the description of single events was already criticized at the end of 1942, when it was said that, "It is not allowed to feed the reader only with episodes." Only after the war did this development come to a head, when single representations were forbidden altogether as being too "subjective"; then only "objective" representations with Stalin as the center of an all-encompassing strategy were allowed. It is in this direction that one must interpret the indication of the Leningrad party organization in August 1942 that "episode literature" is bad for the readers. Interestingly it includes a comparison with the role of the American media, which, conveniently misunderstood, are cited as a positive example: "In England and America there are special commentators. The people know them and listen to them."[36]

Toward the end of 1942 the specific reorientation of propagandists and agitators began in Leningrad; in various city districts the party held courses for the "schooling and reschooling of propagandists."[37] Even military censorship of the Leningrad front came under intensified scrutiny from the party. The Central Committee criticized "very serious inadequacies," including "the negligent attitude of a number of censors toward their work" and "inadequate secondary controls," which together allowed "politically harmful letters" to pass through the mail.[38] The infractions may not have been particularly severe, but the main point is that a breach of instructions had been noticed and criticized.

Another area subject to ideological change was the regime's attitude toward Jews. This again is not Leningrad-specific, but it fits into the pattern, and the Jewish population of Leningrad was affected. In 1941 *Leningradskaia Pravda* reported on ghettos and murders of Jews by the Germans in Poland and took a definite stand against anti-Semitism.[39] The appeal of the Antifascist Committee to "Jewish Brothers in the whole world" to fight against fascism appeared in *Leningradskaia Pravda* in August 1941. Answers from the Socialist League and the organization Hashomer Hatsair from Tel Aviv on the pages of the same newspaper showed the effort at open-mindedness and solidarity with the international antifascist movement.[40] After the war the committee was disbanded, its members were arrested, and many were killed, and the anti-Semitic repressions increased until Stalin's death in 1953.

A famous example of the ideological twists concerning Leningrad and the blockade legend is the fate of the blockade museum that had been planned already during the war and that was very popular during the short term of its existence. In 1946 the division for culture and propaganda of the gorkom collected information about the literary magazines *Zvezda* and *Leningrad* and the number of visitors to the blockade museum.[41] Soon all three institutions were closed.

❖ ❖ ❖

The role of literature during the blockade was to increase local support for defense, to mobilize the population, especially those who were not strictly organized in some hierarchical structure (above all women), to motivate them to continue, to stabilize the situation in the city, and to supply moral support. Another important function was to document the heroism of the people of Leningrad. How much of this was actually effected by literature is not clear, but this was the agenda set at first partly by writers themselves, then increasingly from above.

To these ends new forms of patriotism were promoted. In addition to Soviet patriotism and the new varieties of Russian patriotism implied in the heroization of certain characters from Russian history, a local patriotism was developed in Leningrad. It consisted of pride in the cultural and historical heritage of Petersburg, of pride in Petrograd as the epicenter of the revolution and the hub of victory in 1919, of love for the Leningrad of one's personal experience, and finally of pride for the heroic defense of the city during World War II. This local patriotism had relatively little to do with the whole of the Soviet Union, with the socialist idea, or with Stalin.

In 1943 the direct appeal to the population became less of a prerogative of Leningrad writers, but even though the emphasis in party guidelines changed, there was still a lingering insistence on subjectivity in the literature, on personal feelings and experiences and on the memory of the siege, as if some authors were claiming the areas of freedom gained during the war.

At the beginning of the war, propaganda appealed to personal, local, and group interests on a fairly subjective level (as in Leningrad) and on an international level (women, Jews, Slavs in various countries). Individuals usually not included in the political process took on a certain relevance, and one might count "the Leningrader" among these. As part of a group these individuals might have gained longer-lasting influence from their brief political relevance at the beginning of the war and were therefore quickly disbanded and even destroyed by the central authorities once they had played their part in defending the country.

The relative ideological freedom that resulted from the chaos after the German attack in 1941 and the necessity of total mobilization at all costs diminished as the military situation in the country stabilized. In Leningrad the utter horror of the first winter, 1941–42, was lightened somewhat in 1942 and 1943 when food could be brought in more regularly and a degree of order was restored in the city. This also meant that central party control from Moscow was reinstated. Local patriotism was not allowed to lose sight of the Soviet Union as a whole, and personal feelings in poetry were not allowed to sound too pessimistic. Even though it is hard to disentangle the mixes of patriotism or to pinpoint the exact dates and degrees of ideological changes, certainly such changes did take place during the war itself. In Leningrad in particular the events after the war and the repressions of 1946 and possibly of 1949 can be traced to a gradual development that began toward the end of the blockade.

Notes

1. For western histories of the siege see Harrison Salisbury, *The 900 Days: The Siege of Leningrad* (New York, 1969); Leon Goure, *The Siege of Leningrad* (Stanford, Calif., 1962); Aileen Rambow, *Überleben mit Worden: Literatur und Ideologie während der Blockade von Leningrad, 1941–1944* (Berlin, 1995); and the chapter by Richard Bidlack in this volume. For the German documents see Max Domarus, *Hitler: Reden und Proklamationen, 1932–1945: Kommentiert von einem deutschen Zeitgenossen* (Munich, 1965); *Hitlers Weisungen für die Kriegsführung, 1939–1945: Dokumente des Oberkommandos der Wehrmacht*, ed. Walther Hubatsch (Frankfurt, 1962); *Das Deutsche Reich und der Zweite Weltkrieg*, vol. 4: *Der Angriff auf die Sowjetunion*, ed. Militärhistorisches Forschungsamt (Stuttgart, 1983); Wolfram Wette and Gerd Ueberschär, *"Unternehmen Barbarossa": Der deutsche Überfall auf die Sowjetunion 1941: Berichte, Analysen, Dokumente* (Paderborn, 1984).

2. For the use of literature as a source for historical and social analysis see Vera Dunham, *In Stalin's Time: Middle-class Values in Soviet Fiction* (Cambridge, 1976); Katerina Clark, *The Soviet Novel: History as Ritual* (Chicago, 1985); Irina Gutkin, *The Novel of Socialist Realism as a Phenomenon of Literary Evolution* (Ann Arbor, Mich., 1991), esp. the introduction, "Socialist Realism as a Form of Cultural Consciousness."

3. For a definition of socialist realism see Hans Günther, *Die Verstaatlichung der Literatur: Entstehung und Funktionsweise des sozialistisch-realistischen Kanons in der sowjetischen Literatur der Dreißiger Jahre* (Stuttgart, 1984).

4. Dunham, *In Stalin's Time*, 7.

5. For an account of the radio committee's work see Aleksandr Rubashkin, *Golos Leningrada: Leningradskoe radio v dni blokady* (Leningrad, 1975). For a discussion of blockade literature from the point of view of literary criticism see *Literaturnyi Leningrad v dni blokady,* ed. V. A. Kovalev and A. I. Pavlovskii (Leningrad, 1973).

6. Erwin Oberländer, *Sowjetpatriotismus und Geschichte: Dokumentation* (Cologne, 1967), 9–50.

7. Iosif V. Stalin, *Sochineniia,* vol. 2, ed. Robert H. McNeal (Stanford, Calif., 1967), 35. For the tradition of hagiographic devices in Russian literature and for the development of cult see Margaret Ziolkowski, *Hagiography and Modern Russian Literature* (Princeton, N.J., 1988); Nina Tumarkin, *Lenin Lives: The Lenin Cult in Soviet Russia* (Cambridge, Mass., 1983).

8. Lynn Hunt, *Politics, Culture, and Class in the French Revolution* (Berkeley, Calif., 1984), 14, 27.

9. Mircea Eliade, *Mythos und Wirklichkeit* (Frankfurt, 1988); Ernst Cassirer, *Philosophie der symbolischen Formen,* vol. 2, *Das mythische Denken* (Darmstadt, 1987); Jean Pierre Vernant, *Mythos ohne Illusion* (Frankfurt, 1984); Roland Barthes, *Mythologies* (Paris, 1957).

10. Nikolai P. Antsiferov, *Byl' i mif Peterburga* (Petrograd, 1924); Ettore Lo Gatto, *Il mito di Pietroburgo: Storia, leggenda, poesia* (Milan, 1960).

11. *Gorod slavy boevoi: Stikhi i poemy, 1941–1945* (Leningrad, 1945), 14.

12. Ibid., 11; see also 12, 23, 29, 34.

13. Ibid., 13–14, 20, 23, 34.

14. Ibid., 149. Berggol'ts quotes from Pushkin's poem "19 oktjabrja"; see Aleksandr S. Pushkin, *Sochineniia v trekh tomakh,* vol. 1 (Moscow, 1985), 355.

15. *Gorod slavy boevoi,* 63.

16. Ibid., 5.

17. Ibid., 89.

18. Ibid., 6–8.

19. Ibid., 20.

20. Ol'ga Berggol'ts, *Leningradskii dnevnik: Stikhi i poemy, 1941–1944* (Leningrad, 1944), 28.

21. Katerina Clark, *The Soviet Novel: History as Ritual* (Chicago, 1985), 107.

22. Tsentral'nii Gosudarstvennii Arkhiv Literatury i Iskusstva, Moscow (TsGALI), fond (f.) 1038, opis' (o.) 1, delo (d.) 2490.

23. For the workings of censorship, see Sidney Monas, "Censorship as a Way of Life," in *Perspectives on Literature and Society in Eastern and Western Europe,* ed. Geoffrey A. Hosking and George F. Cushing (London, 1989).

24. *Gorod slavy boevoi,* 52–58.

25. Ibid., 20.

26. Ibid., 11.

27. Ibid., 126.

28. More direct descriptions of the horror of the situation have only been allowed to appear since the mid 1980s. One of the first was Lidiia Gintsburg, *Chelovek za pismennom stolom* (Leningrad, 1989).

29. TsGALI, f. 1038, o. 2, ed. chr. no. 458.

30. Tsentral'nii Gosudarstvennii Arkhiv Literatury i Iskusstva v Leningrade (TsGALI L), f. 293, o. 2, d. 559.

31. Stalin, *Sochineniia*, vol. 2, 42.

32. TsGALI L, f. 293, o. 2, d. 559.

33. See Aleksandr Prokof'ev's speech at the meeting of the Leningrad writers' union in 1944, published in *Pobeda i mir: Sbornik nauchnykh trudov*, ed. V. A. Shoshin (Leningrad, 1987), 107–11; and critical letters by Vsevolod Vishnevskii, TsGALI, f. 1038, o. 1, d. 2490 and 2239.

34. Leningradskii Partiinii Arkhiv (LPA), f. 24, o. 2, d. 5084, list (l. or ll.) 20.

35. Ibid., f. 25, o. 10, d. 335, ll. 20–24.

36. Ibid., l. 24.

37. Ibid., *Perechen'*, biuro, d. 13, protokol 44, 28.9.1942.

38. Ibid., f. 25, op. 10, d. 335, l. 26.

39. *Leningradskaia Pravda (LP)*, 26 July 1941, 1.

40. *LP*, 26 Aug. 1941, 5 Sept. 1941, 1.

41. LPA, f. 25, o. 10, d. 597, 613.

9

Soviet Russian Wartime Culture: Freedom and Control, Spontaneity and Consciousness

Richard Stites

The mobilization of culture in the Great Patriotic War of 1941 must be seen in the context of the overall dynamic interaction of state policy and popular response. To make the point more clearly, one may compare the relation of state and culture in the Soviet experience to that in the Great War of 1914. Bluntly speaking, these two struggles had little in common except the fact that Germans and Russians fought each other. Two important books and some other recent studies are eloquent on the matter. The German scholar Hubertus Jahn's study of popular culture and entertainment in the visual and performing arts offers a picture of commercial opportunity combined with popular patriotism in the initial phases of war which resulted in a very large and interesting output of culture directly related to the war. As a rule this culture highlighted the bravery of Russian troops, the evil of the enemy, the nobility of the Allies (especially the "martyr nation," Belgium), and the reliability of the home front. This output began to fade after 1915 along with enthusiasm for the war among the population. The Imperial Russian regime, with a few exceptions, played a distinctly minor role in promoting anything like a vast propaganda machine.[1]

The Finnish literary historian Ben Hellman's book on the symbolist poets during World War I goes well beyond its main topic and taps the very core of the cultural intelligentsia's response to the war. That response, though rhetorically patriotic, was couched in mystical formulations of the spiritual superiority of the Russian soul. It seldom touched on the realities of blood and battle. For the Russian intelligentsia, this war was fought in the realms of spirit, soul, and mind, an apocalyptic battle of ideas and national moralities.[2]

My own brief survey of high and popular culture in the War of 1914 emphatically confirms this view.[3] The wartime spy thrillers in print culture and cine-

The singer Aleksandra Staskevièiute (member of the Supreme Soviet of the Lithuanian Soviet Socialist Republic) sings before soldiers of the 16th Lithuanian division, 1943. (O-40441; courtesy of the Lithuanian Archive of Picture and Sound, Vilnius)

ma took the consumer to the front lines and into the machinations of the enemy behind the lines. Hero tales exalted the lancer, the machine gunner, the aviator, and the brave nurse; they vividly described the milieu—troop trains, mountains of corpses, field hospitals. Thoroughly mendacious in exaggerating German atrocities and denying or ignoring Russian brutalities during the Great Retreat of 1915, these works of pulp fiction and movie action melodrama nevertheless engaged the war itself—its material ambiance and its bodily exploits and suffering. After the disasters of 1915, even these genres turned back to the more traditional forms and themes of adventure, high society sexual melodrama, and even comedy. As a whole, the culture produced during the Great War metaphorically illustrates two great gaps: one between the state and the rest of society and one between elite and popular visions of the war.

One of the achievements of Stalinist culture—with all its distortions and banalities—was to close these gaps. The closure, or at least a major rapprochement, of the gap between state and society is well enough known: the monopolization and active guidance of literature and all the arts along the lines of "socialist realism." The machinery created in the 1930s ensured tight censorship, the silencing of dissonant voices, and the direct shaping of the arts, particularly the narrative arts—fiction, painting, opera, drama. The content and formulas of socialist realism closed, or attempted to close, the gap between intelligentsia and people, one might even say between mind and body. In fiction, the model for all the other arts, the intelligentsia was welded to the masses in every struggle—for production and against wreckers. The weld joined two elements of Soviet society. One was a mature mentor, often a learned and seasoned commissar, engineer, or scientist, cool and reserved, ready to shape the energies of the other. And that other was the man or woman of the people—partisan, worker, collective farmer, aviator—hotheaded and locked in a battle against some obstruction, but too spontaneous to pull it off without the counsel of the mentor. However false the jointure, however unconvincing the obstacles and the solutions, this formula created the model for the culture of the Soviet war against the Axis powers between 1941 and 1945.

Soon after the initial shock of the 1941 invasion, social volcanoes began erupting on the Soviet home front. State policy, military operations, and mass reaction to the invasion took numerous forms. The government, party, and police mobilized the people, evacuated personnel and factories to the rear, moved whole segments of the population around on an immense scale, relocated government offices and cultural establishments, including film studios and theaters, and saw to the manufacture of weapons, the transport of troops, and the recruitment of ever fresh levees. As an example of massive direction of human energy, within six months over fifteen hundred large-scale enterprises, including over a hundred aircraft factories, were evacuated; about one-eighth of the nation's industrial assets were dismantled, relocated, and reassembled in the Urals, Central Asia, and Siberia. High school graduates of both sexes enlisted. Villagers melted into the forest and became partisans. Youngsters organized urban spy rings to wreak sabotage on the German garrisons. A million women served in the armed forces, not only in traditional wartime roles of nurses, doctors, and antiaircraft gunners, but also as flyers, soldiers, tankers, and partisans.[4]

Nothing even faintly resembling this occurred during World War I. The regime possessed neither the will nor the power to make such things happen, nor would the population have responded in full array for war. This was partly due to the circumstances at the front. By 1915 the possibility of the Germans plunging into Great Russian territory was real, but at the outer limit of German expansion, they occupied only Poland and part of the Baltic provinces and then got stalled. Scattered atrocities occurred, of course, but nothing like the systematic bestiality that followed in the wake of Operation Barbarossa in

1941. In fact, during World War I, Russian outrages in Poland and Galicia were worse than anything the Central Powers perpetrated on the eastern front. Little of this filtered into Russian popular awareness, except for some publicity about the fate of the Jews who were cruelly used during the retreat of 1915.

In the Soviet war, state officials, propagandists of the Communist Party, and leaders of unions and mass organizations, carefully reading the psychology of the wartime masses, constructed new myths, legends, and cultural icons. Grafted onto the template of socialist realism, they were designed to draw upon the bottomless wells of national pride, to substitute visceral themes about the beloved homeland for the dry, bombastic official patriotism of the prewar period. For reasons both noble and ignoble, they reached out to find the heart of war in every Russian and to make it beat the rhythms of love, hate, anger, and ridicule—all directed toward smashing the "fascist" enemy and saving Mother Russia.

The level of hatred toward the German enemy differed greatly in the two wars. Except among a few circles of the pre-1914 Pan-Slavic intelligentsia, the teutonophobic rage was short-lived. Nothing like the Bolshevik buildup of the "fascist beast" had been present in pre-1914 Russia because, of course, fascism had not yet been born. In the Soviet 1920s the word "fascist" became a floating modifier for virtually any kind of enemy, including even Social Democrats who were seen as nothing more than servants of fascism disguised as socialists. In the 1930s, with Hitler in power in Nazi Germany, the term took on flesh, at least until the Nazi-Soviet Nonagression Pact of 1939. After two years of uneasy alliance it was not difficult to revive the old repulsive images. In order to retain some vestige of a Marxoid political category, the enemy was consistently labeled "fascist invader" by the official press. But eventually the more concrete "German" took over, especially in the hate poetry and journalism of eloquent writers such as Konstantin Simonov and Ilya Ehrenburg. When one sets the cardboard villains of Russian World War I spy thrillers, plays, and films beside the quintessential demons of World War II invaders, the former take on an almost comic hue.

In general accounts of the Soviet Union in World War II, the cultural dimension is still relatively neglected. Only religion and literature have been adequately treated. The expressive life of the wartime experience in communications, creativity, entertainment, the arts, hagiography and legend making, and the memorialization of the war has been addressed in a previous book, which focuses on the resurfacing into public life of emotional and even spiritual expression, recently suppressed or distorted in the media during the 1930s.[5]

Two major cultural-psychological currents were at large during this momentous struggle, coexisting and occasionally clashing. The first was the official style of nationalism, authoritarianism, and hierarchy established in the 1930s—formal, impersonal, pompous, and unnervingly unemotional. It expressed itself in various terms: Stalinism, *partiinost* (high ideological consciousness and dedication to political business), socialist realism (the fantasy world of 1930s art that required folkloric structures and idealistic messages), heroicized traditional history, revolutionary glory, and proletarian robustness. Perhaps only the Russian adjectives *offitsioznyi* and *kazënnyi* can convey the terms of expression that in English suggest words like official, state, declamatory, inflated, bureaucratic, operatic, stylized, melodramatic, posed, monumental, utopian, and panegyric. The style was burdened with values of official boast and state talk as illustrated in the radio voices of Yurii Levitan and other announcers, government communiqués, *Pravda* headlines and editorials, and some films, songs, music, plays, graphics, and legends.

While such state-suffused cultural expression exists in all modern societies with mass communication, in the Soviet Union it was exceptionally amplified and hypertrophied, beyond even that of the Third Reich. The "public sphere" that usually lies between private discourse and official culture was unusually narrow because its basis—civil society—was almost eliminated by the nationalization of industry and all business, the collectivization of the countryside, the fear engendered by police, purge, and terror, and the swelling of the state. The small public sphere of expression—mass culture—was never wholly free of state content, even though much of it was very popular in terms of consumption. Needless to say, much that was private, unofficial, semiofficial, and countercultural remained outside the reach of the state, but its public utterance was severely restricted.

An acceptable aspect of unofficial and semiofficial cultural style rose to ascendance after the initial shock, however, and clearly expressed the feelings of a people at war. In vivid contrast to the official style, it was emotional, personal, relaxed, earthy, natural, spontaneous, autonomous, expressive, and honest about death, suffering, heroism, and hate. Wartime culture reflected the partial relegitimation in Soviet public culture of personal life, intimate feelings, interior authenticity, and even quasi religiosity that had been muted during the "optimistic" thirties. Even the official party organ, *Pravda*, was, in the words of Jeffrey Brooks, "opened to new voices and new images of soldiers, partisans, civilians, and citizens."[6] Nina Tumarkin, interviewing veterans, tells of the sense of freedom that many participants felt on the outbreak of war. She quotes survivors saying that "those were our finest hours, the most brilliant time of our lives."[7] For those people the horrors, recalled with equal vividness, did not blot out the golden glow of that memory. Suffering and perhaps fear led to a passionate exaltation of Russian nature, its people, history, culture, and ancient religion. Art in every form could not fail to intersect with the changing mood.

Ironically enough, but not surprisingly, the popular culture of World War I had contained more bombast than emotional authenticity. Battlefield fiction and songs, including contrived hero stories, were suffused with "hurrah patriotism," particularly at the beginning of hostilities. Like the French, the Russians were planning to bivouac outside Berlin in no time at all. Heroic legends—not all of them false—were spun around individuals such as Kuzma Kryuchkov, who allegedly killed eleven German soldiers with his lance.[8] In World War II, the Red Army and the Soviet partisans had their share of individual exploits as well, but the "collective"—particular units, cities, and guerrilla bands—was much more prominent in the hagiography. Although some women went into combat during World War I, there were no partisan martyrs like Zoya Kosmodemyanskaya.

Many sources attest to the relative loosening of intellectual and creative controls in the years of the German occupation and the life-and-death struggle for national and state survival. Sad and terrible as it is to say, the war seemed to unleash creativity and create a kind of relieved joy. "When war flared up," wrote Boris Pasternak, "its real horrors and real dangers, the threat of a real death, were a blessing compared to the inhuman reign of fantasy, and they brought relief by limiting the magic force of the dead letter."[9] As the composer Dmitrii Shostakovich recalled, "the war helped. The war brought great sorrow and made life very hard. Much sorrow and many tears. But it had been even harder before the war, because then everyone was alone in his sorrow."[10] Those who did not collaborate with the enemy—the vast majority under occupation as well as those outside the occupied zones—formed a community of deep and shared sorrow as well as a nearly unanimous hatred of the enemy, which helped to reshape national consciousness to an extent that the old revolutionary élan could never again dislodge.

The notion of a "holy war" is almost oxymoronic, given war's essence and purpose. But almost all nations, particularly those who are attacked and invaded, try to sanctify the struggle. The USSR—with its Russian core—was no exception. The ideology of communism could not always evoke sacred feelings among the masses. Marxism, though not abandoned, was downplayed for most of the war: the Comintern was abolished, and patriotic slogans replaced international proletarian ones in an acceleration of the "nationalization" of Bolshevism that had first glimmered in the 1920s and then rose more rapidly in the 1930s. Significant is the fact that the official name of the war, the Great Patriotic (or Fatherland) War, did not contain the words "communist" or "Soviet." Wartime patriotism was couched in terms of reverence for the land, its history, and its treasure house of culture—all supporting the belief in the virtue of the Russian and Soviet peoples and the hideous bestiality of the German invader who sought their annihilation.

The Russian land as the matrix of home and family provided the central metaphor for wartime mood and culture. Germans lusted after Russian Earth, went the slogan; let them each have six feet of it. The land, with its familiar rivers, steppes, meadows, and endless birch forests, was a permanent backdrop to wartime culture. The motherland (*rodina*)—often represented in graphic art as a maternal figure—became an object of unabashed idolatry. Popular songs evoked simplicity and family happiness (real and imagined), with occasional visions of a rustic cabin or a hometown street. The memorable film song "Dark Is the Night" sings of bullets whistling across the steppe in fierce battle while far away the soldier's wife wipes away a tear beside the cradle of their child. Women were often represented as defenseless and menaced or victimized by a German. There was nothing tendentious about this: women and children were being slaughtered in cold blood by the thousands, a practice graphically exhibited in films of the period such as *She Defends the Fatherland* (1943), *Zoya* (1944), and *Rainbow* (1944). But women were also engaged in combat, a fact poorly reflected in official culture except for this trinity of thematically limited partisan women movies.

Heroes of the historical homeland were quickly reenlisted in the war effort. The 1938 film *Alexander Nevsky*, banned during the Nazi-Soviet Pact, was taken off the shelf and reissued after the invasion. Great military heroes of the medieval and tsarist past were refurbished: Nevsky in film, Kutuzov in drama, Suvorov on posters. Parallels with 1812 were heavily underlined. Dmitrii Moor's poster, "Then and Now, 1812–1941," foregrounded Hitler with a Napoleonic silhouette lurking behind him. The film short *Incident at the Telegraph Office* (1941) shows Napoleon sending Hitler a message: "I have tried it. I do not recommend it." All of this was as formal and contrived as the creation of hero cults at the time. Abstract populations, such as cities, were heroized for their endurance or resistance; Leningrad, Brest, Kiev, Odessa, Sevastopol, and Stalingrad were eventually named Hero Cities.[11] Mythic cults of human heroes and martyrs were woven around the Twenty-Eight Panfilov men, the Five Sailors of Sevastopol, the Young Guard of Krasnodon, and Captain Gastello, who plunged his burning plane into an enemy armored column. Two stand out as the most famous: Alexander Matrosov, who allegedly threw his body across a German machine-gun nest, and Zoya Kosmodemyanskaya, who was tortured and hanged by the Germans early in the war. Both heroic images were stamped into the devotional life of wartime and postwar Russia through poetry, drama, radio, movies, photos, statues, and children's tales, and both are now subject to searching revision by historians.

Rosalinde Sartorti has examined the demythologizing of war heroes and their alleged exploits, asking the question, Which is more important, the "truth," or the truth that was believed? She argues that these heroes were in a sense created by the masses, whose aesthetic and moral demands help craft the deed and the person honored for doing it. Studies of the press also show that real people, "little" men and women, were being watched, interviewed, and chronicled without the mediation of the state. The radio and news correspondents who humanized and desolemnized their material—particularly Vasilii Grossman, Konstantin Simonov, and Ilya Ehrenburg—were the most popular with civilians and soldiers alike. It is interesting that many serious fiction writers served at the front alongside professional journalists—a thing that did not, to my knowledge, occur in Germany or the United States (where the most famous correspondent, Ernie Pyle, was a professional newsman, distant in psychology and style from a writer like Ernest Hemingway who had served in Spain). Jeffrey Brooks, in describing wartime *Pravda,* speaks of "new images of soldiers, partisans, civilians, and citizens," autonomous and sentient beings in contrast to the puppet-like figures interviewed on construction sites in the 1930s. State heroes were thus balanced by real ones—ordinary people caught up in the grimness of war. The space occupied by the cult of Stalin—now in temporary decline—was filled by popular heroism. And when heroism involved death, this was faced with honesty and dignity.[12]

The precious storehouse of Russian classics was linked with the national liberation. Novels and stories flooded the reading market. Tolstoy's *War and Peace*—now read for its promises—was issued in huge print runs and read by actors over the airwaves in a series of thirty radio shows. The same author's *Sevastopol Tales* was given a radio reading during the siege of that city. Many nineteenth-century novels, poems, and plays were read over the radio and thus perhaps became a part of mass culture for the first time. Soviet creative artists appeared on radio talk shows—as the composer Shostakovich, the writer Alexei Tolstoy, and the actor Nikolai Cherkasov (who had played the title role in the film *Alexander Nevsky*) did together—to appeal for a defense of Russian culture against the marauding enemy.[13]

Classical music was exalted as never before. In war-racked cities, the most mournful strains of Chaikovsky filled the concert halls and airwaves, and concerts were aired live from the Bolshoi theater. The journalist Alexander Werth recalled with astonishment "the extraordinary emotional atmosphere that summer, for instance at any routine Tchaikovsky concert—as though all Russian civilization were now in deadly danger. I remember the countless tears produced on one of the worst days in July 1942 by the famous love theme in Tchaikovsky's *Romeo and Juliet* Overture." Werth was puzzled by this. Yet any student of the sociology of music (or any sensitive listener for that matter) knows how easily music that conveys sorrow, even on a wholly unrelated theme, can release feelings and tears about one's own immediate grief. In a time of war or immense tragedy, personal grief can become part of a collective national lament. Soviet composers turned their talents to war-related subjects, Shostakovich's "Leningrad" Symphony being the most famous and most emotionally cathartic of these. Classical music lorded it on the airwaves, becoming in fact a popular art. This had been prepared for by the immediate efforts of cultural leaders to expose workers to "monographic" concerts of classical music right after the Revolution and by radio broadcasts of music education in the 1930s. Beethoven, Mozart, and Bach—though German—were not banished (as they were in some concert halls during World War I); on the contrary they were used by artistic leaders to draw a line between "true and good Germans" and Nazis.[14]

The Germans also sacralized music, treating it as a popular as well as a national art. In the combat film drama *Stukas* (1940), two of the heroes play Chopin on the piano between raids against the French, even though, I have been told, public performance of Chopin's music was outlawed in German-occupied Poland, Chopin's homeland. The two aviators also play Wagner's *Rhine Journey*, arranged for two hands. When later in the film a young pilot becomes shell-shocked, he is cured by a performance of this music at Bayreuth where his nurse points out to him "the beauty of the German land." In another movie, *Wunschkonzert* (1942), a domestic scene shows the playing of Beethoven's *Pathétique* sonata (which has to be identified to the listeners on screen) as the camera cuts to the marching feet of booted soldiers on the street below. Art, nation, and heroism became a natural linking in popular imaging. But the "classics" in general were given much more widespread dissemination in the USSR than in other belligerent nations. This was because officially produced mass culture lacked sufficient emotional power, and the authorities preferred the "clean," respectable emotionalism of the classics, which induced reverent pride—but not a direct individual stake—in the homeland, to that of popular culture from below.

Wartime radio deepened the bond among Soviet citizens who listened to the open expressions of love, loneliness, despair, fear, and hope contained in letters to and from the front. Vladimir Yakhontov, a reader-actor, said, "living without listening to the radio was impossible. Radio informed, signalled and guided us, kept kin and loved ones linked together." Its programming helped to reshape national identity by fusing information, culture, and emotionalism into a picture of a just and martyred people beleaguered by an evil force.[15]

Frontline entertainment brigades of actors, singers, ballet dancers, folk musicians, and circus acts regaled the troops in mixed genre shows right behind the fighting lines. Some 45,000 men and women serving in 3,720 brigades performed over 400,000 concerts at the front. But these itinerant artists—like their counterparts in the American USO (United Services Organization)—had somewhat more freedom and could be more responsive to immediate needs of the soldiery than could those working in the print media or on the air. Time and again, the state bodies that organized these companies tried to "direct" their repertoires and comportment, not always with success. Performers often hesitated to take their frothy wit or sassy song from the civilian stages of home to the roar and flame of the fighting lines. Yet they were always requested by frontline audiences to perform as they had on stage in the prewar days. The armed forces wanted songs of love, elegies of home, salty jokes, and anything that reminded them of home and normal life—certainly not politics and battle themes.[16] It is not at all paradoxical that Russian and other Soviet soldiers and sailors adored two kinds of music from the entertainment brigades above all: Russian folk songs and American jazz, either unmediated in the band of Edi Rozner or in the more adapted and sanitized versions of Leonid Utësov's band. Since the United States was an ally of the USSR in this war, the two wholly normal tastes of the ordinary eclectic consumer could be equally accommodated—an accommodation that would vanish in the postwar period.

The theme of hate was naturally prominent in the cultural offering. News about German atrocities introduced anger and loathing into high and popular culture. "With these hands of mine," wrote the poet Alexei Surkov about the Germans, "I want to strangle every one of them." Konstantin Simonov's "Kill Him" was the culmination of a frenzied rage: "Kill a German, kill him soon / And every time you see one—kill him." Ehrenburg poured his racist abhorrence and contempt for the Germans into the pages of Red Star, the military paper that was devoured by the soldiers. Poster art depicted the Wehrmacht forces as rodents, insects, monkeys, pigs, and hyenas—beasts without feelings, sadistic brutes. The hate message was often conveyed through gross ridicule of Hitler, his minions, and his troops. They were portrayed in circus frontline shows and in graphic art as doomed descendants of Napoleon or "Winter Fritzes," blue-skinned and shivering, unaccustomed to the Russian frosts and addicted to stealing women's garments. Circus clowns had only to recostume the old targets of the revolution: Kerensky, White officers, and fat capitalists.[17]

Three related phenomena reflect the deepening of the emotions in the stress of war and uncover dormant or suppressed layers of the human spirit: religion, populism, and folk culture. Stalin abolished the League of the Godless (founded in the 1920s) and arranged a temporary truce with the Orthodox Church; in return, the Metropolitan of Moscow publicly announced in 1942 that Stalin was "the divinely anointed leader of our armed and cultural forces leading us to victory over the barbarian invasion." Church reopenings were attended by multitudes of devout believers. The regime proudly communicated news about fund-raising efforts by churchmen and congregations to purchase tanks for the army; Ehrenburg openly described people praying; and Simonov wrote poetically and movingly of "the simple crosses on Russian graves." The earthy populism so endemic to the Russian manner was revived and displayed in the soldiers' mass response to the most popular epic poem of the period, Alexander Tvardovsky's *Vasily Tërkin*, a tale about a coarse, witty, and humane soldier—the universal "little man" in the ranks who personified for the masses the notion that this was a war of the people. Folk singing and folk ensemble performance, though still bearing marks of its artificial styling, rose to the full amplitude of popularity in the patriotic war, erupted into a wave of festivals, and swelled majestically in the years to come, reflecting the depth of national feelings ignited by the struggle for existence.[18]

Propaganda and official pomposity never disappeared, of course. One finds it even in the genuinely popular and emotional films: in the final frames of *She Defends the Motherland*, the heroine stands on the gallows from which she has just been rescued and in her exalted speech mixes human feelings with clichés from the press as Soviet planes soar overhead. In *Zoya*, after the heroine is hanged, her smiling face is superimposed against Soviet flying aircraft and tanks rolling westward to victory. After Stalingrad, grandiloquent motifs of victory and military might suffused the media; and after the even greater battle of Kursk, resolemnization ensued on a vast scale. In response to these battlefield victories in 1943 and 1944, and in reaction to the sweeping spontaneity of popular emotion, the Soviets began reintroducing motifs of triumphalism and military might into the media on a vast scale: parades, the salute, epaulets and rows of medals for officers, and inflated communiqués. On the day of victory over the Germans the surgeons of official culture began to excise the great heart that had beat so spontaneously in the cauldron of battle. Wartime songs and films were, to be sure, repeated again and again for decades. But they were sanitized and passed through a filter of piety and self-congratulation that burnt out much of the original spirit of wartime culture. The multipurpose myth of war and victory extended down the years; but the heart of war had become a valentine for the state.

Neither this nor the stilted official cult of the war could stanch human memories of grief, fear, pride, heroism, and loss. This memory rang with the clarion sound of war for two generations. Understanding a nation's experience of war is often difficult for outsiders. War creates myth and memory embodied in great art and popular culture, and the persistent recollection of the moods it evoked in the minds of millions continued to configure attitudes. The human losses in this war were forty times greater than those of Britain and seventy times those of the United States—greater indeed than those of all the belligerents combined. Soviet people may not have known these comparative figures, but they knew through family memory as much as through public reminders that their collective suffering was colossal. The persistent recollection of the war in the minds of millions continued to configure cinema, songs, performance arts, and fiction long after 1945. For decades, Soviet people were constantly barraged by the regime with war images; but the solemnized memory sponsored by the government did not always converge with the actual recollections of the people.[19]

What did soldiers expect of the postwar period? Probably a return to the imagined joys of prewar peacetime life. A campaigner wrote to his wife in 1942 that every day would be like the movie *The Great Waltz*.[20] It was not to be. A major backlash took place against satire, modernism, jazz, and "unpatriotic" or "rootless" elements (such as Jews). The purge of certain war novels (especially Fadeev's *Young Guard*) is well known. The entire postwar cultural pogrom—sometimes called the *zhdanovshchina* after its principal witch-hunter—was as much a reaction against wartime spontaneity, intimacy, emotionalism, and displays of eclectic desire for both native Russian and western entertainment forms as it was a reaction to the cold war. But the cold war and the perceived threat from the West certainly added a strong element of paranoid xenophobia. The replacement of the Holy War by the cold war brought a flourish of Russian chauvinism and anticosmopolitanism, a retightening of ideological orthodoxy and control, an austerity program that was covered over with a glistening cultural smile and the escalation of the Stalin cult to unprecedented heights. Consciousness reasserted itself over the

spontaneity born of battle, hardship, heroism, and adventure. But once un-
leashed, the genie could not be thrust back into the bottle; when Stalin died,
new waves of cultural "authenticity" in the high and popular arts resurfaced.

Notes

1. Hubertus Jahn, *Patriotic Culture in Russia during World War I* (Ithaca, N.Y., 1995).

2. Ben Hellman, *Poets of Hope and Despair: The Russian Symbolists in War and Revolution (1914–1918)* (Helsinki, 1995).

3. Richard Stites, "Days and Nights in Wartime Russia," in *European Culture in the Great War: The Arts, Propaganda, and Entertainment*, ed. Aviel Roshwald and Richard Stites (Cambridge, 1999).

4. John Barber and Mark Harrison, *The Soviet Home Front, 1941–1945: A Social and Economic History of the USSR in World War II* (London, 1991), 59–76, 127–32; Anne Griesse and Richard Stites, "Russia: War and Revolution," in *Female Soldiers—Combatants or Noncombatants? Historical and Contemporary Perspectives*, ed. Nancy Goldman (Westport, Conn., 1982), 61–84; Reina Pennington, *Women, Wings, and War*, Ph.D. dissertation (University of South Carolina, 2000).

5. Richard Stites, ed., *Culture and Entertainment in Wartime Russia* (Bloomington, Ind., 1995).

6. Jeffrey Brooks, "*Pravda* Goes to War," in Stites, ed., *Culture and Entertainment*, 9.

7. Nina Tumarkin, "The War of Remembrance," in Stites, ed., *Culture and Entertainment*, 204.

8. On the cult of Kryuchkov see Jahn, *Patriotic Culture*.

9. Boris Pasternak, quoted in Geoffrey Hosking, *A History of the Soviet Union* (London, 1985), 276.

10. Solomon Volkov, ed., *Testimony: The Memoirs of Dmitri Shostakovich*, trans. Antonina Bouis (New York, 1979), 135.

11. For a case study of the sanctification of cities see Karl Qualls, "The Rebuilding of Sevastopol," Ph.D. dissertation, (Georgetown University, 1999).

12. Rosalinde Sartorti, "On Heroes and Heroines," in Stites, ed., *Culture and Entertainment*, 176–93; Louise McReynolds, "Dateline Stalingrad: Frontline Correspondents," in Stites, ed., *Culture and Entertainment*, 28–43; Brooks, "*Pravda* Goes to War," 9–27.

13. James Von Geldern, "Radio Moscow: The Voice from the Center," in Stites, ed., *Culture and Entertainment*, 44–61.

14. Ibid.; Alexander Werth, *Russia at War, 1941–1945* (New York, 1964), 410; Robert Rothstein, "Homeland, Home Town, and Battlefield," in Stites, ed., *Culture and Entertainment*, describes how a female sound engineer could not record the famous film song, "Dark is the Night," because of her tears falling on the equipment, and of a chorus who could not get through "Dnieper Song" without weeping (87, 89). Those who lived

in the United States during the war will recall perhaps how the music of Grieg, Dvorák, and Chopin, among others, was used to elicit sympathy for occupied peoples. And of course it worked.

15. Vladimir Yakhontov, quoted in Von Geldern, "Radio Moscow," 55.

16. For troop entertainment see Stites, "Frontline Brigades," in Stites, ed., *Culture and Entertainment*; I. N. Sakharova, ed., *Iskusstvo v boevom stroiu: Vospominaniia, dnevniki, ocherki* (Moscow, 1985).

17. Argyrios Pisiotis, "Images of Hate in the Art of War," in Stites, ed., *Culture and Entertainment*, 141–56.

18. See Richard Stites, *Russian Popular Culture: Entertainment and Society since 1900* (Cambridge, 1992), 98–122.

19. Nina Tumarkin, *The Living and the Dead: The Rise and Fall of the Cult of World War II in Russia* (New York, 1994).

20. *The Great Waltz* was a prewar Hollywood musical based on the life of the nineteenth-century Austrian operetta and waltz composers, Johann Strauss, father and son. This and other American movies were captured by Soviet troops at various stages of the war.

Part 3

Soldiers' Attitudes and Behavior

10

Soviet Soldiers and Officers on the Eve of the German Invasion: Toward a Description of Social Psychology and Political Attitudes

Mark Von Hagen

Problematica and Historiography

Among the persistent riddles for historians studying the Soviet Union during the Second World War has been the initially disastrous performance of the "invincible" Red Army against the *Reichswehr* in the summer of 1941; the front-line Red Army virtually collapsed in the face of the German invasion, and millions of Soviet soldiers surrendered and were taken prisoner. During the Khrushchev "thaw," Soviet scholars and military memoirists blamed the early defeats on the nation's lack of preparedness for the war; they alloted the overwhelming portion of blame to Stalin and his immediate entourage and defended the honor of the "genuinely" military men, the generals and marshals who eventually won the war. The debate about the state of Soviet preparedness on the eve of the German invasion focused on prewar foreign policy decisions, the critical element of surprise, the relative manpower strengths and deployment policies, prewar military doctrine and organization, the levels of military technology, and, importantly, the consequences of the purges on the officer corps.[1]

The debate in the Soviet Union under Gorbachev and since picked up where the earlier debate left off;[2] particularly younger historians, however, have abandoned the practice of distinguishing Stalinists from anti-Stalinists in the military-political leadership. The disastrous performance, they argue, was not the fault of one man, Stalin, nor his immediate associates; instead, they have launched a radical questioning of the entire Soviet sys-

Execution of partisans by German troops in 1943. (Courtesy of the Bilderdienst Süddeutscher Verlag, Munich)

tem and its rules of operation.[3] Moreover, they have effectively expanded the notion of preparedness to include salient features of the political economy and, still gropingly, the social psychology of the Soviet population.[4] In the new intellectual space opened up by the radicals' assaults, even more "establishment" writers[5] began to leave behind the clichés of Stalinist literature about "unity of state and people" and to raise the important issue of the relationship of the regime to society.[6]

The new developments inside Russia come at a particularly fortuitous time for scholars outside Russia as well. Non-Russian historians are exploring the complex relationships between various social groups and the Soviet regime during the 1920s and early to mid-1930s.[7] The new post-Soviet studies, combined with greater access to archives for all scholars, now make possible exciting work on the behavior of soldiers and civilians during the crucial period immediately preceding and following the German invasion. Not surprisingly, perhaps, the new work reveals a rich range of responses—from enthusiastic, patriotic support through passive neutrality and conformism to clearly anti-Soviet resistance.[8]

Although most scholars and memoirists have acknowledged the importance of morale in the prewar army as a factor in the initial performance against the

Germans, discussion of this key issue has been limited to impressionistic accounts and has not been based on solid scholarly studies. Soviet historians most often approached their subject from a narrowly military vantage point, that is, they viewed the army as somehow isolated from the society and political regime it served.[9] Certainly after 1934, however, when the Red Army grew steadily to a genuinely mass force (reaching 5.5 million by mid-1941), life in the military could not help but reflect most, if not all, of the social conflicts and tensions that characterized the everyday world of Soviet civilians. But even before the mid-1930s, indeed beginning during the Civil War, the Bolshevik leadership deliberately tried to fashion a new form of civil-military relations that would ensure the revolutionary regime a loyal armed force by preventing military men from recreating the isolated caste relations of the Imperial Army.[10] Just as historians should not isolate the moral factor in the army from other technical and logistical matters, so too should they not view the lives of millions of soldiers and officers in isolation from Soviet society nor from the political economy of which the army formed an integral component. Where regime, army, and society most keenly intersect is the field of political attitudes and social psychology.[11]

Data and Sources

The earlier, cursory discussions of the morale of Soviet troops usually were based on one of several sources, each of which presented special opportunities and difficulties for the historian. First, important conclusions were extrapolated from the evidence of the severe measures introduced in the Soviet Army after the German invasion, most conspicuously, the 12 September 1941 order to create *zagradotriady,* the special NKVD detachments assigned to prevent desertion by threatening soldiers with certain death by machine-gun fire if they thought to flee the front lines of combat.[12] In the absence of documents chronicling the decision making that led to these orders, historians have been forced to second-guess the reasoning behind these measures; consequently, their assumptions about the Soviet political system have played a substantial role in filling the logical gaps.

A second important source has been German records of the behavior of Soviet POWs and German impressions of Soviet soldiers in combat.[13] German military men had their own scores to settle after the war; German politics and Soviet-German relations left their peculiar marks on this type of evidence.[14] Finally, a few scholars have tried to recreate the situation inside the prewar Soviet army on the basis of the postwar memoirs of Soviet commanders. In general, however, Soviet historians and memoirists have ignored the interwar period or, at best, given the prewar years cursory treatment in prefaces or introductions. More important have been the political constraints shaping the former generals' and marshals' narratives, constraints that have forced rewrites of key episodes or the complete omission of important information.[15]

Even these sources, problematic as they may be, suggested that one ought to apply differentiated criteria to judgments about troop morale and combat performance. The behavior of Soviet soldiers and Soviet peoples varied from region to region, within regions, and from one period to another. Today we have substantially more evidence, this time from Soviet army archives and from a new set of published reminiscences, that reinforces those earlier impressions of a wide variety of responses.[16]

The primary focus of this chapter is a comprehensive concept from the practice of Soviet political workers in the army known as "the political-moral condition" of military units. The concept embraced a wide range of phenomena, including "objective" information about the socioeconomic background of servicemen, their level of education, their ethnic identity, and party or Komsomol membership. Political workers recorded other data in the realm of social psychology that were far less "objective," including any overheard statements soldiers and officers might have made about the army or political system of the Soviet Union, any registered cases of individual or collective protest, and a very broad category of disciplinary infractions and "extraordinary occurrences" (*chrezvychainye proisshestviia*), ranging from automobile accidents and explosions to suicides and drunken behavior or debauchery. Because the Soviet term "political-moral condition" was understood to be much more comprehensive than it might appear from such a laconic formulation, and because the term has little meaning for nonspecialist readers, I have chosen to translate it as "political attitudes and social psychology."

Data pertaining to these matters were recorded primarily by the political staff of the army—the Political Administration and later the Main Administration of Political Propaganda of the Red Army—but also by the Special Departments (*osobye otdely*) of the NKVD that were an integral part of internal intelligence in the army. In addition, officers were expected to contribute their impressions of soldiers and fellow officers. The main sources for the characterizations that follow are the regular reports on political attitudes and social psychology (*polit-doneseniia*) from the various data-collecting agencies within the army and a series of top secret reports that were the result of high-level meetings of the Party Central Committee, the Army High Command, and the Political Administration following the near disastrous performance of the Soviet army in the Finnish War of winter 1939–40.[17]

During those meetings, stenographers recorded often frank discussions of earlier campaigns at Lake Khassan, Khalkhin-Gol, eastern Poland, as well as in Finland. These campaigns, together with the brief Romanian campaign in the summer of 1940, provided the first evidence of combat readiness for regular units of the Soviet army.[18] The high command, officers, and political workers offered a diagnosis of the most urgent problems of Red Army life and training, and then elaborated and partially implemented several measures that became known as the Timoshenko reforms, after the new people's commissar of defense who replaced Voroshilov in May 1940 following the Finnish campaign.

Ultimately, a judgment about the combat readiness and condition of troop and officer morale on the eve of the German invasion must involve an evaluation of the success of the Timoshenko reforms in changing certain fundamental aspects of Soviet army life.[19] By way of a preliminary conclusion, I have come to agree more with the radical critics of the Soviet system that the Timoshenko reforms not only failed, but most likely could not have succeeded, war or no war. Despite the existence of an alternate military command cohort in Timoshenko, Shaposhnikov, and the generals who would soon fight the major battles of World War II, and despite their genuine attempts to remake the army as quickly as possible, they failed to change the institutional and political principles that shaped army life because they did not understand what really needed changing, namely, the entire political, economic, and social system that fed the army. Among other significant shortcomings, the reformers failed to address the crippling role of the NKVD inside the army; therefore, even within the army itself those reforms ran into formidable obstacles. The Soviet military leadership, in accepting tacitly or even unwillingly the basic outlines of the political, social, and economic structures of the Stalinist order, foreclosed any genuine restructuring of military life.[20]

The Political Economy of Army Life

Historians and publicists have highlighted the disastrous performance of Soviet soldiers in the first weeks and months after the German invasion as evidence of not only cowardice but disloyalty, if not justified resistance, to the Soviet regime.[21] The instances of panic during combat and mass surrender to the Germans, however, are very complicated matters. Until we know more about prewar political attitudes, we can not insist upon any close linkage between combat behavior and political loyalty;[22] rather, I will try to disaggregate several aspects of army life in the late 1930s to begin to understand the reactions of Soviet soldiers during the first weeks of war.

During the early autumn of 1939, Nikita Khrushchev, as a member of the Military Council of the Kiev Military District, took an active role in the military operations in eastern Poland. According to his memoirs, the entire operation required two to three days and proceeded without any serious complications.[23] Khrushchev's account reproduces the official press version that the Soviet people learned; archival documents tell a different story. Despite the low number of casualties, the reports and analyses prepared for the Army High Command following the campaigns in the Far East, eastern Poland, and the Finnish War were near unanimous in expressing alarm at the poor performance of troops and officers. The official casualty report after two weeks of the campaign in western Ukraine listed only 167 killed and wounded, 38 of these killed and 116 wounded in actual combat. But the director of the Political Administration of the Ukrainian Front, Erokhin, reported widespread panic and other "serious negative phenomena," as a result of which seven hundred troops had been placed under arrest.[24] A participant in the Belorussian campaign also painted a very different picture from Khrushchev's in his diary. One Lt. Anatolii Matveev, who served in both the Belorussian and the Finnish campaigns, noted that despite minimal resistance from hostile Polish forces, Soviet soldiers were poorly prepared, Soviet officers failed to coordinate operations, orders from above frequently changed, and both soldiers and officers engaged in extensive looting. Matveev claims that troops were often forced to move ahead without directions in unknown territory, that many officers could not read a map, and, consequently, units frequently lost their way.[25]

Despite the usual self-congratulatory press accounts of Soviet performance in the Finnish campaigns, the evidence from the archives suggests another picture here as well, namely, panic among troops and very high Soviet losses. The casualty figures for the Finnish War remain a subject of controversy.[26] The war lasted 105 days and demonstrated above all else the poor state of preparedness of Soviet troops to engage in combat operations in difficult climatic conditions.[27] L. Z. Mekhlis, in his relatively new capacity as director of Political Administration, oversaw the formation of the notorious *zagradotriady* to prevent the flight of Soviet soldiers from the front lines of combat. The poor performance of Soviet troops is confirmed in Lt. Matveev's diary.[28]

According to the high-level diagnoses, the major contributing factor to panic was the general lack of preparedness for actual combat conditions. This involved two important components, a training one and a psychological one.[29] The major conclusions reached by the high-level meetings that reviewed the evidence of combat performance for these campaigns was that everywhere in the army disorganization and slovenliness reigned, that troops exhibited poor discipline and succumbed easily to panic and desertion in confusing situations, that officers failed to demonstrate initiative, and that officers and troops were ill-prepared for real battle conditions because their training had been limited to classroom exercises. Soldiers and officers had little experience in digging trenches, conducting camouflage operations, crossing rivers, and, especially crucial during the Finnish campaign, skiing. As a consequence, soldiers and officers were simply unfamiliar with many basic tasks that would confront them in a real war.

Perhaps the single most often repeated characterization of combat training in the Red Army in the second half of the 1930s—and extending well beyond the first months after the German invasion itself—was *shapkozakidatel'stvo*, a pejorative term suggesting a carelessness and lack of discipline and authority grounded in a false sense of superiority or invincibility and linked to the *kraskomchvanstvo* of earlier generations, who equated professionalism negatively with the restoration of Imperial Army values. Shapkozakidatel'stvo, literally "hat-tossing," described everything from military doctrine to the process of recruitment. The confusion that characterized most army life was a consequence of all sectors of the army falling down on the job, from supply organs who failed to deliver necessary goods to engineering units who had not thought through such basic matters as how to get across minefields.[30]

There were some explanations for the poor training that were easy and politically safe to identify. One was the persistent staff shortfalls, which had become more severe since the purges and since the increasingly rapid expansion of Red Army numbers since 1934.[31] The major consequence of the shortfalls was that basic combat training functions were not adequately performed; manpower was typically diverted to other noncombat tasks such as construction. At the end of 1940, Timoshenko soberly concluded that the official report on the army's condition that had been commissioned by the Commissariat did not tell the whole story of the manpower problems. "Things are much worse," he wrote.[32]

The poor discipline that Soviet soldiers exhibited during the recent campaigns was further diagnosed as a consequence of incorrect relations between officers and troops.[33] At least until the autumn of 1940, when a new, stricter disciplinary code was issued in the army, officer-soldier relations continued to be characterized as relatively loose and informal (army critics referred to them by the pejorative *panibratskie otnosheniia* [buddy relations]).[34] The informality had positive and negative sides. For example, soldiers captured by the Germans generally spoke well of their commanding officers and somewhat less well of political officers. But the informality also expressed itself in a certain lack of respect for officers' authority, on the one hand, and arbitrary behavior of officers toward subordinates, on the other hand. Arbitrary punitive practice, another example of shapkozakidatel'stvo, was widespread in an environment lacking clearly defined parameters of behavior, a system of predictable punishments and rewards, and mechanisms to appeal sanctions that were considered unjust.

The lack of respect for officers was in part the consequence of the purges (certainly in the opinion of many officers), but also of the ever-widening social gap between officers at the top of the command hierarchy and soldiers and junior officers at the other end. Indeed, many officers fell during the purges because soldiers or political workers initiated proceedings against them on the grounds of their "uncommunist lifestyles." Throughout the 1930s, the highest officers enjoyed more and more privileges in Soviet society, most visibly in the form of expensive residences and vacation homes and their access to well-provisioned officers' clubs and resorts.[35] They also won immunity from certain types of criminal and civil prosecution. In an army traditionally lacking in the middle ranks of noncommissioned officers, distant officers and political officers increasingly came to be regarded as part of the bosses, the "them" (*oni*) of the Soviet elite, and less part of the "people."

Other factors contributing to the poor performance were more sensitive and collectively make up what has been called the pathology of the Stalin regime.[36] These features typically show up not in higher-level reports, but in soldiers' and officers' overheard comments. For example, soldiers and officers panicked because they were not informed about battleground conditions. Political workers recorded officers' and soldiers' complaints about the excessive secrecy in the Red Army. "No one informs us where the enemy is, what his strength is, whence we should wait for him," protested one officer. Another claimed that his troops were less well informed about what was happening on their own fronts than they would have been at home on their kolkhoz.[37]

The cult of secrecy reflected the inordinate power of the Soviet security police, whose agents interfered at every level of army life, from recruitment to officer promotions,[38] and who participated in combat situations as martial-law authorities, for example in the territories annexed from eastern Poland and northern Romania.[39] An important but less tangible consequence of the power and practice of the Soviet security police was felt in recruitment policies. Local military commissariats not only processed recruits for the Red Army during the annual call-up, but they were additionally responsible for OGPU-NKVD recruitment. At least beginning in the early 1930s, and no doubt more intensively following 1934 when the OGPU-NKVD expanded rapidly, army authorities frequently complained that they were regularly assigned the second-best recruits.[40] The struggle with the security police over the best recruits, combined with the already exclusionary class and political principles that were applied during annual recruitment drives, deprived the military of the best available cadres, at least by Soviet criteria; for example, the statistical average of years of education in the army remained low, as did the indices of physical fitness.

Of course, the culmination of the process of power accumulation by the security police as far as the military was concerned was the purges of 1937–39, and it was the purges that more than anything else eroded officers' authority.[41] By the beginning of 1940 as many as 70 percent of regimental commanders and more than 70 percent of divisional commanders had held their positions for all of one year.[42] (The disruption in career advancement patterns and continuity resembled the confusion introduced by the mass promotion of *vydvizhentsy* (those who were moved out) to management positions in industry during the First Five-Year Plan; the campaigns also recalled the earlier atmosphere of mutual distrust and denunciation.) Officers were commanding large units for which they had no preparation or experience.

The typical response of disoriented soldiers and junior officers after the arrests of Tukhachevskii and Iakir was, "Whom to trust then? How can I know, when a commander gives an order, whether it is good or bad?" Indeed, when commanders were replaced in rapid succession on the sole grounds that they had been unmasked as "enemies of the people," soldiers and junior officers could only look on in bewilderment. The disorientation resulted in a decline in discipline and an increase in the number of accidents and suicides. Smirnov spoke of an "astronomical figure of 400,000 extraordinary occurrences" between 1 January and 1 May 1937.[43] During 1938, 1,178 servicemen were killed and 2,904 were wounded in accidents and from self-inflicted wounds.[44]

Among the political workers many were not only disoriented, but feared for their own futures and tried to leave their jobs as quickly as possible.[45] The atmosphere of fear paralyzed party life in the army. Communists frequently refused to recommend servicemen who wanted to enter the party's ranks for fear that they might turn out to be enemies of the people. Secretaries of party organizations denounced nearly every communist in their organization as a safeguard against their own potential incrimination for lack of vigilance.[46] Such an atmosphere extended into the first months of the war itself, when officers denounced one another after the disastrous defeats.

Officers who had been purged, even after they were restored to their previous positions, could not enjoy the same authority as they had before their dismissal. And soldiers did not respect the authority of those who had taken the places of arrested officers. The responses to the purges varied considerably. For those who believed the accusations of treason and espionage to be true, the purges probably had not gone far enough. "We have to chase from our ranks all former officers [in the Imperial Army]," was one typical response. "I trust no one now, only Comrades Stalin and Voroshilov." For those who did not believe the accusations to be true, they could only conclude the worst about what was happening in the country's political leadership. A few soldiers expressed doubts in the leadership's judgment. "We were taught again and again to memorize the Marshals of the Soviet Union," said one A. E. Platonov, "and now one by one they are being removed as enemies of the people." A Lieutenant Filin asked, "why did Stalin let Trotsky go? He should have been shot. Why were not Tukhachevskii, Gamarnik, and the others not unmasked earlier? If they didn't know, that means they were working poorly; but if they knew, then why put them in such senior positions?"

Other soldiers expressed the sentiments that were being echoed in foreign capitals and among foreign military attachés. "I don't know how we will fight if the capitalist countries declare war against the Soviet Union. I, for one, don't believe a single commander. After all you can't believe them, if such big people as Gamarnik and Tukhachevskii have turned out to be spies and terrorists." In July 1937 a political worker in the Kiev district reported to Borisov that soldiers were expressing outright defeatist sentiments. "Why should we do exercises if the fascists will defeat us anyway?" one asked. Another from the same district concluded that "there's no way we can do anything now anyway. They know our military plans and documents, and they will win in the war." Punitive measures were often taken against soldiers and commanders who dared to doubt the invincibility of the Red Army and who predicted defeat by the Germans.[47]

Military Doctrine, National Politics, and Soviet Patriotism

The purges were but one source of the defeatist attitudes that had penetrated into Red Army ranks by the eve of the German invasion and very likely contributed to the high incidence of panic and perhaps also to the cases of collaboration by many Soviet citizens in German-occupied territory. Paradoxically, defeatist attitudes were also rooted in Soviet patriotic propaganda both in and out of the army, particularly the myth of the invincible Red Army and the moral righteousness of Soviet international behavior. Consequently, the surfacing of defeatist attitudes was as much of a surprise to the leadership as was the poor combat performance, since the initial response of civilians and military personnel to the earlier campaigns had been very positive.

The first announcements by the Soviet government about the campaigns in eastern Poland and Finland were greeted with widespread enthusiasm among the Russian-Ukrainian majority troops and their relatives.[48] According to political workers' reports and the letters to and from Soviet soldiers, the population apparently accepted the official version of enemy provocation, serious threats to Soviet national security, and the mission to "liberate" the "occupied" territories from their "White Guard" Polish or Finnish overlords. Soldiers referred to Finland as "a pig rooting around in the Soviet truck garden"; the Polish lords (*panowie*) were depicted as oppressors of "our blood brothers in western Ukraine and western Belorussia." Finland and Poland were treated as illegitimate small powers that had brought the wrath of the mighty Soviet state down on themselves. In the case of the campaigns in eastern Poland, soldiers articulated a version of Russian-Ukrainian revanchism reformulated in the rhetoric of proletarian internationalism with unambiguous motifs of vengeance for the Polish War of 1920.[49]

These expressions of Soviet patriotism had clear chauvinistic and great-power imperialist overtones, which were reinforced by the widespread acceptance of the official myth of the invincible Red Army. This myth was elaborated in films, songs, and all patriotic education. Most damaging of all was the military doctrine that seemed to flow logically from these official delusions: Defense Commissar Voroshilov's insistence that a future war would be fought on the enemy's territory and victory would be swift and with minimal bloodshed.[50] During the 1930s the predominant image of future war was one in which the Soviet Union was attacked by lightning forces of a probably German army, but within minutes Soviet troops would respond with overwhelming force and destroy the enemy.[51] Of course, the reverse side of the myth was a systematic belittling of the strength of all potential enemies, but especially that of the Germans. German commanders were portrayed as incompetent and arrogant, whereas German soldiers, as members of the international proletariat, were believed to be ready to rise up against their bourgeois overlords and join their allies, the Soviet people.[52] Any alternative vision of a future war that was predicated on even minimal Soviet difficulties was denounced by other writers as "defeatism" and often followed up by NKVD harrassment or persecution.[53]

The myth of the invincible Red Army, a heightened sense of the moral and political superiority of the Soviet Union, and the Voroshilov doctrine defined the orientation of political propaganda and indoctrination in the army and society at large. The result of this false sense of confidence and systematic denigration of potential enemy strength was a general lack of serious concern with military and psychological preparation for future war, especially a long-term defensive one. In the disastrous Finnish and eastern Polish campaigns, official myths suffered considerable erosion. The Political Administration eventually concluded that Soviet soldiers and commanders had performed poorly in the Finnish campaign in large measure because they had been led to a virtually "pacifist" view of future wars; that view was the consequence of systematic exaggerations of the weakness of the world capitalist system and of the strength of the Red Army.[54] But even the attempts by L. Z. Mekhlis and his successor A. I. Zaporozhets to overcome the admittedly harmful psychological consequences of the pre-1939 propaganda of Red Army invincibility failed to uproot the wishful thinking that pervaded all levels of the military command.[55]

At a conference in 1940, the deputy director for political affairs in the artillery administration, G. K. Savchenko, gave eloquent testimony to how little things had changed and also how pervasive was the atmosphere of denunciations and mutual fear. Savchenko had spent three months in Germany and had a far higher opinion of German military capabilities than the current propaganda line allowed, but he dared not utter these thoughts aloud. "If I gather my assistants and speak positively about the ways foreign armies work, I know in advance that of the ten present nine will write denunciations of me."[56] But a gap emerged between the propaganda image of the German army and their actual performance. The continuing success of the German army in Europe, particularly during the summer of 1940, demoralized sectors of the officer corps and troops. In July 1940, after the fall of France, cadets and soldiers in the Kiev district feared that Germany would defeat the Soviet Union because German military technology was superior to Soviet technology and because the German soldiers had such good morale. Such defeatist sentiments were another consequence of the now considerable cracks that had emerged in the official myths.

When the Finnish army offered fierce resistance to the Soviet invaders and when Soviet losses steadily climbed, soldiers and officers expressed clear anxieties and doubts about their mission.[57] The NKVD kept track of negative phenomena; despite the clear risk involved in expressing such sentiments, several commanders and soldiers spoke out against the Finnish War, declaring it to be unjust and claiming that the people and army do not want to fight such a war.[58] During the Romanian campaign of the summer of 1940, a soldier (described as having a higher education) was charged with anti-Soviet agitation for the following statement: "The policy of the Soviet state is peaceful only in words; in fact it is aggressive and annexationist. It forced a war on Poland, Finland, and now Romania. We are cannon fodder."[59] Most alarming were political officers' reports of a rise in the frequency of attempts by soldiers to kill commanding officers.[60]

In general, as the terms and meaning of the Soviet-German Nonaggression Treaty gradually reached the troops and officers,[61] military men experienced a profound sense of disorientation and, in some quarters, outright cynicism. Many officers and political workers, after all, had fought in the Spanish Civil War, and many more had identified positively with the Soviet support of the republicans against the fascists.[62] Suddenly the criticism of fascism abated; the hierarchy of enemies was rearranged. England and France were treated as instigators of war and Germany as the seeker after peace. "Now," complained one instructor at the Military Engineering Academy, "you don't know what to write or how to write; before we were instructed in the antifascist spirit, and now the opposite." Another officer was overheard by the NKVD to have said, "Germany is the country of fascism. We communists are waging a struggle against fascism, and all information coming from the newspapers is on the side of Germany." Still other soldiers wondered how Stalin and Molotov could permit themselves to be photographed next to the "most evil enemies of the people," Joachim Von Ribbentrop and Friedrich Gaus. Now that the Soviet Union supported fascism, Germany would be able to seize all the little countries, and the hands of the Soviet Union would be tied. The NKVD registered many such reactions to the new course in foreign policy.[63] The glaring contradictions between pre- and post-pact political education also induced outright cynicism. When a soldier asked his political worker, "What sort of war is this we have now, the second [imperialist] or some other kind?" the political worker answered, "there's no point in counting imperialist wars. . . . When the war's over, a [party] congress will convene, and they'll tell us what type of war it was."[64]

The military campaigns before the German invasion eroded official Soviet myths in other key aspects as well. The isolationist domestic policies of the Stalinist regime had helped to shape a defensive Soviet patriotism that was buttressed by comparisons with a fictional outside world. Many soldiers and officers believed that life in the Soviet Union was better than anywhere in the world and that the Soviet state was the incarnation of progress and justice. The invasion of eastern Poland in the fall of 1939 threatened that fragile and large-ly illusory worldview. Instead of the backward economy they had been led to expect, they saw abundant consumer goods and foodstuffs of considerably higher quality than they knew from the Soviet Union. Among the negative phenomena that alarmed the Ukrainian front command was the feverish pur-chase by officers and soldiers of nonessential goods in large amounts, includ-ing alarm clocks, tablecloths, and ladies' shoes.[65] Commissars were concerned about the political consequences of the campaign; many soldiers were reported to have begun praising the "bourgeois lifestyle."[66]

Preliminary Conclusions and Considerations

The evidence from the Red Army's campaigns before the German invasion suggests a far more complex picture than has been previously presented. It is difficult to determine how widespread was the erosion of myths and the emer-gence of defeatist or anti-Soviet attitudes during this period for several reasons. The evidence for the erosion comes almost exclusively from political workers' reports and military men's denunciations of one another to the NKVD. Still, these reports were taken seriously by the political and military high command when they convened their emergency meetings after the Finnish War. A more fundamental difficulty in assessing how political attitudes evolved during the final prewar years is our general ignorance about Soviet popular attitudes dur-ing the 1930s and in the initial war years. What were the elements of Soviet patriotism, and how were those elements understood, adapted, or rejected by diverse groups in the Soviet population?

By way of preliminary and altogether unsurprising conclusion, I propose that the soldiers who met the initial German onslaught were a heterogenous group. The majority of Red Army men, the Russians and Ukrainians, shared some degree of Soviet patriotism and commitment to the political and social order of the Soviet state. Of course, an officer who had chosen for himself a lifelong career in the Soviet army was likely to have a far greater attachment to the political and social system than would a common conscript who was also typically younger than the officers; however, it was the officer corps and political workers who fell in the greatest numbers during the purges, so their confidence in their futures had been considerably shaken.

As conscription was extended more widely in the second half of the 1930s to include many more non-Russians and non-Ukrainians, as well as Ukraini-ans and Belorussians who recently had lived under Polish or Romanian rule, the type of patriotism that had been devised by the political workers for an earlier, smaller, more ethnically homogeneous Red Army found less effective resonance. Furthermore, when military commissariats began almost immediately to conscript local youth in the annexed provinces for service in the Red Army, they encountered not only large numbers of unwilling new citizens, but they also quickly discovered that even those who were willing had dramatically different notions about politics and the Soviet Union.[67] In general, political workers were skeptical about the loyalty of soldiers recruited from the recently annexed territories of former eastern Poland, Romania, and Czechoslovakia. These recruits had been exposed to years of anti-Soviet attitudes in their local communities and in state propaganda; moreover, they had not been brought up in the agencies of socialization common for Soviet youth by the mid-1930s, such as the Young Pioneers, Komsomol, and Soviet school system.[68]

Finally, judgments about patriotism and combat readiness based on the wars of annexation that were waged on non-Soviet territory (Finland, eastern Poland, northern Romania) can be extended only with great caution to the type of war that Soviet soldiers fought on their own territory when Germany invaded in June 1941.

Notes

I gratefully acknowledge the fellowship support of the International Research and Exchanges Board and the Alexander von Humboldt Foundation (Bonn) as well as the invaluable assistance of the staff of the Russian State Military Archive (formerly the Central State Archive of the Soviet Army).

1. The Khrushchev-era debates centered around the publication and later condemnation of Aleksandr Nekrich's *22 iiunia 1941* (Moscow, 1965); see the critical review that set the tone for all later comments, G. A. Deborin and Major-General B. S. Tel'pukhovskii, "V ideinom plenu u fal'sifikatorov istorii," *Voprosy istorii KPSS* 9 (1967), 127–40.

2. For surveys of the debates over military history in particular, see the excellent accounts by Hans-Henning Schroeder, "Die Lehren von 1941: Die Diskussion um die Neubewertung des 'Grossen Vaterlaendischen Krieges' in der Sowjetunion," in *Der Zweite Weltkrieg: Analysen, Grundzuege, Forschungsbilanz,* ed. Wolfgang Michalka (Munich, 1989), 608–25; and "Weisse Flecken in der Geschichte der Roten Armee," *Osteuropa* 5 (1989), 459–77. See also A. N. Mertsalov and L. A. Mertsalova, *Stalinizm i voina: Iz neprochitannykh stranits istorii (1930–1990-e)* (Moscow, 1994). For the general context of the military debates, see the surveys of the Soviet *Historikerstreit* in R. W. Davies, *Soviet History and the Gorbachev Revolution* (Bloomington, Ind., 1989); R. W. Davies, *Soviet History in the Yeltsin Era* (London, 1997); Walter Laqueur, *Stalin: The Glasnost Revelations* (New York, 1991); Mark Von Hagen, "Stalinism and the Politics of Post-Soviet History,"

in *Stalinism and Nazism: Dictatorships in Comparison,* ed. Moshe Lewin and Ian Kershaw (Cambridge, 1997).

3. The most notable such attack, at least in the vehement tone of the author's rejection of the Soviet system and its values, is the work of Boris Sokolov, *Tsena pobedy, Velikaia otechestvennaia: Neizvestnoe ob izvestnom* (Moscow, 1991).

4. Outside Russia, scholars are adopting similarly exciting approaches to the Soviet political economy treated as a system. Under Michel Foucault's influence, Gabor Rittersporn and Stephen Kotkin have analyzed the political economy of the 1930s by revealing its unspoken rules, assumptions, blind spots, and dysfunctional aspects. See Gabor Rittersporn, *Simplifications staliniennes et complications sovietiques: Tensions sociales et conflits politiques en URSS, 1933–1953* (Paris, 1988); Stephen Kotkin, *Magnetic Mountain: Stalinism as Civilization* (Berkeley, Calif., 1995).

5. See for example the biography of Stalin by the late Dmitrii Volkogonov, *Triumf i tragediia* (Moscow, 1990); Iurii Kirshin, "Dukhovnaia podgotovka sovetskogo naroda k voine," unpublished manuscript, n.d.

6. Among Soviet historians, the orthodox view had held that despite the traumatic shocks of the 1930s, the Soviet people were "united in spirit," and this unity was a major source of Soviet victory. Curiously, this position unites historians who otherwise differ on their assessment of Stalin. On one side of the argument, those critical of Stalin highlight the spiritual unity of the Soviet people to deprive Stalin of any credit for winning the war; that is, the Soviet people, not the Soviet system, won the war in spite of Stalin. See Volkogonov, *Triumf i tragediia,* and Kirshin, "Dukhovnaia podgotovka." On the other side are those who, while acknowledging the damage done by the purges, still want to give Stalin primary credit for preparing the country for the war; they explain the "spiritual unity" of the people as one of the perhaps paradoxical consequences of Soviet educational, cultural, social, and economic policies. These latter scholars point to the social mobility of workers and peasants, the increased access to cultural goods, the dedication to socialist ideals, and the further unifying effect of the growing threat of fascism and imperialism to the Soviet people.

7. Here I have in mind the work of historians following the lead of Moshe Lewin and Sheila Fitzpatrick. See Moshe Lewin, *The Making of the Soviet System* (New York, 1985); Sheila Fitzpatrick, *Education and Social Mobility in the Soviet Union, 1922–1934* (New York, 1979).

8. For a similar reconsideration of British wartime morale see Angus Calder, *The Myth of the Blitz* (London, 1991).

9. This was true not only for military historians; elsewhere party historians wrote about the Communist Party in isolation from social and economic developments, historians of Soviet society rarely paid attention to politics—all this despite slogans that affirmed the unshakable unity of party and army, or army and people. See A. P. Nenarokov and O. V. Naumov, "Glazami amerikanskogo istorika," *Voenno-istoricheskii zhurnal* 12 (1990), 60–66.

10. For the early history of the Red Army see John Erickson, *The Soviet High Com-*

mand: A Military-Political History, 1918–1941 (London, 1962); Mark Von Hagen, *Soldiers in the Proletarian Dictatorship: The Red Army and the Soviet Socialist State* (Ithaca, N.Y., 1990).

11. For some suggestive parallels in German history, see Omer Bartov, "Soldiers, Nazis, and War in the Third Reich," *Journal of Modern History* 63 (March 1991), 44–60; Omer Bartov, *Hitler's Army: Soldiers, Nazis, and War in the Third Reich* (New York, 1991). Bartov warns against "the tendency to overlook or underestimate the importance of the intimate ties between the army, the regime, and society."

12. The relevant documents were published in full in *Voenno-istoricheskii zhurnal* 8 (1988), 73–79.

13. Among others, see F. W. von Mellentin, *Panzer Battles* (Norman, Okla., 1956); Kurt von Tippelskirch, *Die Geschichte des zweiten Weltkriegs* (Bonn, 1954); Franz Halder, *Kriegstagebuch*, 3 vols. (Stuttgart, 1962).

14. See Manfred Messerschmidt, "Juni 1941 im Spiegel deutschen Memoiren und Tagebuecher," unpublished manuscript, 1991; Olaf Groehler, "Zur Einschaetzung der Roten Armee durch die faschistische Wehrmacht im ersten Halbjahr 1941, dargestellt am Beispiel des AOK 4," *Zeitschrift fuer Militaergeschichte* 7 (1968), 729–35; Andreas Hillgruber, "Das Russland-Bild der fuehrenden deutschen Militaers vor Beginn des Angriffs auf die Sowjetunion," in *Zwei Wege nach Moskau: Vom Hitler-Stalin-Pakt zum Unternehmen Barbarossa*, ed. Bernd Wegner (Munich, 1991), 167–84.

15. For the difficulties of using Soviet war memoirs see Seweryn Bialer, *Stalin and His Generals* (Boulder, Colo., 1984), esp. 15–44.

16. Among the most revealing memoirs, those of Konstantin Simonov have played a key role in the discussions. See Konstantin Simonov, *Glazami cheloveka moego pokoleniia: Razmyshleniia o I. V. Staline* (Moscow, 1990). Soviet and post-Soviet historians and several journal editors have been publishing fascinating archival documents from the army and party high command. I have based much of what I argue in this paper on the unpublished manuscript by Kirshin, "Dukhovnaia podgotovka," and Volkogonov's biography of Stalin, *Triumf i tragediia*. Finally, I was able to work in the Russian State Military Archive during the summer of 1990 and the winter of 1991 and gained access to thousands of pages of previously classified materials, primarily focusing on the Kiev and Kharkov Military Districts in the interwar years, the latest documents dated May 1941.

17. After the war, the Central Committee of the Party convened a special military meeting in the Kremlin (March 1940). This was followed by an expanded session of the Main Military Council; a meeting of high-level political workers convened by Mekhlis, 21 April 1940; and a highly critical report on the People's Commissariat of Defense, 12 November 1940. For the accounts of these meetings, I rely almost exclusively on Kirshin, "Dukhovnaia podgotovka," and Volkogonov, *Triumf i tragediia*, who, in turn, cite archival holdings in the Central Archive of the Ministry of Defense (TsAMO) and the Russian State Military Archive (RGVA). Also N. F. Kuz'min, *Na strazhe mirnogo truda* (Moscow, 1959), 269–74.

18. The earlier campaigns, conducted during the period when the Nazi-Soviet Pact was observed, had been largely ignored by Soviet historians. We have the best evidence for the campaigns in eastern Poland and Finland, somewhat less for the campaigns in the Far East, and very little on the Romanian and Baltic campaigns of 1940. For the Finnish campaign, scholars have long had a remarkable set of documents in V. Zenzinov, *Vstrecha s Rossiei: Kak i chem zhivut v Sovetskom Soiuze: Pis'ma v Krasnuiu Armiiu* (New York, 1944). During the summer of 1940 Zenzinov traveled to Finland; the Finnish government gave him limited access to the letters and personal papers found on the bodies of Soviet soldiers who had died during the Winter War.

19. Defenders both of the Stalinist order and the non-Stalinist military alternative, each for different reasons, assert that the German invasion in June 1941 caught the Red Army in the midst of the Timoshenko reforms, which, therefore, were not given an adequate chance to remedy the primary ills of the preceding period. The Stalinists thereby demonstrate that the Stalin system was flexible in devising self-correcting mechanisms once a sober analysis was made of the situation; the anti-Stalinists assert that once the Stalinist clique of Voroshilov and his cohort were removed from power, the army was able to put its own house in order, but that Stalin's errors in judging the German threat once again undermined the military's ability to do this in time to prevent further disaster.

20. John Erickson arrives at a similar evaluation of the Timoshenko reforms, but for different reasons. See Erickson, *Soviet High Command,* 552–60. See also Rittersporn, *Simplifications staliniennes,* for a parallel argument about the inability of the Moscow party leadership to reform what they perceived to be irregularities and inefficiency in the local party organizations.

21. This is especially the argument of Sokolov, *Tsena pobedy,* but also of Gennadii Bordiugov and Aleksandr Afanas'ev, "Ukradennaia pobeda," *Komsomol'skaia pravda,* 5 May 1990.

22. A rich but far from conclusive literature on panic among troops touches little on political attitudes. See the classic work by S. L. A. Marshall, *Men against Fire* (New York, 1947); John Keegan, *The Face of Battle* (London, 1976). On the performance of American soldiers in battle, see the collection of essays by S. A. Stouffer et al., *Studies in Social Psychology in World War II,* vol. 2, *The American Soldier: Combat and Its Aftermath* (Princeton, N.J., 1949). See also Anthony Kellett, *Combat Motivation: The Behavior of Soldiers in Battle* (Boston, 1982); Ben Shalit, *The Psychology of Conflict and Combat* (Westport, Conn., 1988).

23. N. S. Khrushchev, "Vospominaniia," *Ogonek* 30 (1989), 10–11. Only at L'vov did a question arise as to who would occupy the city; through negotiations with the German command, the Soviet side acceded to German claims on the city and subsequently withdrew.

24. Reports sent from Erokhin to Pozhidaev, between 15 Sept. and 9 Oct. 1939, RGVA, fond (f.) 25880, opis' (o.) 4, delo (d.) 35, listy (l. or ll.) 53, 102–6.

25. See the unpublished manuscript prepared by Valerii A. Savin, "Dnevnik leitenanta Krasnoi Armii," based on the diary of Anatolii Matveev, a lieutenant who served in the Belorussian and Finnish campaigns. The diary was found among the collection on the Soviet-Finnish War, RGVA, f. 34890, o. 14, d. 84, ll. 130–205. Staff performance on the Ukrainian front was criticized in an extensive internal memorandum dated Oct. 1939, RGVA, f. 25880, o. 4, d. 2, ll. 57–61. Officers up and down the ranks failed to demonstrate the slightest initiative, preferring merely to transmit orders and instructions from above.

26. At the end of the war, a figure of 207,608 dead and wounded was released, but *Pravda* in 1989 raised that figure to 246,000; another Moscow paper asserted that the real figure is 289,510. *Pravda,* 30 Nov. 1989, 6; *Argumenty i fakty* 45 (1989), 8.

27. Georgii Zhukov claims that, following the disastrous showing of the Soviet army in the Winter War, Stalin took fright and replaced Voroshilov as commissar of defense with Timoshenko. Vladimir Karpov, "Marshal Zhukov," *Znamia* 11 (1989), 82.

28. Matveev concluded that the Finnish campaign demonstrated that the army had had to learn most important matters in the course of the fighting, that the infantry performed poorly, and that the reserve soldiers were cowards. Finally, he noted that there was too much futile bravery (*naprasnoi smelosti*) and drinking, especially among officers. See Matveev's diary, RGVA, f. 34890, o. 14, d. 84, ll. 130–205.

29. The psychological component will be discussed in the next section on national politics, patriotism, and military doctrine.

30. L. Z. Mekhlis, in an unpublished highly critical report entitled "The Lessons of the War in Finland," identified what he saw as "chronic disgraces," many of which had been clear from the campaigns in Khassan, Khalkhin-Gol, and Poland; but the General Staff had failed to act upon them and, as a result, despite constant inspection visits and damning reports, nothing had changed. RGVA, cited in Iurii Kirshin, "Die sowjetischen Streitkraefte am Vorabend des Grossen Vaterlaendischen Krieges," in *Zwei Wege nach Moskau,* ed. Bernd Wegner (Munich, 1991), 379–80. During April 1941 General Meretskov, the deputy commissar of defense, was sent to inspect the combat readiness of the Kiev Special Military District. Nearly three-quarters of a year after the implementation of the Timoshenko reforms, the inspection revealed that much, if not most, of what had been diagnosed as shortcomings during the painful sessions following the Finnish War had not been remedied. "Materialy inspektirovaniia boevoi podgotovki voisk sviazi okruga," 21 Apr. 1941, RGVA, f. 25880, o. 4, d. 450, ll. 1–3. Since the summer of 1940 new training programs had been introduced that were designed to reflect the lessons learned from recent wars in Europe and Asia. The Kiev District High Command concluded that most of the initial results had been negative and that the district as a whole was not operationally prepared for a genuine combat situation. The Commissariat also sent out inspection teams in March 1941 and found similarly disconcerting conditions in the Leningrad, Ural, and Orel Military Districts. "Materialy," 18 Apr. 1941, ibid., ll. 83–85.

31. As of 12 November 1940, the shortfall was determined to be 21 percent of desired staffing levels. By the eve of the war, more than 102,000 officers' positions were unstaffed, including a 17–25 percent shortfall in the western frontier districts. See "Akt o prieme NKO," 12 Nov. 1940, TsAMO, f. 72, o. 173022, d. 3, ll. 208–374, cited in Kirshin, "Die sowjetischen Streitkraefte," 390. See also Roger Reese, "A Note on a Consequence of the Expansion of the Red Army on the Eve of World War II," *Soviet Studies* 41:1 (January 1989), 135–40. Reese argues that the rapid expansion and the transition to a more technologically sophisticated army played a crucial role in the poor performance of the second half of 1941.

32. Document dated 20 Dec. 1940, RGVA, f. 4, o. 14, d. 2742, cited in Kirshin, "Die sowjetischen Streitkraefte," 355.

33. Many of these analyses resemble similar discussions of discipline before and during the Frunze reforms in the mid-1920s. See von Hagen, *Soldiers in the Proletarian Dictatorship,* 183–270.

34. Many officers welcomed the harsh new regulations as a long overdue corrective to the "pseudodemocratic vestiges in the army, that had shaken [*rasshatyvaiushchikh*] discipline in the past." See the comments by a military writer, S. Krasil'nikov, "Perestroika boevoi podgotovki Krasnoi Armii," *Znamia* 6 (1941), 164.

35. Kirshin, "Die sowjetischen Streitkraefte," 291, cites RGVA figures from the Administrative-Economic Sector of the Main Administration of the Commissariat. For example, at the end of 1936 and the beginning of 1937, tens of thousands of rubles were allocated to purchase furniture for the high command. Tukhachevskii was allocated 67,363 rubles for furnishings, Gamarnik 46,451 rubles, Iakir 33,235 rubles.

36. See Lewin, *Making of the Soviet System,* 304.

37. RGVA, cited in Kirshin, "Die sowjetischen Streitkraefte," 435–36.

38. See Bernd Bonwetsch, "Stalin, the Red Army, and the 'Great Patriotic War,'" in *Stalinism and Nazism: Dictatorships in Comparison,* ed. Moshe Lewin and Ian Kershaw (Cambridge, 1997), for the persistence of these patterns of pathology in military life, where perverse notions of political loyalty were prized over military competence, until at least late 1942 or early 1943.

39. On the NKVD role in eastern Poland, see the extensive documentation from Hoover Archives, Collection: Poland, Government-in-Exile, Ministerstwo Informacji i Dokumentacji (Poland MID), box 2; also the official plans for establishing Soviet power issued to army political workers. On the NKVD in Northern Romania, see RGVA, f. 25880, o. 4, d. 5, ll. 1–5.

40. See the frequent correspondence about annual recruitment drives in RGVA, f. 25899, o. 3, d. 1572, ll. 279–82, 354–61, 371–84.

41. For a review of the literature on the purges' impact, see Bernd Bonwetsch, "Die Repression des Militaers und die Ensatzfaehigheit der Roten Armee im 'Grossen Vaterlaendischen Krieg,'" in *Zwei Wege nach Berlin,* ed. Bernd Wegner (Munich, 1991), 404–24.

42. *Velikaia Otechestvennaia voina Sovetskogo Soiuza: Kratkaia istoriia* (Moscow, 1965), 40.

43. Oleg F. Suvenirov, "Vsearmeiskaia tragediia," *Voenno-istoricheskii zhurnal* 3 (1989), 43. During a meeting of the political staff in August 1937, Stalin asked P. A. Smirnov, Gamarnik's replacement as director of the Political Administration, how the Red Army had reacted to the unmasking of "the bands of spies." Though Smirnov claimed the general reaction was positive, he noted "very many negative and blatantly counterrevolutionary statements. These attitudes, generally, are along the lines that the authority of the leaders of the party and state has been undermined, as has the authority of the officer corps." Smirnov then reported that "moments of disorientation have seized a certain part of the leadership, who have lost their will and let go of the reins."

44. Ibid., 44.

45. On the fear that reigned among high-ranking officers after the summer of 1937, see L. Nikulin's description of K. A. Meretskov's anxieties. L. Nikulin, *Tukhachevskii: Biograficheskii ocherk* (Moscow, 1964), 194. Meretskov was arrested, then later returned to the army, together with several other commanders and commissars, including K. K. Rokossovskii, A. V. Gorbatov, and L. G. Petrovskii.

46. In one rifle division of the Kiev district, the political worker, Mamonov, reported that 50 percent of the communists in his party organization had been accused of one thing or another, but most of the charges could not be confirmed. RGVA, cited in Kirshin, "Die sowjetischen Streitkraefte," 346.

47. "Dokladnye zapiski i doneseniia o politiko-moral'nom sostoianii chastei KVO," 1 Jan.–31 Dec. 1937, RGVA, f. 25880, o. 4, d. 42, ll. 227–28, 264, 415; RGVA, cited in Kirshin, "Die sowjetischen Streitkraefte," 344, 348.

48. When the government announced the formation of volunteer ski battalions, applications came in at the rate of ten for every one place. Parents refused exemptions for their only remaining sons. Leningrad Party Archives, f. 24, o. 12, ed. khr. 30, l. 46; and RGVA, cited in Kirshin, "Die sowjetischen Streitkraefte," 62–63.

49. See "Doklad o boevykh deistviiakh 6–oi armii i provedennoi partpolitrabote v boevoi obstanovke," 15 Oct. 1939, RGVA, f. 25880, o. 4, d. 2, ll. 164–74. Typical comments included the following: "I will beat the Polish *pans* [lords] mercilessly; I will remind them how they beat my father and brother in 1920 and how I felt the riding-crop"; "Thank you, comrade Stalin, for allowing us to liberate the Ukrainian and Belorussian peoples from the Polish lords."

50. Voroshilov began enunciating this doctrine in 1928 and developed it in succeeding years at various party and military meetings, for example, the ninth congress of the VLKSM (All-Union Leninist Young Communist League [Komsomol]) in 1931. See *Sovetskie Vooruzhennye Sily* (Moscow, 1987), 194; *Krasnoarmeiskii polituchebnik* (n.p., 1931).

51. The most succinct expression of Voroshilov's doctrine in literature was a short story by Nikolai Shpanov, "Pervyi udar: Povest' o budushchei voine" (The first blow:

a story about a future war) *Znamia* 1 (1939), 36–119. A German air assault begins at 5 P.M., but Soviet airspace is completely freed of German airplanes within a half-hour. Within another eleven hours the land battle ends victoriously for the Soviet forces. Shpanov's view of a swift and clean Soviet victory with virtually no Soviet bloodshed was repeated in songs, poems, and army political work.

52. See Il'ia Ehrenburg's memoirs about the first period of the war. Konstantin Simonov and Il'ia Erenburg, *V odnoi gazete . . . Reportazhi i stat'i, 1941–1945* (Moscow, 1979), 88.

53. When E. Henri predicted not only the German invasion of the USSR but also the direction of the major blows, a reviewer retorted that the author had erred in his assumption that the Red Army and the Soviet people would permit the enemy into the frontiers of the motherland. He reminded Henri that the Red Army would strike the enemy on his own territory. See *Literaturnoe obozrenie* 3 (1989), 69; E. Henri, *Hitler over Europe* (New York, 1934).

54. Following an authoritative meeting of High Command and Main Political Administration in April 1940, Mekhlis decreed a reform of political work. See "O perestroike partiino-politicheskoi raboty," *Propagandist i agitator* no. 17 (1940), 1–4. The GUPPKA (Main Administration of Political Propaganda of the Red Army) also issued several more orders to reform the methods of military propaganda. See, for example, *Propagandist i agitator* nos. 221, 240, 69, 188, 219.

55. In his draft directive following the Finnish War, Zaporozhets persisted in portraying the German army and society as on the verge of a revolt or mutiny due to the severe social and economic pressures that the war had placed on the German nation. See also General Staff intelligence reports from as late as 19 May 1941, which persisted in dismissing the German threat. RGVA, cited in Kirshin, "Die sowjetischen Streitkraefte," 488–90.

56. Mekhlis, chairing the meeting, sardonically replied, "You're exaggerating, but two to three would indeed denounce you." RGVA, cited in Kirshin, "Die sowjetischen Streitkraefte," 491.

57. Zenzinov, *Vstrecha s Rossiei,* chap. 7; see also Savin, "Dnevnik leitenanta Krasnoi Armii."

58. During the war, the Political Administration reported what it deemed alarmingly high rates of desertion, self-mutilation, and flight from the battlefield. RGVA, cited in Kirshin, "Die sowjetischen Streitkraefte," 293, 310–11.

59. "Svodka na 27. VI. 1940," RGVA, f. 25880, o. 4, d. 5, ll. 285–86. Other soldiers justified their refusal to serve because a motherland that allowed their families at home to starve was not worth fighting for. For other reports on soldiers refusing to fight out of protest against Soviet domestic or foreign policy see ibid., ll. 303, 305.

60. See "Svodka No. 006," RGVA, f. 25880, o. 4, d. 5, ll. 303–6, 6 July 1940, for numerous reports of arrests for "terrorist threats," soldiers threatening to kill their commanding officers.

61. Mekhlis, as director of the PUR (Red Army political administration), in his directive no. 0246 (11 Sept. 1939), sent political workers extensive instructions about how to "work through" the treaty and the new international situation in army units. The required texts included Molotov's speech announcing the treaty in *Pravda*, 1 Nov. 1939; *Molodoi bol'shevik* 4 (1940), 55; *Molodoi bol'shevik* 7 (1940), 1.

62. Many memoirists write of the widespread popularity of the Spanish republican cause and the sense that the Soviet Union was pursuing a noble and just policy in supporting the loyalists. See Petr Iakir, "Bud' nastoiashchim, syn!" in *Komandarm Iakir: Vospominaniia druzei i soratnikov* (Moscow, 1963), 221–23.

63. RGVA, cited in Kirshin, "Die sowjetischen Streitkraefte," 96–98, 487; see also Bialer, *Stalin and His Generals*, 128–29.

64. At the meeting of political workers convened by Mekhlis in spring 1940, one of the participants, Solov'ev, told this story to illustrate the corrosive impact of the Nazi-Soviet Pact on army morale. RGVA, cited in Kirshin, "Die sowjetischen Streitkraefte," 415.

65. Troops sent letters home to relatives requesting them to sell whatever they could (including clothes and livestock) and to send them the money to buy goods in the western provinces. See the unsigned copy of Timoshenko's order, Sept. 1939, RGVA, f. 25880 o. 4, d. 35, l. 107; commissar Zelenkov's secret order, 14 Nov. 1939, RGVA, f. 25880, o. 4, d. 34, l. 288; for evidence of looting see RGVA, f. 25880, o. 4, d. 2, ll. 19, 30–33, 36, 37–40.

66. Timoshenko, as commander of the Ukrainian front, complained that officers and soldiers were filling local stores and buying up goods for which they had no conceivable use on the front line; furthermore, they were buying goods in amounts clearly not for personal use. This behavior besmirched the dignity of a Soviet soldier and undermined the prestige of the army and Soviet state in the eyes of the local population. Timoshenko warned than any further such behavior would be punished severely. Soviet reports are confirmed in Polish sources; see Hoover Archives, Poland MID, box 2, folder 6.

67. RGVA, f. 25880, o. 4, d. 2, ll. 30–33; Zenzinov reports that Karelian draftees in the Soviet army harbored great resentment against the Soviet regime and fled to the Finnish side at the first opportunity. Zenzinov, *Vstrecha s Rossiei*, 14.

68. The large issue of Soviet patriotism requires a great deal more investigation. When political instructors in the Red Army and Soviet school teachers turned to the recent past for inspirational material, they most obviously could point to the period of heroic struggle during the Revolution and Civil War. But civil wars are not ultimately reliable founts of patriotic lessons, especially in a multinational state such as the Soviet Union. When the army expanded its recruitment pool to include more and more non-Slavs, the patriotism of the Civil War found less and less resonance. Not only did Russians often fight other Russians as we might expect from a genuine civil war, but whole peoples seceded from the Russian centralized state and existed as independent,

albeit short-lived and often compromised, states; furthermore, the "regathering of the Russian lands" was in large measure a military reconquest, with the Red Army repeating the work of centuries of tsarist generals. As long as the popular memory of the civil war survived, that formative period of the Soviet state could have but an extremely circumscribed appeal. True, historians could point to examples of multinational unity against foreign or "class-alien" elements, but the greater truth was interethnic hatred and violence during the early years.

11

Soviet Women as Comrades-in-Arms: A Blind Spot in the History of the War

Susanne Conze and Beate Fieseler

"One afternoon in January 1945 I was standing in the doorway of a peasant's cottage; a few small-caliber shells had just landed in the village street. Then, in the low ground between the snow-covered hills, I saw a file of men slowly advancing. It was the first detachment of the Red Army. It was led by a young woman, felt-booted and carrying a submachine gun."[1] This was Czeslaw Milosz's first view of the advancing Soviet army in Poland in the late winter of 1945. We know nothing else about this young woman; perhaps she died ten minutes later, perhaps she lived to see her own grandchildren grow up. She has no name in history. This faceless female soldier, somehow put into a position of leadership in a Soviet platoon, symbolizes the great variety of roles women filled in the armed forces of the USSR and the way their achievements and sacrifices have gone virtually unrecorded.

Who was the Soviet fighting woman? What was her public image, and what were her private thoughts and hopes? We can only begin to address these questions.

The Forgotten Combatants

Women have participated in war probably as long as there has been war. Russian females had to take part in the defense of their homeland against Mongols, Poles, Swedes, French, and Germans for centuries before 1941.[2] There were ample stories, fictional and nonfictional, of women who fought in the Russian Civil War. In the USSR during the 1920s and especially the 1930s the regime promoted decidedly mixed messages about what women should be and do, but the idea that they should defend their country with guns or airplane controls in hand never disappeared. However, World War II threw the ques-

Belorussian female partisans in Minsk. (R91918; courtesy of the Bundesarchiv, Koblenz)

tion of what women's roles should be into stark and deadly relief; the people and government of the Soviet Union tried to work through this issue at a time when the country's survival depended on its resolution.[3]

As a rough estimate, more than a million Soviet women served in the Red Army or in partisan units.[4] Five hundred thousand of these women saw duty directly at the front and carried weapons.[5] At the high point of female participation, in 1943, women made up 8 percent of the Soviet armed forces.[6] At the beginning of the war, women joined the army in noncombatant and rather traditional capacities. Great numbers were found in the medical sector,[7] while others worked for the communication, transport, and intelligence services, and as political officers.[8] Over the course of the war, however, the boundary between fighting and nonfighting female tasks became increasingly blurred, as Milosz's squad leader demonstrates. Even nurses carried guns and used them while rescuing wounded soldiers; they too were often wounded or killed.[9]

Due to severe losses and extreme manpower shortages, women as comrades-in-arms appeared at the front beginning in mid-1942. Soon they mastered nearly all military specialties in all-female as well as in mixed combat units and served on all fronts.[10] On the initiative of the record-holding flier Marina Raskova, three female air regiments were put together and trained in 1941.[11]

Two of them later received the honorary title of "guard."[12] The proportion of women was greatest in the air defense forces, where they made up 24 percent of all personnel,[13] but they also joined the ground forces as snipers, machine gunners, and tank crew members. Only a few women served in the navy. In addition to their military duties, all these women were expected to lead in giving first aid to their wounded male comrades.[14]

Beginning in the spring of 1942, on the basis of decisions of the State Committee of Defense (GKO), the Communist Youth League (Komsomol) carried out five mobilization campaigns for female Communist Party members.[15] Conscription took place sporadically and according to need in spring and fall 1942, in 1943, and again in 1944.[16] In addition to those who volunteered, about five hundred thousand young women were recruited into the Red Army without, incidentally, being tested for fitness and physical strength.[17] In the beginning, only those with specialist qualifications (as pilots, for example) were accepted, but subsequently the call to arms was extended to all childless women between eighteen and twenty-five years of age not engaged in work vital to the war effort.[18]

There was never a uniform policy on conscripting and promoting women in the armed forces. Partly for that reason, data on age, rank, and nationality of female combatants are missing or remain vague. But the majority seem to have been very young and to have occupied low ranks in the military hierarchy. Not many female soldiers received training as noncommissioned officers, and only in exceptional cases did they gain admission to officer courses,[19] not a surprising situation given the low proportion of women in all supervisory positions across the country.[20] There is little information on how practical problems for women in the armed forces, for example regarding housing, hygiene, and uniforms, were solved, or on how well or badly the integration of women into the army proceeded.[21]

With regard to orders and honorary decorations, female military personnel seem to have fared proportionately worse than their male counterparts.[22] Eighty-six women received the "Hero of the Soviet Union" medal, the highest military award, but many of them were decorated only posthumously. Twenty-six won the title for partisan warfare, twenty-one were air force crew members, and fifteen belonged to the medical sector, but only five snipers, four machine-gunners, and two tank drivers got the award.[23]

Even fifty years after the end of the war, the critical and detailed quantitative as well as qualitative story of these women remains to be written. In all the thousands of books dealing with the war that appeared in the Soviet Union, the largely male historians were not in a hurry to integrate the experience of women into

their accounts. Female soldiers do not figure prominently in Soviet encyclopedias, nor do they appear as leading characters in contemporary novels or films
dealing with the Soviet Union during World War II.[24] The first two pioneering
scholarly studies on the subject were published in the Soviet Union only in the
early seventies.[25] To this day, the history of women as comrades-in-arms has not
become part of the general history of the war. This was of course also due to
the fact that most official Soviet treatments approached the war from a rather
narrow military-technical perspective; that is, they left people out altogether,
as had become the rule during Stalin's time.

Thousands of war memoirs or biographical sketches of participants were
published during the later years of the Khrushchev "thaw," the term applied
to the relative liberalism and loose censorship of 1962–65. The voices of women
soldiers were included in such volumes, but not according to their former
proportions in the army. Instead, the first- and third-person accounts concentrated on outstanding heroines. Especially prominent were the stories of those
who had lost their lives at the front or in partisan warfare. Interestingly, the
1960s, when such articles appeared, were the first time after World War II when
female specialists again were mobilized into the Soviet armed forces in large
numbers.[26]

Women's combat service was episodic, and females constituted only a small
minority within the Red Army. However, women's roles in the war deserve
attention and analysis, first because they highlight the ambivalence of Soviet
myths, traditions, and practice regarding women. Second, new appearances
and deeds by women in the armed forces led, if only to a certain extent, to a
rethinking of what "masculine" and "feminine" mean. Finally, the way people dealt with women's roles during the fight with the Germans says much
about the relationship between women, men, and the state in the Soviet Union
during its darkest hours.

The Preparedness of Women for the War

Soviet women were not pioneers in assuming combat roles. Already during the
First World War female soldiers had volunteered for the Imperial Army and
fought in the front lines.[27] The provisional government in 1917 even agreed to
the formation of regular women's battalions, largely to shame male soldiers,
who were deserting in great numbers, back into action.[28] When civil war broke
out in Russia following the Bolshevik coup d'état of October 1917, tens of thousands of women joined the Red Army. They made up 2 percent of its members and carried out a wide range of tasks, including fighting against the coun-

terrevolutionaries.[29] Their performance was seen as a first proof of the complete equality of the sexes that the Bolsheviks had put on their agenda.

To bolster women's commitment to the Revolution and to help memorialize the brutal struggle of the Civil War, female fighters emerged in Soviet literature as exemplars of courage and dedication to the cause, while at the same time they did not lose their "femininity" and were often described as beautiful. The new Soviet hero, male or female, had to have a politically conscious mind in a handsome body. Thus in Mikhail Sholokhov's *And Quiet Flows the Don* (1928), the Bolshevik machine-gunner Anna Pogoodko is "of a full, healthy figure, perhaps a little round-shouldered, and not particularly beautiful except for her great, strong eyes, which endowed all her face with a wild beauty." When she becomes deeply upset after her first taste of combat, her comrade Bunchuk takes her in his arms, wipes away her tears, and says, "Don't let your thoughts turn that way [to fear]! Take them in hand. You see now; although you said you were brave, the woman in you has won." When Bunchuk catches typhus, Anna nurses him back to health by herself. Later they become lovers: "Bunchuk felt not only the caress and fire of a woman beloved, but the warm, full-flowing care of a mother."[30] Of course Anna is eventually killed, sacrificing herself in battle. Leaving aside the temptation to analyze this romance in Freudian terms, it reveals all the demands that the male-dominated regime placed on women during the war: they should be beautiful, tough, soft, brave, mothers to the men, nurses, and if the circumstances were right, good with weapons.[31]

The ideal of the "New Soviet Woman" as it emerged from the pages of *Kommunistka*, the journal of the communist women's section (*zhenotdel*) during the 1920s, was the fully emancipated, female revolutionary who devoted her whole life to building socialism.[32] While her role in the Soviet workforce gained in prominence over the course of the decade, topics such as sexual liberation were abandoned in favor of more traditional values. Then, in accordance with the more restrictive laws of 1936 on abortion and divorce, a new image of women was propagated, which concentrated on her role in the family.[33]

Nevertheless, since the early thirties women had been called upon to take up typical "male jobs" in the industry or in the machine-tractor stations of the countryside, which supplied heavy equipment to the collective farms. On a more general scale, the threat of war, the struggle against external and internal enemies, however "real" they might be, were the conditions that shaped everyday life for Soviet citizens long before the German invasion. Thus patriotism and a spirit of sacrifice and hero worship were central aspects of Soviet propaganda in the prewar period, and they helped to facilitate the population's readiness for the demands of war.

Woman-as-fighter was thus not an image or issue that appeared in Soviet life for the first time in 1941. Before the war Soviet domestic propaganda did not deny but rather encouraged the prospect of women bearing arms. Depictions of females defending their country changed over time in the mass circulation press. What were the major changes, and why did they occur? The main sources for such images were journals for women like *Rabotnitsa* (female worker) and *Krest'ianka* (female peasant), as well as one for soldiers, *Krasnoarmeets* (male soldier). How did women respond to role models they saw, and how far did their self-perception differ from the official message? Female partisans and medical personnel have been omitted for the purposes of this study, which will concentrate exclusively on participants in combat.[34] Long before recruitment of women into the armed forces actually started, paramilitary training for women and girls was conducted on a wide scale. It was mainly organized by the Society for the Cooperation in Defense and Aviation-Chemical Development (*Osoaviakhim*) which had been founded by the Komsomol in 1927.[35] Instruction followed the demands of civil defense. It informed the participants about biological, bacteriological, and chemical warfare and trained them in the use of gas masks, proper conduct during bomb attacks, first aid, and the use of firearms. Women could take examinations in different fields, for example as snipers, and receive badges.[36] Moreover, the international success of the record-breaking fliers Polina Osipenko, Marina Raskova, and Valentina Grizodubova had a mobilizing effect on numerous young women, who joined aviation clubs in order to emulate their brave example.[37]

All these activities were extensively covered between 1938 and mid-1941 on the pages of *Rabotnitsa*, the journal for working women, as well as in *Krest'ianka*, which addressed the female peasant. Articles and photographs acquainted the readers with model Osoaviakhim groups or training courses. Women were encouraged to establish similar crews and to assert themselves in defense matters, if necessary, against reluctant collective farm directors.[38] Reports on women who had mastered the skills of sniper, aviator, or paramilitary trainer alternated with articles dealing with successful working or peasant girls. These stories usually followed a fixed pattern: quite ordinary women performed extraordinary tasks because they regarded it as their patriotic duty to engage in defense activities. Thus, even an average working or peasant woman who had devoted her spare time to developing additional skills could become a hero and gain some recognition.[39] Aside from working women, this propaganda addressed housewives, soldiers' wives, schoolgirls, and female students, to whom paramilitary training was offered as an opportunity to compensate for their "unproductiveness." Thus it also opened a new field of activity for the former participants of the movement of public-spirited middle-class wives (*obshchestven-nitsy*) which lost momentum by 1938.

Following the lines of the Stalin constitution of 1936, according to which the emancipation of women was completed in the Soviet Union, female partici-pation in defense training appeared as something ordinary, as a well-defined task of every Soviet woman. It highlighted the close ties between the female population and the Red Army, while it helped to strengthen the bonds with "Comrade Stalin" and the Soviet homeland. The permanent threat to the So-viet Union from capitalist states served as legitimation for military training of Soviet women. They too, it was said, should be able to defend the achievements of their country in building up socialism, especially because their emancipa-tion as women would be at stake in case of an attack.[40]

Women's international struggle against fascism was an oft-repeated topic in *Rabotnitsa* during 1938, which contained a number of reports on armed performance of women during the Spanish and Chinese civil wars. In addi-tion to preparing Soviet women to perform similar tasks in case of war, the journal conveyed to the female reader the notion that because of her greater degree of emancipation, she was expected if need be to fight better and hard-er against fascism than her sisters in Spain and China.[41] Therefore the target butts during sniper training carried the inscription "Fascist."[42]

As soon as the Hitler-Stalin Pact was signed in 1939, this motto was no longer used in defense training, and reports on the female struggle against fascism ceased to appear in *Rabotnitsa*. Instead the conflict with Japan as well as the Soviet-Finnish Winter War gained in importance. *Rabotnitsa* now carried ar-ticles on brave Soviet nurses who had served on the Finnish front,[43] while *Krest'ianka* reported on the "liberation" of western Ukraine and White Rus-sia from bourgeois Poland. Even if female military performance in the ranks of the Red Army was not directly referred to, articles like these certainly helped to prepare women for the situation of war.[44] To sum up, despite extensive press coverage of paramilitary training programs for women, the Soviet model of "complete" emancipation did not aim at calling women to arms on a mass scale. Only in emergency cases should they defend their village, factory, or house against an aggressor; they were not supposed to participate in regular army action. Nevertheless, the USSR's women still trained to be pilots and sharpshooters; the leadership wanted women to be all things to all men. Dur-ing the "Great Retreat" (from 1934 onward) propaganda returned largely but never completely to middle-class values and images of women as keepers of the family hearth.[45] Thus in the years just before the German invasion, Soviet women faced a mixture of traditional male chauvinism and exhortation to achieve as much as men did. In this sense women were well prepared for the contradictions of their varied roles in the war.[46]

Images of Women in Soviet War Propaganda

During the first phase of the war, widely circulated propaganda images did not prepare women for regular combat service. On the contrary, they focused on the working or peasant women who had to replace men in heavy industry and the collective farms. The message was, "men to the front, women to the home front." Yet Soviet women did in fact gain ground in former male domains. The average percentage of women in the industrial workforce rose from 39 percent in 1940 to 51 percent in 1945, although their share varied in different branches.[47] Accordingly, the demands of war led to fundamental changes in the composition of the workforce not only in the industrial but also in the agricultural sector of the Soviet economy.[48] As a result of the general upheaval, productivity sank drastically. In this situation, dominant propaganda themes were to mobilize all people who were able to work, improve their qualifications for new jobs, and spur them to record achievements. Accordingly, in 1942 a frequent propaganda image of the ideal woman was that of an ordinary yet outstanding worker or peasant who excelled in a traditionally masculine job. This motif appeared in the mass circulation press, in journals for women, and in resolutions adopted by many groups for International Women's Day (8 March). During sowing and harvest months, articles and photographs dealing with peasant women became predominant over portrayals of female industrial workers. This was also true for the year 1943, when the state strove to end a crisis in agriculture.[49]

Especially at the beginning of the war, one of the most persistent images of women in Soviet posters was that of the mother.[50] Female figures appeared not only in symbolic form as allegories of the motherland (*rodina-mat'*)[51] but as real people, too. Posters showed a mother who had sent off her son to the front,[52] depicted defenseless women accompanied by children, or portrayed women as victims of the German aggressors.[53] In addition to their efforts in industry and agriculture, and matching this widespread motherly image, Soviet women were expected to knit stockings and gloves for the soldiers and to send parcels and letters to the front in order to strengthen the morale of the Red Army. Exemplary letters of women to their sons or husbands were published in the press.[54] At the same time, propaganda articles encouraged women to participate in civil defense, for example in air surveillance, fire departments, or barrage balloon units. On the whole, propaganda images of women with regard to their role at the Soviet home front were highly functional, and they corresponded well to the demands of the state and the necessities of the war economy.

Was this also true for the combat woman? To what degree can we speak about congruence between public interest, widely circulated ideal image, and reality in her case? At the beginning of the war, Soviet representatives abroad made clear that the socialist state did not plan to use women for regular frontline duty. In an interview with foreign journalists who seemed to have doubts about this point, the wife of the Soviet ambassador to Washington said in July 1941 that there were nothing like women's battalions in the Red Army, which, she maintained, had not even existed during the Civil War. Instead, women worked for the defense of the country, and if they served at the front at all, it was only in the medical sector, communications, or supply services. The main task of the Soviet woman, she said, was at the home front, where she should replace men at the workbench and take care of the children.[55] A few days later this view was emphasized in another article, which was also published in the *Information Bulletin* of the Soviet embassy:

> No woman is allowed to attempt work injurious to her as a woman. Especially, none is called to serve in the regular ranks of the Red Army and Navy. Only in the confusion of the Civil War of 1917–1920, and perhaps today with some guerilla forces behind the German lines, have individual women seized rifle and grenade and stepped into the ranks with their husbands and brothers. Some women technical workers are serving at the front with Soviet troops today. Besides doctors and nurses there are considerable numbers of telephonists and radio operators in the communication service and some women chauffeurs in the transport service. There are also women specialists with the engineering corps and a few women fliers. Many of these women have already behaved gallantly under fire. But in general the women of the U.S.S.R. are fighting this war by taking over the civilian occupation of their menfolk.[56]

Regular service of women in the ranks of the Red Army was rejected on the grounds that men and women had different "natural" features, which should not be overruled: "The ordinary Russian woman is heroic in her own feminine sphere of life. . . . There was a time when we tried to copy our menfolk in every way. Women were trained in marksmanship; they learned to operate machine-guns and ride cavalry horses. But a stop was put to this. In our country we have enough men to do these jobs. But there are branches of defense where women can do more and better."[57] What the ambassador's wife had in mind was the medical sector, air defense of cities, and donating blood for the front.

In close agreement with this negative attitude toward regular combat service of women, the medical sector and partisan warfare were the only fields of activity to receive some attention with regard to mobilization of women in the Soviet mass-circulation press during the first year of the war. *Rabotnitsa,* for example, published an article in August 1941 under the heading "Fighting Female Comrades," which was full of praise for some heroic nurses who had rescued wounded soldiers while under fire.[58] This and similar articles encouraged young women to emulate their example.

Reports on female soldiers, however, did not appear in the Soviet press at home or abroad before 1942. The main function of such articles was to document or to justify a recent development rather than to stimulate it. While in the pages of *Pravda,* the official newspaper of the Communist Party, female combatants never figured prominently during the course of the war, *Rabotnitsa* began to report on them in early 1942. The article "Heroines of Sevastopol'" mentions a machine-gunner, Nina Onilova, whose heroism in the city's defense was portrayed as an example for other women. This tradition, the story noted, reached back to Dasha Sevastopol'skaia, who had excelled in the Crimean War (1854–55).[59] Interestingly, before early 1942 female historical predecessors were rarely used for propaganda purposes, even though Russian history could boast of other cases of female bravery.[60] The mobilizing character of articles on fighting women became more apparent only in the middle of the year, with an affirmative report on a husband-and-wife tank crew. Sevastopol' again figured in numerous references to women serving there as snipers or machine-gunners.[61] In July 1942 an article on two female snipers, Maria Baida and Liudmila Pavlichenko, finally called directly upon the female reader to pick up a weapon: "Learn to shoot like the death sniper Liudmila Pavlichenko. She is indeed an example of courage and boldness."[62]

From the pages of *Krest'ianka* a quite different picture emerges. Fighting women were mentioned only in connection with partisan warfare. Since the readers of this journal were peasants, the reasons for this rather selective pattern of propaganda are clear. Rural women were supposed to replace men in agriculture, where the lack of manpower was greatest. In case of German occupation, however, they were expected to join partisan units or at least to support their activities. A typical exhortative example is an article of February 1942 that depicts the heroic struggle of Soviet female partisans, nurses, and peasants in defending their homeland against the fascist threat. The report ends with a call to greater achievements during the forthcoming harvest.[63] Even if the journal also published some photographs and brief reports on combat women after mid-1942, they remained an exception rather than the rule. While the Soviet press and pro-Soviet media in the United States frequently reported on Pavlichenko,[64] the most famous woman sniper of World War II, *Krest'ianka* devoted only one photograph, but no article, to her in 1942.[65]

Generally speaking, in contrast to *Rabotnitsa*, a mobilizing character is not perceptible in *Krest'ianka*'s coverage of female soldiers either in 1942 or in 1943. This does not suggest that the female peasant was still considered "backward" in comparison with the woman worker, merely that her patriotic duty was defined in different terms. Instead of joining the front lines, she was expected to stay in the hinterland, be it as a collective farmer or as a partisan.

Despite the fact that *Rabotnitsa* came out less often after 1943, reports on combat women tended to increase in this journal.[66] Women now appeared more often as active fighters, for example as bomber pilots, snipers, or tank drivers. The aviators of an all-female night bomber regiment especially gained in prominence, as did its founder Marina Raskova after her death in December 1942. In January 1943 *Rabotnitsa* published her obituary, which called to mind the record flight of 1938; yet her initiative in creating three all-female aviation regiments in fall 1941 was omitted.[67] The 46th Guards Regiment was referred to for the first time only later that year, in an article on its commander Evdokiia Bershanskaia.[68]

Almost all reports on combat women followed the same pattern. *Rabotnitsa* carried many articles on female soldiers and on prominent heroines, but they always concentrated on outstanding individuals. Women's organizing achievements were often slighted or ignored. At the same time the journal carefully avoided publishing a comprehensive account of women's activities in the front lines, not to mention their actual experience. Figures relating to the proportions and ranks of females in the army were also conspicuous by their absence. While individual pilots or tank crew members did receive some recognition,[69] the general military performance of women was obviously considered a subject too delicate to deal with explicitly. The same pattern prevailed in articles on the occasion of International Women's Day or in a report on the exhibit "Women in the Great Patriotic War," which was held in Moscow's House of Soviets in spring 1944. As was the custom, it praised the achievements of Soviet women at the front, yet their actual numbers and concrete activities remained in the dark.[70]

Thus, despite the official acknowledgment that famous heroines received for their feats at the front, the state tended to conceal or downplay the much wider and more organized scale of women's military participation. In contrast to the civil defense activities that every Soviet woman was expected to master, regular female combat service was not encouraged in propaganda, even though it was not systematically concealed. Such service remained the business of out-standing individuals, not of women as a group, and was referred to only as long as the extraordinary wartime situation continued.

Even more than the print media, the visual arts contributed to masking the fact that hundreds of thousands of women were actually fighting in the front lines. During the course of the war, posters and other graphic or figurative depictions of combat women were almost absent, while even representations of armed female partisans remained rare. They thus lacked the immortaliza-tion of the "unknown," average male soldier.

Judging by their representation in contemporary print media or on stamps, for example,[71] the Soviet state never considered combat women a desirable mass movement or an integral part of the Red Army. Instead, such women were depicted as isolated cases, however numerous they might have been. It is not clear whether the regime adopted this stance to cover up the harshness of ev-eryday life at the front, to assuage popular resentment against women in com-bat, or to stop calls for women's mass recruitment into the armed services. In any event, the limited representation of combat women reflected male unease about women's participation in the fighting.

Several factors may have contributed to the more extensive coverage of fe-male combatants on the pages of *Rabotnitsa* than in *Pravda*. According to Soviet sources, already in the first days of the war recruiting centers received thousands of applications from young women who desperately wanted to go to the front, but they were rejected.[72] One female Komsomol member wrote, "I know how to handle a rifle and wish to fight . . . in the front ranks. My heart is brimming over with hate toward the Nazis. It is better to spill blood in defending one's honor than to go down on one's knees before Hit-ler."[73] It seems she had learned her lessons well a few years earlier. The same was true for the female defendants of Sevastopol', who indeed acted in ac-cordance with the heroic images of Soviet women that *Rabotnitsa* had helped to introduce in 1938.

By 1942, female combatants had actually created a new and taboo-breaking reality, which could not simply be dismissed by a women's journal. Moreover, this was exactly the time when the Red Army, suffering from severe losses, had begun to accept women as recruits, although with considerable hesitation, mistrust, contempt, and even hostility. The new propaganda images not only served to mobilize women for the front, they also aimed at strengthening the home front, and last but not least they may have been published in order to spur the fighting spirit of male soldiers.

How did the literary-artistic journal for Soviet soldiers and sailors, *Krasnoarmeets-Krasnoflotets* (Male Red Army soldier–Male Red sailor),[74] cope with the fact that women had joined the ranks of the Red Army? Since they had volunteered and were recruited for duty at the front on a mass scale, this development could hardly be ignored completely. Therefore it was covered in articles and short stories. As in the case of the women's press, these reports usually concentrated on individual feats, while a number of photo essays were devoted to the manifold duties of women on the home front. Already in prewar times the journal had paid attention to female achievements and published autobiographical statements by Raskova and Osipenko.[75] On International Women's Day in the spring of 1938, a woman-aviator appeared on the front page, and a uniformed woman carrying a gun appeared on the back page.[76] From 1942 to 1944 the number of females featured on the cover of *Krasnoarmeets* increased considerably,[77] but this trend came to an end in 1945. The illustrations that did appear concentrated not on women soldiers, as one might have expected, but presented the readers with a wide range of different images. Only four of the fourteen illustrations depicted woman soldiers,[78] two showed a nurse, two were devoted to partisans, while six dealt with women as victims or civilians.

What do the presentations of war heroines tell us about their reasons for joining the Red Army as combatants? Motivation was rarely mentioned in the sources, but when it did appear, it often had to do with patriotism and revenge for Nazi atrocities. Usually readers were told that the portrayed woman had lost her husband, father, brother, child, or another dear person in the war. Hence her feelings of revenge came from personal motivations: the Germans had ruined her life. From a psychological point of view, these were conceivable reactions, while for propaganda purposes they certainly helped to make the women appear more humane than cruel. In other cases, the resolution to go to the front was described as a rather spontaneous decision that was made immediately after the German invasion. In that event, the preeminent goal was to defend the motherland, where every Soviet woman could lead a "quiet and happy life" thanks to the achievements of the Soviet Union with regard to the emancipation of women.

As a rule, the younger female soldiers were generally described as pretty, charming, energetic, brave, and courageous, but at the same time as ordinary people. Older women in the ranks often appeared in their capacity as mothers: "Herself a mother, Marina Raskova in her battle plan defends the mothers and children of the Soviet country from the beasts of prey in the shape of men, from the murderers of mothers and children."[79] It was said about the tank driver Mariia Vasil'evna Oktiabr'skaia that she "was like a true mother" to the soldiers around her.[80]

On the one hand, the descriptions of combat women as feminine and motherly perhaps made it easier for the female readers to identify themselves with the war heroines, who matched the motherly image of the "true Soviet woman" as it had emerged since the mid-thirties. On the other hand, however, the accentuation of their femininity tried to keep the "natural" hierarchy of the sexes intact, which was actually put into question by the armed performance of women at the front. In consideration of the fact that combat women had to cope with oversized greycoats, boots, and ill-fitting uniforms, the palliative purpose behind such incantations of femininity becomes even more obvious. When the Belorussian journalist Svetlana Aleksievich conducted a series of interviews with former female soldiers in the mid-eighties, most women complained about their forced defeminization at the front. This, they maintained, was one of the hardest things to endure.[81]

Memoirs and Biographies of Combat Women

What did the women themselves or their biographers tell us about their reasons for joining the army? Beyond the officially acceptable patriotism and hatred for the Nazi aggressors, highly personal motivations often appeared to lead women to such an extraordinary step. Their reasons could include a longing for a fuller life, for adventures, or their determination to emulate famous heroines like Raskova.[82] Such unpolitical driving forces were usually masked by slogans such as "Death to the fascists" or "Everything for the defense of the homeland," which clearly served as an outward legitimation of women's unconventional decision to take up a weapon. While they lacked any clear idea of what it meant to fight in the front lines, something probably also true for young male soldiers, some of these women seem to have had doubts about their future role as wives and mothers in Soviet society. Perhaps they had been looking for a way to express their discontent with traditional family life already, but only with the outbreak of the war did they get a chance to escape: "And now I'm on the threshold of adult life and what do I see: An amethystine foggy remoteness is expanding in front of me; it allures me with unknown pleasures, it offers tempests on the open sea, tranquillity in a haven of rest. I feel a strong man's hand on my shoulder, a child embraces me. Yet, what I'm really craving for is storm!"[83] This is what Nina Kosterina, who lost her life in late

1941 during a mission behind the enemy's lines, noted in her diary on 23 May 1940, a year before the war broke out.

In contrast to this rather militant spirit, typical of autobiographical sketches by women who joined the Red Army, biographies of war heroines usually abound with descriptions of their femininity and outer appearance. Take, for example, a title such as "The Commander with Thick Eyelashes."[84] Usually we learn much about the soft and pretty faces of the female soldiers, their sad eyes, their love for embroidery, and their never-ending ability to support their male comrades.[85] If we take such texts at face value, young women constantly posed as sisters or daughters of the soldiers, while mature women were received as mothers.[86] The reader is made to believe that the "nation at war" was in fact one big family fighting against the German invaders. If it was all a family business, women were supposed to be welcomed, and they could even be expected to take up a weapon in order to defend the hearth of the symbolic family of the state with Father Stalin as the patriarch.[87]

As in all traditional families, Soviet front women were often depicted as the bearers of culture within the army. In 1942, for example, President M. I. Kalinin told a meeting of political workers of the Moscow Air Defense Front that women soldiers had not only directly strengthened the army but had also influenced the performance and behavior of male soldiers. They had had a civilizing effect on the army. Moreover he claimed that conditions of barracks and the appearance of male soldiers had improved, and that the men were now reading more.[88] Yet before a group of former female soldiers in July 1945, Kalinin maintained that the war represented the final step in the emancipation of women.[89] This was perhaps the last time when both sides of the coin with regard to military performance of women were displayed in public. Only the traditionalist view with respective propaganda images was to survive in the Soviet Union, in order to accentuate a new myth according to which Soviet postwar society was now "returning to normalcy."[90]

In fact, Soviet women soldiers had contributed significantly to winning the war, but they did not succeed in serving as role models and in adding a career in the military to the list of acceptable opportunities for Soviet women. On the contrary, even before the war came to an end their achievements were no longer mentioned in public. In his speech on the occasion of the anniversary of the October Revolution, for example, Stalin praised the contribution of Soviet women to the war effort, but he mentioned only those at the home front, completely omitting the nearly one million who actually had served at the front.[91]

Captured female Red Army soldiers, 19 August 1941. In German propaganda of the time they were called "gunwomen." (Courtesy of the Bilderdienst Süddeutscher Verlag, Munich)

In a deeply symbolic step back to Soviet-style "normalcy," female combatants, who had suffered a higher porportion of losses than male soldiers, were not allowed to participate in the great Moscow Victory Parade:[92]

> The ten best aircrews from our regiment were selected to take part in the Victory Parade in Moscow. How we all waited for this occasion! We dreamed of flying over Red Square in brand-new machines that had just left the assembly line, and of the announcer Levitan's voice proclaiming to the entire city of Moscow: "A group of dive bombers from the 125th M. M. Raskova Borisov Guards Bomber Regiment, Orders of Suvorov and Kutuzov." So far, we have not been spoiled by war correspondents and photographers, who in fact paid us scant attention. Whether this was

a military secret, or whether there were other reasons, the existence of our dive bomber female regiment was not at all publicized. And, therefore, our wish to gain some publicity by means of our participation in the planned air show was fully justified. But the air show did not take place due to bad weather. Instead, we were charged with ferrying our PE-2s to other units.[93]

Most of the women who had served in the Red Army were demobilized after the war, except for a number of instructors, physicians, interpreters, and political officers. Thus it was made unmistakably clear that the government considered their military performance an expedient in times of trouble, but in principle as contrary to female "nature." This also seems to be the message President M. I. Kalinin had in mind when he advised a gathering of demobilized women soldiers, "Equality for women has existed in our country since the very first day of the October Revolution. But you have won equality for women in yet another sphere: in the defense of your country, arms in hand. You have won equal rights for women in a field in which they hitherto have not taken such a direct part. But allow me, as one grown wise with years, to say to you: do not give yourself airs in your future practical work. Do not speak of the services you rendered, let others do it for you. That will be better."[94]

When the war came to an end, women could not but notice that their contribution was systematically obscured and ignored. This policy must have made it difficult if not completely impossible for them to develop a collective identity as women soldiers of the Great Patriotic War. Instead, they were expected to return to their well-known dual role as workers and mothers and actively participate in the struggle for reconstruction of the devastated country, including accelerated replacement of the massive war losses, which was facilitated by a strict pronatalist policy.[95] For the time being, there was neither recognition nor relaxation of tension and release from obligations and constraint for the demobilized Soviet women soldiers.

Soviet women participated in World War II in many different capacities: they carried out drudgery at the home front, but they also joined partisan units, served as medical and technical personnel in the front lines, and fought as regular soldiers in the ranks of the Soviet army. However, these front women soon disappeared from most public commemoration and writing about the war; they did appear wearing their medals at celebrations on Victory Day, 9 May, and continue to do so. But for the most part their story was kept alive only in the oral tradition, a powerful but private stream of memory. This chapter has tried to demonstrate that that outcome was not due to any poor performance on their part or to their small number relative to male fighters, but was the result of systematic displacement in public discourse. We have analyzed some of the ways in which Soviet propaganda tried to mask the front-line experience of hundreds of thousands of women. While females' armed performance could hardly be ignored completely as long as the war dragged on, Soviet diplomacy, the print media, and the visual arts set the tone for creating the long lasting myth of the "Great Patriotic War," which in terms of the fighting was once again depicted as a pure male event, brimming with patriotism, heroism, and bravery. Women nearly always appeared when they were protected by or were appealing to men for help. Through such barren stereotypes the individual harsh and distractive battlefront experiences of real people, whether men or women, were consciously obscured.

Notes

1. C. Milosz, *The Captive Mind* (1953), trans. Jane Zielonko (New York, 1990), viii.

2. See for example N. A. Durova, *The Cavalry Maid: The Memoirs of a Woman Soldier of 1812*, trans. J. Mersereau Jr. and D. Lapeza (Ann Arbor, Mich., 1988). See also notes 5 and 28 below.

3. Many thanks go to Daniela Calamini and Barbara Falk (Ruhr-Universität, Bochum) for skillful bibliographical assistance. For an overview of American, British, German, and Soviet women's military performance during World War II, see D. Campbell, "Women in Combat: The World War II Experience in the United States, Great Britain, Germany, and the Soviet Union," *Journal of Military History* 57 (1993), 301–23.

4. V. S. Murmantseva, *Zhenshchiny v soldatskikh shineliakh* (Moscow, 1971), 9; K. J. Cottam, "Soviet Women in Combat during World War II: The Rear Services, Partisans, and Political Workers," in *Soviet Armed Forces Review Annual*, vol. 5. (Gulf Breeze, Fla., 1981), 275; J. Erickson, "Soviet Women at War," in *World War II and the Soviet People: Selected Papers from the Fourth World Congress for Soviet and East European Studies, Harrogate 1990* (New York, 1993), 50; R. Pennington, "Offensive Women: Women in Combat in the Red Army," in *Time to Kill: The Soldier's Experience of War in the West, 1939–1945,* ed. P. Addison and A. Calder (London, 1997), 249.

5. A. E. Griesse and R. Stites, "Russia: Revolution and War," in *Female Soldiers—Combatants or Non-Combatants? Historical and Contemporary Perspectives,* ed. N. L. Goldman, (Westport, Conn., 1982), 73.

6. K. J. Cottam, "Soviet Women in Combat in World War II: The Ground/Air Defense Forces," in *Women in Eastern Europe and the Soviet Union,* ed. T. Yedlin, (New York, 1980), 115. In the partisan movement, however, women accounted for 25 percent of all participants. Pennington, "Offensive Women," 255.

7. Women made up 100 percent of the nurses, 43 percent of the paramedics and military surgeons, and 41 percent of all frontline doctors. Griesse and Stites, "Russia," 70.

8. Cottam, "Soviet Women in Combat in World War II," 115; Erickson, "Soviet Women at War," 50.

9. Griesse and Stites, "Russia," 71.

10. Cottam, "Soviet Women in Combat during World War II," 275. These were the 586th Fighter Regiment, the 587th Short-Range Bomber Regiment, and the 588th Light Night Bomber Regiment. For more detailed information see K. J. Cottam, *Soviet Airwomen in Combat in World War II* (Manhattan, Kans., 1983).

11. Cottam, *Soviet Airwomen*, 8.

12. Cottam, "Soviet Women in Combat in World War II," 118.

13. Cottam, "Soviet Women in Combat during World War II," 290; Pennington, "Offensive Women," 254.

14. Erickson, "Soviet Women at War," 61; Cottam, "Soviet Women in Combat in World War II," 117–18.

15. S. Conze, "Kämpferin—Arbeiterin—Heldenmutter: Die Frau in den Anforderungen des Sowjetstaates, 1941–1945," Master's thesis (Ruhr-Universität, 1992), 53.

16. A. E. Griesse, "Soviet Women and World War Two: Mobilization and Combat Policies," Master's thesis (Georgetown University, 1980), 29; Pennington, "Offensive Women," 251.

17. Griesse, "Soviet Women and World War Two," 29.

18. Cottam, "Soviet Women in Combat during World War II," 275; Pennington, "Offensive Women," 261.

19. Erickson, "Soviet Women at War," 66–67; Griesse and Stites, "Russia," 72–73.

20. Women made up only 2.6 percent of collective farm directors in 1940, for example. As late as 1956 women were only 1 percent of Soviet enterprise directors. Gail Warshofsky Lapidus, *Women in Soviet Society: Equality, Development, and Social Change* (Berkeley, Calif., 1978), 179, 183.

21. Griesse and Stites, "Russia," 74–75.

22. V. S. Murmantseva, *Sovetskie zhenshchiny v Velikoi Otechestvennoi Voine* (Moscow, 1974), 264–71; Conze, "Kämpferin," 65.

23. Pennington's figures differ slightly, but point in the same direction. R. Pennington, "'Do Not Speak of the Services You Rendered': Women Veterans of Aviation in the Soviet Union," *Journal of Slavic Military Studies* 9 (1996), 124.

24. Of the seventy-eight films made during the war, none showed females performing combat roles in the army. Yet several movies made use of female partisans as leading characters. P. Kenez, *Cinema and Soviet Society, 1917–1953* (Cambridge, 1992), 195–200; R. Stites, *Russian Popular Culture: Entertainment and Society since 1900* (Cambridge, 1992), 99, 112–16. The same was true for the writings of the well-known war correspondents Ilya Ehrenburg, Vasilii Grossman, and Konstantin Simonov, and for postwar fiction about the Great Patriotic War. Pennington, "'Do Not Speak of the Services You Rendered,'" 143, 138.

25. These were Murmantseva, *Zhenshchiny v soldatskikh shineliakh* and *Sovetskie zhenshchiny v Velikoi Otechestvennoi Voine*.

26. M. D. Leibst, *Women in the Soviet Armed Forces* (Washington, D.C., 1976), 4.

27. Griesse and Stites, "Russia," 63–65.

28. R. Abraham, "Mariia L. Bochkareva and the Russian Amazons of 1917," in *Women and Society in Russia and the Soviet Union,* ed. L. Edmondson (Cambridge, 1992), 124–44.

29. B. E. Clements, "The Birth of the New Soviet Woman," in *Bolshevik Culture: Experiment and Order in the Russian Revolution,* ed. A. Gleason, P. Kenez, and R. Stites (Bloomington, Ind., 1985), 220; R. Johnson, "The Role of Women in the Russian Civil War (1917–1921)," *Conflict* 2:2 (1980), 201–17.

30. M. Sholokhov, *And Quiet Flows the Don,* trans. S. Garry (New York, 1966), 425, 431, and 496.

31. For another strong, beautiful, dedicated communist woman who is able to face danger, see Dasha Chumalova in F. Gladkov's *Cement* (1925), trans. A. S. Arthur and C. Ashleigh (New York, 1980).

32. Clements, "Birth of the New Soviet Woman," 227.

33. R. W. Thurston, "The Soviet Family during the Great Terror, 1935–1941," *Soviet Studies* 43:3 (1991), 557–58.

34. For a detailed analysis of the construction and deconstruction of the myth of partisan-martyr Zoia Kosmodemianskaia see R. Sartorti, "On the Making of Heroes, Heroines, and Saints," in *Culture and Entertainment in Wartime Russia,* ed. R. Stites, (Bloomington, Ind., 1985), 176–93.

35. F. Seidler, *Frauen zu den Waffen? Marketenderinnen, Helferinnen, Soldatinnen* (Koblenz, 1978), 208.

36. Women were eligible for the following badges: *Voroshilov-strelok* (Voroshilov-rifleman), *Gotov k trudu i oboronu* (Ready for work and defense), *Gotov k sanitarnoi oborone* (Ready for medical aid in case of defense), and *Protivovozdushnaia i khimiche-skaia oborona* (Antiaircraft and chemical defense). See I. Vasil'ev, "Shire razvernut' oboronnuiu rabotu," *Krest'ianka* (*K*) 14 (1939), 7. For the close ties between the general advancement of sports-mindedness in women and paramilitary training programs see "Bud' gotov k trudu i oborone," *K* 7 (1941), 16; "Znachenie fizicheskoi kultury dlia zhenshchin," *K* 11 (1941), 21.

37. V. Hardesty, *Red Phoenix: The Rise of Soviet Air Power, 1941–1945* (Washington, D.C., 1991), 48–49.

38. "Shire razvernem oboronnuiu rabotu," *K* 3 (1939), 20–21; A. Serov, "Bolshoi interes k oboronnoi rabote," *K* 24 (1939), 24; I. Sharonchikov, "Ovladeem novymi spetsial'nostiami—izuchim voennoe delo," *K* 5 (1940), 18.

39. This type of propaganda, which spread the message that "Every woman can do it," continued the tradition of two of the most notorious hero cults of the mid-1930s, that of aviation heroes ("Stalin's falcons" or "fledgling children") and that of production heroes (*Stakhnovites*). For a detailed discussion of these cults see K. Clark, *The Soviet Novel: History as Ritual* (Chicago, 1985), 114–35; L. H. Siegelbaum, *Stakhanovism and the Politics of Productivity in the USSR, 1935–1941* (Cambridge, 1988), 210–46; R. Maier, *Die Stachanov-Bewegung, 1935–1938: Der Stachanovismus als tragendes und ver-*

schärfendes Moment der Stalinisierung der sowjetischen Gesellschaft (Stuttgart, 1990), 177–95.

40. "Budem krepit' oboronu SSSR," *K* 11 (1939), 14–15; I. Vasil'ev, "Shire razvernut' oboronnuiu rabotu," *K* 14 (1939), 7; "Osoaviakhim—moguchii rezerv Krasnoi Armii," *K* 3 (1941), 13; "Budem gotovy k oborone," *Rabotnitsa (R)* 16 (1940), 3.

41. V. Vasil'ev, "Zadachi zhenshchin v oborone strany," *R* 24 (1938), 8–9.

42. S. Engel, "Pervaia professiia," *R* 25 (1938), 12.

43. "Kak my byli samuraev," *R* 21 (1939), 6; I. Kurchavov, "Patriotki," *R* 4 (1941), 7; A. Prigozhin, and V. Kandratenia, "Voenvrach," *R* 4 (1941), 9; E. Vasil'eva, "Na frontakh," *R* 10 (1941), 15.

44. "Pis'ma sovetskikh patriotov," *K* 22/23 (1939), 43; I. Tambovtsev, "Boi za Grodno," *K* 3 (1940), 4–5.

45. For the movement of the obshchestvennitsy and the women's journal *Obshchestvennitsa,* founded in 1936, see S. Fitzpatrick, "'Middle-Class Values' and Soviet Life in the 1930s," in *Soviet Society and Culture: Essays in Honor of Vera S. Dunham,* ed. T. L. Thompson and R. Sheldon (Boulder, Colo., 1988), 31–32; R. Maier, "Die Köchin krempelt die Ärmel hoch—Frauen im Stalinismus," *Mitteilungen des Instituts für Wissenschaft und Kunst* (Vienna) 45:3 (1990), 8–15; Siegelbaum, *Stakhanovism and the Politics of Productivity,* 241–42. For the response of a former obshchestvennitsa see E. N. Domokhoziaika Velichko, "Sanitarnaia druzhina," *R* 4 (1938), 10.

46. For a detailed analysis of the changing image of peasant women in Soviet political art from 1920 to the 1930s that also led to an amalgam of the old and new see V. E. Bonnell, "The Peasant Woman in Stalinist Political Art of the 1930s," *American Historical Review* 98 (1993), 55–82.

47. *Women in the USSR, Brief Statistics,* ed. Central Statistical Board of the Council of Ministers of the USSR (Moscow, 1960), 35–36.

48. G. M. Smith, "The Impact of World War II on Women, Family Life, and Mores in Moscow, 1941–1945," Ph.D. dissertation (Stanford University, 1990), 89; B. E. Clements, "Later Developments: Trends in Soviet Women's History, 1930 to the Present," in *Russia's Women: Accommodation, Resistance, and Transformation,* ed. B. E. Clements, B. A. Engel, and C. D. Worobec (Berkeley, Calif., 1991), 271; R. T. Manning, "Women in the Soviet Countryside on the Eve of World War II, 1935–1940," in *Russian Peasant Women,* ed. B. Farnsworth and L. Viola (Oxford, 1992), 220.

49. The daily newspaper *Pravda,* for example, in 1942 carried twenty-five photographs of working women, but only eight of peasant women. In 1943, however, the ratio was eleven to nineteen.

50. Stites, *Russian Popular Culture,* 100, 111–12.

51. See for example the most famous Soviet war poster, "Rodina-mat' zovet" (The motherland calls) by I. M. Toidze, 1942, and the sequel of 1943, "Za rodina-mat'" (For the motherland).

52. "Bei krepche synok" (Fight harder, my son), by I. A. Serebrianyi, 1941.

53. "Boets, Osvobozhdii ot fashistskogo gneta" (Soldier, rescue us from the fascist yoke), by B. V. Ioganson, 1943; "Syn moi, ty vidish doliu moiu—gromi fashistov v sviatom boiu" (My son, you see my fate—destroy the fascists in this holy war), by F. Antonov, 1943.

54. See for example *R* 24 (1941); 26 (1941); 27 (1941); 3 (1942); 6 (1942); 16 (1942); *K* 10/11 (1944).

55. *Information Bulletin,* ed. Embassy of the Union of Soviet Socialist Republics, Washington, D.C., 18 July 1941, 14.

56. *Information Bulletin,* 24 July 1941, 9.

57. Radio interview with Litvinov's secretary, in *Information Bulletin,* 19 Mar. 1942, 2.

58. "Boevye podrugi," *R* 24 (1941), 3.

59. E. Gyrdymova, "Geroiny Sevastopol'ia," *R* 4 (1942), 7–8.

60. Even if that tradition was not frequently referred to in official statements, Marina Raskova put herself in a line with historic figures such as Nadezhda Durova, who had posed as a man in the war against Napoleon. When a play based on Durova was staged in 1942, Raskova told the women pilots whom she was training: "Well, girls, someday there will be plays written and mounted about us. We have been summoned to continue the glorious tradition of the Russian woman-soldier." Quoted in Cottam, *Soviet Airwomen,* 3–4.

61. "Istrebitel' tankov," *R* 8 (1942), 6.

62. "Na frontakh otechestvennoi voiny," *R* 14 (1942), 8–9.

63. "Zhenshchina—boevaia pomoshchnitsa frontu," *K* 4 (1942), 1.

64. "Na frontakh otechestvennoi voiny," *K* 10 (1942), 12–13.

65. Her presence in American pro-Soviet media was due to a visit to the United States as a member of a Soviet student delegation in October 1942. "Lieutenant Liudmila Pavlichenko to the American People," *Soviet Russia Today,* Oct. 1942, 8–10.

66. In 1942 *Rabotnitsa* had twenty issues with sixteen pages each; in 1943 nine issues with sixteen pages came out, whereas in 1944 there were only eight issues with sixteen pages. In the beginning, reports on women at the front concentrated on nurses, yet over the course of the war this topic lost its dominance.

67. "Pamiaty geroicheskoi docheri naroda," *R* 1 (1943), 7. Obituaries in *Information Bulletin* also do not mention her initiative explicitly: "An exacting and strong-willed commander, an able and sensitive teacher, an experienced organizer, Marina Raskova helped many girl fliers to become experts in air combats." *Information Bulletin,* 19 Jan. 1943, 8.

68. M. Martynov, "Kommandir gvardeiskaia polka," *R* 3 (1943), 12.

69. See for example "Slavnaia doch' Urala," *R* 12 (1943), 8; S. Gal'pern, "Doch' rodiny," *R* 6/7 (1944), 12; "Geroi Sovetskogo Soiuza," *R* 10/11 (1944), 10–11.

70. E. Valina, "Na zashchite rodiny," *R* 4/5 (1944), 9; "Sovetskaia zenshchina na zashchite rodiny," *R* 2/3 (1945), 4.

71. I. Zbarskii, "Miniatiurnye pamiatniki," *R* 4 (1945), 2.

72. Griesse, "Soviet Women and World War Two," 27–28; Erickson, "Soviet Women at War," 59–60.

73. Murmantseva, *Zhenshchiny v soldatskikh shineliakh*, 4.

74. It was published twice monthly.

75. M. Raskova, "Nachalo druzhby," *Krasnoarmeets* 3/4 (1939), 18–22; M. Raskova, "Kak ia stala letchitsei," *Krasnoarmeets* 5 (1939), 18–20; P. Osipenko, "Vysotnye polety," *Krasnoarmeets* 10 (1940), 7–11.

76. *Krasnoarmeets* 4 (1938). A similar photograph of a woman in uniform was published on the back page of *Krasnoarmeets* 5 (1941), probably also on the occasion of International Women's Day.

77. *Krasnoarmeets* 5/6, 11, 13, 15, 22 (1942); 12, 16, 19, 23/24 (1943); 5, 9/10, 17/18, 19, 23/24 (1944). This tendency decreased in 1945, when only two covers (5, 7/8) showed a female figure, a telephone/radio operator and a tank driver, respectively.

78. It is interesting that they were not portrayed in combat action, except for one example (17/18 [1944]) that showed a man and a woman behind a machine gun. But the woman is holding field glasses (19 [1943]) or a flag (23/24 [1943]). Only the most famous woman, the sniper Pavlichenko, was honored by a photograph on the front page. (11 [1942]).

79. *Information Bulletin*, 19 Jan. 1943, 7.

80. Golubeva, "Geroi Sovetskogo Soiuza," *R* 10/11 (1944), 10.

81. S. Alexijewitsch, *Der Krieg hat kein weibliches Gesicht* (Hamburg, 1989), esp. 153–82.

82. See for example Kh. Dosponova, *Pod komandovaniem Raskovoi: Vospominaniia voennogo letchika*, (Alma-Ata, 1960), 5; *Poka stuchit serdtse: Dnevniki i pis'ma geroia Sovetskogo Soiuza Evgenii Rudnevoi* (Moscow, 1958), 7–11; M. P. Chechneva, *Samolety ukhodiat v noch* (Moscow, 1962), 7–8, 14.

83. N. Kosterina, *Das Tagebuch der Nina Kosterina: Moskau, 1936–1941* (Frankfurt, 1981), 99. Another reason why Kosterina joined the armed forces was to try to save her father, who had been arrested during the Great Purges, by means of her bravery (121).

84. A. Vyatskiy, "The Commander with Thick Eyelashes," in *The Golden-Tressed Soldier*, ed. and trans. K. J. Cottam, (Manhattan, Kans., 1983), 164–72.

85. See for example Cottam ed., *The Golden-Tressed Soldier*, 50, 99, 107, 164, 169, 181, 192, 255.

86. See for example ibid., 58, 68, 71, 104, 110, 135, 160, 197, 209, 255, 267, or the following quote in Cottam, *Soviet Airwomen*: "Our girls were great—We all loved them in a brotherly manner" (48). See also Pennington, "'Do Not Speak of the Services You Rendered,'" 134.

87. For a discussion of the Stalinist myth of the "great family" see Clark, *The Soviet Novel*, 114–35.

88. Cottam, "Soviet Women in Combat during World War II," 290.

89. M. I. Kalinin, *On Communist Education: Selected Speeches and Articles* (Moscow, 1953), 428.

90. For a discussion of postwar nonrelaxation and the reasons why a return to normalcy did not occur before Stalin's death see S. Fitzpatrick, "Postwar Soviet Society: The 'Return to Normalcy,' 1945–1953," in *The Impact of World War II on the Soviet Union,* ed. S. J. Linz (Totowa, N.J., 1985), 129–56.

91. Pennington, "'Do Not Speak of the Services You Rendered,'" 143.

92. Pennington, "Offensive Women," 260.

93. G. I. Markova, "Youth under Fire: The Story of Klavdiya Fomicheva, a Woman Dive Bomber Pilot," in Cottam, *Soviet Airwomen,* 124.

94. Kalinin, *On Communist Education,* 428.

95. Soviet pronatalism began as a policy in the 1930s but became strengthened after the war. Lapidus, *Women in Soviet Society,* 235–39.

12

Cauldrons of Loyalty and Betrayal: Soviet Soldiers' Behavior, 1941 and 1945

Robert W. Thurston

German and other Axis invaders captured more than three million Soviet prisoners from 22 June 1941 to the end of the year.[1] This roundup, the catastrophic loss of territory in the same period, and the claim that as many as one million Soviet citizens donned German uniforms during the war have led numerous authors to conclude that Red Army troops did not want to fight for their country, or more precisely for its regime. Supposedly the cumulative effects of terror and coercion made soldiers prefer surrendering to Hitler to fighting for Stalin. Similarly, the civilian population is said to have welcomed the Germans as liberators in the first months of the war; it was only the occupiers' stupid and brutal treatment of civilians that turned them against the Reich. This reversal, an appeal to traditional nationalism and patriotism, and even more coercion on the part of the Soviet party-state, the argument goes, produced the margin of victory.[2]

Previous chapters of this book, however, as well as some of my own earlier work,[3] have argued that issues of loyalty and disloyalty to the Stalinist regime are difficult to untangle, but that considerable evidence indicates that voluntary support for the Soviet state predominated. Dissatisfaction and welcome for the Germans had many causes, among them a tragic hope that Hitler would accommodate nationalist aspirations in Eastern Europe. To give one telling example, the invaders found a relatively warm greeting in the ethnically Ukrainian areas of former Poland, incorporated into the USSR in 1939, where Ukrainian nationalism had run high before the war. But as German troops crossed into the "old" Soviet Union, they noted a distinctly less cordial welcome.[4] This trend undercuts the argument that Soviet people embraced the attackers out of hatred for Stalinism; if that had been so, the warmth of the greeting would have risen, not fallen, across the old frontier. Certainly some people expected

After the liberation of Kerch' on 4 April 1944, the returning inhabitants of the city find their murdered relatives. (B0215/56/2; courtesy of the Bundesarchiv, Koblenz)

and hoped for a better life under the Germans. But that attitude did not characterize at least the younger and urban sectors of the populace.[5]

It is usually the studies concerned primarily with the Terror of the late 1930s or with Stalin's regime, not with the war, that conclude that in 1941 disloyalty reigned in the Red Army (RKKA). Studies of the war itself, however, often speak favorably of Soviet soldiers' will to fight from the start and ascribe early German victories to other causes.[6] The figure of one million citizens of the USSR donning German uniforms needs to be examined across chronological, geographical, and political dimensions. No systematic study of Soviet morale in World War II exists, nor are there theoretical or comparative treatments of the subject.

This chapter provides some background on the Red Army up to the summer of 1941 and then examines morale in the first months of combat. This early period presents the best opportunity to study Soviet performance before word of German treatment of prisoners and civilians became widely known and thus might have bolstered the will to fight.[7] Finally, a separate section will discuss Soviet prisoners of war and their decision after the end of the fighting to return to their homes or to stay in the West. To examine these topics is to look at how soldiers felt about their regime in the war's early stages and at its end, which provides a new means of probing the extent of support for Stalinism. This chapter also offers new ways of understanding the devastating pressures that the war exerted upon people's bodies and psyches.

In sifting the factors that influenced Red Army morale in the early combat, one major issue is how much the surrenders or collaboration with the Germans stemmed from hatred of the Soviet system and how much from more strictly military or wartime difficulties. The second category was vast. To begin with, the purges of army officers in the late 1930s continued to have a deeply negative effect, leaving major gaps among military leaders and educators. Another source of trouble in the officer corps by the time of the German invasion was the tremendous expansion of the Red Army. In 1936 its standing strength was about 940,000 men; in 1941 it numbered nearly five million. At least 255,000 new officers were needed to command the added troops, not counting losses in the fighting of 1938–40 in the Far East, Poland, and Finland.[8] Thus beyond the destruction of thousands of officers in the Terror, hundreds of thousands of others had to be found and trained before the Germans came. Serious problems also weakened the military education these men received.[9]

Another difficulty was that as the Soviet military expanded and attempted to cope with the impact of the Terror, it simultaneously switched rapidly to new weapons and tactics. New generations of tanks, planes, and rockets were adopted after about 1937, and the army was reorganized from territorial units into more divisions on active duty. Often the training that men had received for one kind of weapon was irrelevant to the arms they actually had to use when war broke out.[10]

A brief look at Soviet performance in other fighting before June 1941 provides perspectives on behavior during the German invasion. In July and August 1939, the Red Army defeated a Japanese division at Nomonhan or Khalkin-Gol, located on the Manchurian-Mongolian border. The losers "admitted, grudgingly, that the Soviets were a first-class opponent."[11] No morale problems appeared among Soviet participants at Nomonhan; they had hardly been reduced to uselessness or treason by Stalinism.

Yet the Red Army performed poorly in the Finnish War, from November 1939 to March 1940, despite the fact that about a million Soviet troops faced two hundred thousand Finnish soldiers.[12] The reasons for the dismal showing lie mostly in the peculiar conditions of the struggle and inadequate or improper Soviet preparation. The RKKA was not trained for deep snow conditions, and it was overly mechanized for the given terrain. Invading columns were limited to the roads, while the Finns skied through the forests they knew so well to attack from the flanks or rear. The long winter nights, heavy snowfall, and persistent fog all greatly limited Soviet aviation.[13] Still, individual Red Army soldiers and units displayed remarkable courage and determination to fight. The Finns were deeply impressed with Soviet soldiers' spirit, if not their combat abilities.[14]

By June 1941, when the German invasion began, gaping defects still characterized Soviet preparedness, or lack of it. To cite just a few examples, most units did not have wireless communication; they had to string wire within their ranks or to the next unit to communicate. Where wireless was available, many officers did not know how to handle it. The Russians had more tanks than the Germans, but in mid-1941 only a small number of those in the frontier area were the new models, 508 KVs and 967 T-34s in all, according to the official Soviet history of the war. Of the old tanks, only 27 percent were in working order by 22 June.[15] And those that could move and fight probably could not do so for long; many of the old models had only a four-hour engine life before major repairs were needed, and that was in peacetime.[16] Training was also defective or too short in many cases.[17]

For their part, the Germans possessed significant advantages. The attack began on virtually the longest day of the year, so that German aircraft could bomb and conduct reconnaissance for the majority of each twenty-four-hour cycle. The German army had the benefit of broader recent experience gained in Poland and Western Europe. The Wehrmacht had planned carefully for the attack.

Where terrain was less favorable for German tanks and aircraft, as in the Baltic region with its forests, streams, and swamps, Soviet troops acquitted themselves relatively well. The steppes of Ukraine, however, were perfectly suited to large-scale tank operations. Here poor command-level leadership also played a role. In southern Ukraine, however, the more competent hand of General M. P. Kirponos and the fact that he had some time to prepare for the enemy led to better Red Army performance.[18] On the Belorussian front, located in the center and astride the route to Moscow, Soviet units bore the heaviest German attacks and fared poorest. Yet if Red Army soldiers were able to retreat into heavy woods or marshes, they sometimes fought on for months or even years.[19]

When the RKKA had a chance to dig in and resist from well-prepared positions, it often resisted stubbornly. One example is the defense of the Brest fortress, which held out for several days after the Germans had swept around it. On the walls, Russians wrote messages about their determination to die rather than surrender. One was scratched into the plaster with a nail: "We are three men from Moscow—Ivanov, Stepanchikov, and Shuntiaev. We are defending this church, and we have sworn not to surrender. July 1941." Below that was written, "I am alone now. Stepanchikov and Shuntiaev have been killed. The Germans are inside the church. I have one hand-grenade left. They shall not get me alive."[20] Most of these men kept their word; few prisoners were taken in the fortress.

But what about the 3.35 million who were captured in 1941? They can be divided into two major groups: those who were surrounded and those who were not. Capture usually involved "cauldrons" (*Kesseln*), rings closed around Soviet units by the Germans that summer and fall. The thirteen major cauldrons netted an estimated total of 2,465,000 prisoners, or almost 74 percent of all Soviet soldiers captured before the end of 1941.[21] Many other, lesser encirclements obviously took place, so that all but a small minority of the year's prisoners of war (POWs) were caught in this fashion.

Once German armor closed a ring, tanks, infantry, and the Luftwaffe sliced the trapped forces to pieces. Red soldiers were cut off from the rest of the army as well as from supplies of food and ammunition. Often water became scarce. Soviet air drops were greatly limited by German air superiority. Nevertheless, German units frequently reported that strong resistance lasted for days in the Kesseln.[22] Given these circumstances, the argument that surrendering troops acted out of disloyalty is unacceptable. Obviously their morale was shattered, but that resulted from a situation in which they had struggled for days against great odds, often with little or nothing to eat and no way to shoot back.

Red Army men often rejected surrender even when they had cause to give up. In the Kiev entrapment in September, a "high percentage" of the surrounded troops threw away their weapons, a German report stated, to try to pass as civilians and cross through enemy lines to the *east*, back to Soviet-held territory.[23]

Other German units also reported desperate Red Army attempts to break out of rings. Panzer Group I, for example, noted that on 8 August a "squadron" attacked an SS division and was "fully destroyed."[24] The 26th Infantry Division encountered similar resistance near Filipovskoe at about the same time.[25]

Even when a cauldron did not develop, German air superiority gravely injured Soviet morale. One veteran recalled that at first the Germans had complete control of the air and that there was widespread terror of dive-bombing among his comrades. "You felt that every plane was coming down at you," he said. "It made a very terrible impression to see the German planes coming over

every day flying quite freely and unafraid, taking photographs without interference and scouting and looking around."[26]

During his interrogation by the Germans on 19 July, Stalin's son Iakov Djugashvili, a senior artillery lieutenant, underscored this problem. He told his
captors that the speed, exactness, and organization of the German forces had
made a profound impression on Soviet soldiers. They especially feared the
Luftwaffe's attacks on troops moving to the front, so that Djugashvili felt it
was more dangerous to be marching than to be in ground combat.[27] German
and Soviet commanders alike recognized that air attacks behind RKKA lines
greatly facilitated the invaders' progress.[28]

The caliber of replacement troops also contributed to the Soviet debacle. The
most battle-worthy formations of the standing army had been deployed at or
near the front,[29] and these suffered immense casualties in the first assaults.
There were other well-trained troops available, but until October 750,000 of
these were held in the Far East for fear of a Japanese attack. Thus many of the
soldiers sent against the Germans were poorly trained. Among replacements
for the 275th Artillery Division brought up between 3 and 5 September, for
example, were "many older untrained people." Having been issued weapons
and uniforms, they marched directly into battle.[30] A commissar's diary found
by the Germans in early August noted that "many reservists are traitors and
there are many more deserters among them than among men called earlier."[31]
But probably these deserters or poor fighters were not traitors to begin with;
they were simply woefully unprepared for combat.

On occasion incompetent officers and the high casualty rate among good
and bad officers alike turned the men into leaderless mobs. One captured
Russian reported, "We were surrounded, thanks to our stupid commanders,
and then the Germans started to pound us. Night and day they flew over us
and bombed us. We were completely disorganized. Our leaders were dead or
fled and without them we were absolutely useless."[32]

A former Soviet colonel mentioned another problem regarding officers. "In
the first months of the German attack," he claimed, "many officers were under suspicion by their very [own] troops, by the very soldiers they had to command. Some of the officers were killed by their own troops who thought that
they were spies."[33] He did not explain this remark; it may be that such soldiers
believed too well in the existence of "enemies of the people" before the war.
Or perhaps such murderous troops decided that their officers were traitors
because of the horrendous slaughter and confusion on the Soviet side.[34]

Cauldron or no, given any sort of officers or none at all, horrendous supply
problems occurred regularly. One bizarre desertion involved five Jewish sol-

diers, former Romanian citizens from Bukovina. "Rations are bad," they told the Germans; "you get no bread from the unit. Everyone crossed the Dnepr unwillingly, because they were terribly afraid of being hungry there."[35] Desertion by Jewish troops was in vain, for German practice dictated their quick execution.

Captured in August in Estonia, a sailor who remained in the West after the war remarked, "on the Russian front there had been no bread, no meat, etc. Is there any wonder why so many Russian soldiers were taken prisoner?"[36] Surrendering to the Germans obviously seemed better to many men than starving to death.

Besides these problems, the heavy Red Army losses took a toll on soldiers' spirits. Willingness to fight was high at first, a Major Konov told his interrogators. But as time went on the combination of losses and retreat drove feelings down.[37] Casualties were often staggering; one prisoner reported 70 percent losses in the 190th Artillery Division.[38] The German First Mountain Division's dispatches mentioned laconically that from 22 to 26 June, "The small number of prisoners is explained by the fact that in the hard battle most of the enemy were shot."[39] The same division reported that around Vinnitsa from 18 to 20 August it took about 200 prisoners but killed about 850.[40] It is easy to imagine the spirits of the 200 survivors just before they were captured.

The truly remarkable feature of the war's early months is that the Red Army did not collapse. Despite all the Soviet troops' problems, the Germans spoke regularly of their "hard," "tough," or even "wild" resistance. Such phrases did become somewhat ritualistic, but the field reports are almost entirely free of fancy rhetoric, the approach we would expect from exhausted men writing close to the front. Nor were these documents for public consumption; they were meant for other soldiers and professional purposes. This same recognition of Soviet determination to resist appears as well in the diary of General Franz Halder, the chief of the German Army General Staff, who wrote only for himself. Indeed, Halder was one of several Germans who viewed Soviet resistance as much tougher than anything his side had faced in Western Europe.[41]

It is certainly true that a fair number of Soviet participants who later emigrated spoke of low morale at the time of the invasion and linked it to disloyalty.[42] Such people might be expected to show antipathy toward the Stalinist regime and to denigrate the land they left behind in order to provide themselves with a strong psychological underpinning for their departure.[43]

Another great difficulty in assessing why any Soviet citizen was disloyal, not only during the war but at any point in time, lies in trying to determine when and how that stance arose. Some of the people who remained in the West after the war rather than going back to the USSR, and who preferred the term "nonreturnee" to "emigré," indicated in interviews that their antipathy to Soviet rule stemmed from the Revolution of 1917 or the Civil War period. "The motherland was no longer mine from the first days of the October Revolution," explained one former POW.[44] The alienation from the USSR felt by such people stemmed more from the devastation of the Russian Civil War or a visceral hatred for socialism than from experiences under Stalinism.

But it is also true that numerous emigrés noted enthusiasm for the Soviet cause in June 1941.[45] Even several POWs who had grown up in anti-Soviet families reported fighting "with all their strength right up to the moment of capture."[46] They had surrendered only because of circumstances.[47]

A large number of the USSR's citizens entered German military service during the war. In many accounts these people are lumped together with others who had connections to the tsarist empire but had never lived under Soviet rule. One such ill-starred group consisted of certain Cossacks, either emigrés from the period of the Russian Civil War or their children, who volunteered for service with the Wehrmacht under the delusion that they could live the dream of the old, prerevolutionary days after a German victory. Cossacks, not an ethnic group but a centuries-old military caste largely of Russian and Ukrainian descent, had enjoyed various privileges under the tsars. By February 1945 the Wehrmacht had gathered enough Soviet and emigré Cossacks to form a division under the command of the seventy-two-year-old general Petr Krasnov, who had fought against the Red Army in the Russian Civil War and had left Russia after the Bolshevik victory. Of the eighteen thousand men in Krasnov's division, however, more than five thousand were German soldiers assigned to it. Like their commander, most of the Cossacks in this unit had not been Soviet citizens.[48]

There were also Georgian units, complete with aristocrats who had been "taxi-drivers in Paris before the war," in German service.[49] Other ethnic groups, for example Balts and "Galicians" (Ukrainians), were allowed to form similar units. Thus the *Osttruppen* (eastern troops) by no means consisted solely of former Soviet citizens. In any event, figures on the number of such citizens who entered combat units on the German side are far from certain. Joachim Hoffmann believes that at least 250,000 Azerbaijanis, Tatars, Turkmen, Armenians, Georgians, and other southern and eastern nationalities, but not Slavic peoples, were in German fighting forces by late 1944.[50] However, the Russian historian Leonid Reschin places the total number of Osttruppen of all Soviet nationalities at no more than 45,000, of which perhaps 60 percent had been POWs, by 1943.[51]

Of the Soviet citizens who joined the Wehrmacht, many were certainly "westerners," people taken into the USSR in 1939–40 from areas of Poland, the Baltic states, Finland, or Romania.[52] Again, national sentiments had often been strong among such groups before the war, only to be dashed and turned into hatred for the Soviet Union when all or parts of those countries were annexed.

The estimated total of one million collaborators working under German direction includes people who took part in combat service, in noncombat roles for the German army as *Hilfswillige* (literally "those willing to help," often shortened to *Hiwis*), and in positions as local officials and police under the German occupation.[53] Probably less than half of these collaborators were ethnically Russian, concludes Mark Elliot.[54] Non-Russian citizens of the USSR, including those who were not "westerners," had often hated Russian governments well back into tsarist history and had become fixated upon the Germans as likely to satisfy old national aspirations. Ukrainian nationalism has already been mentioned. The Germans put these sentiments, which often had little to do with Stalinism or even Soviet rule in general, to use.

The Germans frequently sent former Soviet soldiers to fight partisans behind the front lines; however, significant numbers of these troops, including some from ethnic minorities, disappointed their handlers by defecting back to the Soviet side.[55] This problem occurred despite the fact that the officers were typically German and that each unit had a core of rank-and-file German soldiers. Most Osttruppen were eventually shipped to the western front for labor duties, as it was "risky" to leave them on Soviet territory.[56] Such problems for the Germans in using POWs as troops suggest that when former Red Army soldiers entered the enemy's service, they did so more from a desire to eat and survive than out of anti-Soviet feelings.

The most notorious story of military collaboration centers on the Soviet general Andrei Vlasov, captured in July 1942 after his army was encircled near Volkhov, south of Leningrad. His own behavior does not show particular eagerness to serve the Germans at first: Vlasov wandered in the forest for two weeks after the destruction of his forces before the enemy found him. He sought to elude the invaders yet made no move to resist—which might have been fatal—when they located him.

After using Vlasov as a propaganda tool in the attempt to coax deserters over and to calm the civilian population behind the lines, the Germans in early 1945 allowed him to begin forming a force commonly known as the Russian Army of Liberation (ROA). Units of this largely paper "army," which enrolled perhaps fifty thousand men, saw action against the Red Army on the Oder River on 6 April 1945; on 5 May they turned on their hosts and attacked German troops at Prague.[57] Hoping that the western countries would welcome them despite their service for Germany, Vlasov's soldiers were doomed to a cruel end whenever Soviet authorities got hold of them.

German data show that 5.74 million Soviet troops were captured in the war.[58] Attempting to calculate the percentage that entered German service is difficult. Perhaps 60 percent of the POWs captured in 1941 died before the end of the year; some 1.4 million probably perished before September.[59] Many other prisoners subsequently died or were rendered too weak in captivity to be of any use to their masters, so a high proportion of POWs never had a chance to ask to help the Reich. Still, German documents show that as of May 1944, 1,053,000 POWs remained alive and in custody, of whom 875,000 were working in factories, mines, farms, or elsewhere,[60] usually under abysmal conditions.

Of a total of 5,160,000 prisoners counted by that same time, 818,000 had been released "to civilian or military status." This last group included ethnic Germans (*Volksdeutsche*) captured in the USSR. Adding up the prisoners at work or still alive in the camps, we get a total of 1,871,000 survivors at this point.[61] By May 1944, 3,289,000 POWs were dead or missing; surely few of the second category survived. Christian Streit puts the death toll for the entire war at 3.3 million of 5.7 million Soviet soldiers captured by the Germans.[62]

How did they die? Many were wounded when captured, and some of those would not have survived anyway. The Germans were not prepared for the great numbers they rounded up and may perhaps be excused to a small degree because of the massive problems they faced in trying to house and feed three million of the enemy army at once. Stalin also deserves some of the blame, for he considered the POWs to be traitors and refused to help them in any way or to recognize their existence, even when his own son was captured. The USSR had not signed the Geneva Protocol of 1929 on treatment of prisoners of war, so Red Army men in German hands had no legal protection. However, if the estimate is correct that 60 percent of the 3.35 million POWs captured in 1941, or just over two million, died before the end of the year, then they succumbed before the hard-pressed Soviet government, or any Russian government with the best will in the world, could have gotten aid to them.

The captors, of course, cared nothing for rules in any event. For years Germans had been taught that all Slavs, especially those under communist rule, were *Untermenschen*, a less-than-fully-human but still dangerous breed. Omer Bartov argues that many German soldiers fully accepted this notion;[63] presumably many civilians followed suit. German leaders certainly laid down clear guidelines for behavior toward Soviet people. "Brutal violence" would be needed in Russia, Hitler told his top officers in early 1941.[64] On 30 March he said,

"We do not wage war to preserve the enemy"; in October he remarked that "this enemy consists not of soldiers but to a large extent only of beasts."[65] Earlier chapters of this book have shown what Nazi attitudes led to when the invaders occupied Soviet territory.

The Nazi hierarchy of "races" applied in POW camps as well. At the top were the British and white Americans, while the Soviet troops ranked near the bottom. About 2 percent of western Allied prisoners held by the Germans died, but mortality among Soviet POWs reached 60 to 70 percent.[66] The German authorities made explicit plans in the spring of 1941 to treat Red Army prisoners worse than others;[67] this project succeeded. Surrounded after capture by barbed wire and guards, many POWs never saw the German Reich. They starved or froze along the way, their corpses lining the roads in some areas like stacks of logs. A hundred grams of bread a day was not enough to sustain life if captured soldiers had to walk to their ultimate destinations, or if they rode in open railroad cars, as many did even in winter.[68]

Once in camps in the Reich, the survivors of the journey fared only slightly better. They faced starvation, overwork in mines and factories, disease, and deliberate cruelty.[69] It was a group of Soviet prisoners on whom the Germans first tested Zyklon B gas,[70] the chemical later used to dispatch millions of Jews and others in the death camps. Given all this, it must be a source of wonder that more POWs did not die or that more did not join German ranks.

The last issue to be considered here concerns Soviet citizens who had been in enemy hands but found themselves at the war's end in May 1945 under British or American authority. Many had no choice about their fate, but others had to decide whether to return home or try to remain in the West. The complex of factors involved in these decisions also tells us something about loyalty to the Soviet regime and about the impact of the war on people's thinking.

A rough estimate of five million Soviet citizens in German hands toward the end of the war seems acceptable. Of those, perhaps half were left in western zones.[71] Soviet figures, possibly incomplete, show that 451,561 of that portion did not go home. Here too ethnicity played a major role: while only 31,704 Russians did not return, 144,934 Ukrainians did not, and 109,214 Latvians, 63,401 Lithuanians, and 58,924 Estonians remained abroad.[72] Nationalism and antisocialist feelings often precluded a return to a country that many in these groups did not consider theirs. Among the non-Russians who remained abroad must have been a high proportion of "westerners."

Some people scheduled for repatriation resisted so desperately that they committed suicide as they were about to be forcibly returned. Although some accounts claim that as many as "several thousand" ended their own lives for this reason, the most detailed study of the subject notes only several dozen documented attempts and actual suicides. These were overwhelmingly among POWs who had exchanged life in the invaders' camps for service in the German army, typically in the Russian Army of Liberation. Such men had every reason to expect execution in the USSR,[73] a fate that many Soviet citizens who had not been captured probably considered just.[74]

Like many Cossacks, a large group of "Russians" who resisted shipment to the USSR after the war by British or American authorities had never been Soviet citizens. Such soldiers did not fall under the Yalta accords, which specified the mandatory repatriation of all who had served in the Axis forces to their home countries. They were nonetheless turned over to Soviet authorities.

Other evidence suggests that suicides among POWs often related not to the defects of Stalinism, huge as they were, but to a person's wartime fate or to hatred of the Soviet regime dating from 1917. A study of thousands who did not return concludes that during the war itself "a very large percentage of Soviet emigrés left their homeland under very substantial duress." "Nonreturnees" often confided to their interviewers that they would like to return to the USSR if they could resume a "normal life" there.[75]

But as Soviet citizens stranded in the West at the end of the fighting thought about returning to their native country, many factors worked on their minds. One influence was the terrible blunders of the war's beginning, which had often led directly to capture. One former POW recalled later that in his barracks, reserved for officers, only two of 150 still supported the Soviet government late in the war. "The rest were convinced that our defeats were due to the inability and short-sightedness of our military and our high political command, and were opponents of Stalin's policies and government."[76] This comment suggests that many of the negative feelings in this barracks stemmed less from basic antipathy to Stalin's rule than from the disasters of the war's early stages.

A related issue was the feeling in the German camps that the POWs had been rejected by their own government. A soldier who expressed frustration at his government's "abandonment" of the POWs also told an American interviewer in emigration that "he would never have left the Soviet Union, nor turned in any sense against the regime as a whole, had it not been for the war."[77] A lieutenant captured in 1942 maintained to his postwar interviewer that he never wanted to oppose the Soviet Union and never joined the Russian Army of Liberation. "You do not want to fight against your mother," he said. "But when I saw what had happened, what was happening in the repatriation camps, I found out that it was not a mother any more, but a stepmother. Therefore, I escaped."[78]

Another influence on the decision to return or stay was stories told about the fate of ex-prisoners who again came under Soviet control. Some prisoners asserted that their counterparts taken by the Finns in 1940 had either been shot or sent to work as forced laborers upon their return to the Soviet Union.[79]

Prisoners in German camps had already heard widely, of course, about shootings of men who had been captured but had managed to escape and make their way back to Soviet lines.[80] On 16 August 1941 the army High Command (*Stavka*) issued Order 270, apparently drafted personally by Stalin. Stavka directed that if a "commander or unit of Red Army soldiers instead of the organization of resistance to the enemy prefers to surrender, they are to be destroyed by all means, both on the ground and from the air, and the families of Red Army soldiers who have given themselves up into captivity will be deprived of support and aid."[81] As Stalin's biographer Dmitrii Volkogonov remarked, this was an "order of desperation and harshness."[82] By the time the directive was issued, millions of soldiers had been destroyed or captured, and thousands of square miles had been overrun by the Germans. As yet there seemed to be no way to stop the onslaught. POWs also knew of Stalin's "not a step back" order, issued at the end of July 1942, which forbade retreat without express permission: "You have to fight to your last drop of blood to defend every position, every foot of Soviet territory."[83] Accompanying editorials thundered, "He who does not observe order and discipline is a traitor, *and must be mercilessly destroyed.*"[84] Such orders and statements resulted from a mood of near despair produced by horrendous losses and are not necessarily indicative of Stalin's state of mind at the moment of invasion or of expectations of treason he entertained then.

When ex-POWs and other Soviet citizens who had been under German control returned home, their treatment varied considerably. They were usually taken first to "checking-filtration points"; in general, rank-and-file troops and sergeants were not arrested, excepting those who had been Vlasovites or served the Germans as police. Otherwise, Soviet authorities released low-ranking POWS, although they often had to enter reserve or labor units of the Red Army for a certain period of time. However, returning officers went straight into "special camps" of the NKVD. By 1951, Soviet data show, 4,304,381 citizens had returned to the USSR and had been processed by the authorities. Detailed information on their fate is available for the 4,199,488 who reached their homeland by 1 March 1946: of those, 272,867, about 6.5 percent, remained in the hands of the NKVD, although others went into exile.[85]

Several people who returned after the war from captivity or forced labor later fled to the West; they related that they were imprisoned or under suspicion by the authorities for only a short time.[86] Unfortunately, and despite explicit government policy that returnees were to receive equal treatment with other citizens, they faced discrimination from local authorities and their countrymen.[87] On the basis of this material, it appears that, as in other cases, Stalin (1) was deeply suspicious of whole groups of citizens, especially those who exercised authority; (2) required investigations of their conduct to determine guilt; and (3) presumed guilt among arrestees, who had to prove their innocence.[88] This of course was often difficult or impossible. In any event, the Stalinist regime did not repress the returnees wholesale, but only those found guilty of offenses, albeit in a context of hypersuspiciousness and usually without a fair hearing.

At the end of the war POWs and forced laborers removed to the Reich (*Ostarbeiter*) could reasonably have felt great concern about their future at home following the war, given their knowledge of Order 270 and similar statements. It is therefore somewhat surprising that Soviet citizens held by the Germans often came to understand the possibility of severe treatment at home only after the combat stopped. Perhaps they had erected a psychological defense against the idea that, having fought for their country and having endured the horrors of German captivity, they might now be branded traitors by their own leadership. Whatever the reason for this delayed understanding, one former POW made it clear that his decision not to return "was absolutely absent during the war and came about only after information was learned while in Germany that all POWs were being sent to concentration camps for the rehabilitation of their 'minds.'"[89] "A Red Army officer in a German camp said that at the end of the war, there were many among us who did not wish to return home. To me this attitude seemed absurd, unreasonable, pathological. . . . I was then in command of a group of over 400 persons who wanted to return home immediately. I counted the days, anxiously awaiting the happy moment of going home." Only his treatment just after the war by Soviet authorities changed his mind and caused him to seek refuge in the West.[90]

The same decision, made only because of what happened immediately after the war, appears in other accounts. Another POW heard that people who went back were being "isolated." His sister was tried as a traitor for having been an Ostarbeiter.[91] Such people often believed that they would face punishment back in the USSR. One young woman who had been a forced laborer started to make her way home after May 1945, but in Prague heard "unpleasant news" of what happened to people in her situation. Women like her were called "lovers of the

Germans." She turned around and recrossed Soviet lines back to the West.[92] Another young woman expressed her reasoning simply. Asked, "Did you want to be repatriated?" she replied, "No, I had heard that those who repatriated went to concentration camps." It was at that point that she decided not to return.[93]

Sometimes the decision to remain abroad was based on a dense web of factors. One woman gave "at least three reasons": the West had better living conditions and more freedom; she feared reprisals; and she was influenced by her husband, who was of Polish descent and did not want to return.[94] An ex-prisoner who stayed in the West was the son of a tsarist colonel executed by the Soviet authorities in 1918. An uncle was arrested in 1937; the respondent did not specify his fate. However, as though these disasters were not enough to turn him completely against the regime, he also noted the better living conditions he had seen in Romania and Bulgaria, his mother's arrest in 1948, and the "terrible postwar conditions" in the USSR.[95]

A great variety of considerations bore on the decision to go or stay. The pull of relatives, language, culture, and the possibility of regaining a place in a familiar society were powerful incentives to return. But the threat of punishment and the economic devastation at home, which had never provided a decent standard of living for most to begin with, were strong factors in keeping people in the West. One study based on postwar interviews with ex-Soviet citizens concluded that young people who became disaffected with the regime and remained abroad generally acted from disenchantment with economic conditions at home, especially after seeing some part of Western Europe. These people did not usually mention "an atmosphere of greater personal freedom" abroad as a factor in their decision. Older nonreturnees, however, more often cited "lack of freedom."[96] This division of attitudes tends to support other findings that young people were more loyal, at least before they crossed the boundaries of the USSR for any reason, than older citizens were.[97] Of course, the vast majority of the army was young.

Above all, the sources support the comments of two emigrés on their peers' feelings. One woman said, "I really think that there is not a single DP [displaced person, the term for those stranded in Allied camps after the war without a country to go to] here who would not go back if he could, if it were not for the awful terror." By this the respondent meant not the arrests of the regime's internal "enemies" in general but the repression of those who had spent any time under German control: "if they [nonreturnees] were pardoned, then they would go back."[98] Another man maintained that "if the emigrants here could return without being punished all of them will return. It is a deep mistake to believe that people don't want to return because they don't like the regime.

They don't return because they fear to be punished for the crimes they have committed."[99] Such evidence suggests that Soviet citizens did not widely want to leave the USSR to begin with, and many who had to leave longed to go home at the war's end.

❖ ❖ ❖

Detailed sources on the early months of the war largely describe strong resistance and loyalty in the Red Army as the German invasion unfolded. If and when morale collapsed, leading to surrender, it was due largely to abysmal military conditions. Although various western writers have ascribed Soviet disasters in 1941 mostly to the impact of Stalinist horrors, evidence to the contrary has been readily available. Those horrors were certainly real and far-reaching, but they by no means produced widespread treasonous conduct during the German attack. The early Soviet defeats and surrenders had other, more immediate and tangible causes.

When at the end of the war some former prisoners and Ostarbeiter decided to remain in the West, they did not necessarily act out of hatred for Stalinism. More often they took the devastation inside the USSR into consideration; above all they feared punishment by Soviet authorities. Still, the vast majority did return, and most of them probably went willingly. For the great majority of Red Army soldiers, whether captured or not, World War II on the eastern front was their war, the people's war.

Notes

The author gratefully acknowledges support from the International Research and Exchanges Board, the American Council of Learned Societies, and Miami University's Committee on Faculty Research.

1. Christian Streit, *Keine Kameraden: Die Wehrmacht und die sowjetischen Kriegsgefangenen, 1941–1945*, 2d. ed. (Bonn, 1991), 83, lists 3.35 million prisoners by mid-December. Apparently Streit has attempted to correct for the possibility of double counting by the Germans. Albert Seaton, *The Russo-German War, 1941–1945* (New York, 1971), 208n, simply says the number "exceeded three million."

2. For examples of works that link the high number of prisoners to low morale in general, see Martin McCauley, *The Soviet Union since 1917* (London, 1981), 113; David Mackenzie and Michael W. Curran, *A History of the Soviet Union*, 2d ed. (Belmont, Calif., 1991), 338–39; Nicholas V. Riasanovsky, *A History of Russia*, 4th ed. (New York, 1984), 525; Alexander Dallin, *German Rule in Russia, 1941–1945: A Study of Occupation Policies* (London, 1957), 63. Several works make an explicit connection between the "Great

Terror" of the 1930s and purported low morale of Soviet troops at the beginning of the invasion. See Robert Conquest, *The Great Terror: A Reassessment* (New York, 1990), 456 and 468; Joel Carmichael, *Stalin's Masterpiece: The Show Trials and Purges of the Thirties—the Consolidation of the Bolshevik Dictatorship* (New York, 1976), 189; George Fischer, *Soviet Opposition to Stalin: A Case Study in World War II* (Cambridge, Mass., 1952), 5–6. Fischer introduces the concept of inertness, supposedly the result of Soviet totalitarianism in general, emphasizing terror in the production of this characteristic (122). In his view, Soviet troops were inert and incapable of strong resistance until Stalin reasserted his leadership, at which point the troops and the populace fell back into their accustomed pattern of total obedience.

3. See Robert W. Thurston, *Life and Terror in Stalin's Russia, 1934–1941* (New Haven, Conn., 1996).

4. Ibid., 217–19.

5. Alex Inkeles and Raymond Bauer, *The Soviet Citizen: Daily Life in a Totalitarian Society* (Cambridge, Mass., 1959), 265, 274, write that based on a survey of several thousand Soviet emigres and interviews with more six hundred of them completed after World War II, each succeeding generation of Soviet people was more inclined than the one before it to accept the system as a whole. See also Thurston, *Life and Terror,* chap. 6, 164–98, on industrial workers and their response to the system. For a contrasting view, but one with points of agreement, see Sarah Davies, "'Us against Them': Social Identity in Soviet Russia, 1934–41," *Russian Review* 56:1 (1997).

6. See for example John Erickson, *The Road to Stalingrad: Stalin's War with Germany,* vol. 1 (London, 1975); Paul Carell, *Hitler Moves East: 1941–1945* (Boston, 1964); Alan Clark, *Barbarossa: The Russian-German Conflict, 1941–1945* (New York, 1965); Alexander Werth, *Russia at War, 1941–1945* (New York, 1964).

7. Streit, *Keine Kameraden,* 83 and 86–87, argues that German conduct increased Soviet resistance to the utmost from the beginning. Yet this was not always the case, even in areas occupied by the Germans, for their treatment of civilians varied widely from place to place. See for example "Respublika Zueva," anonymous typescript in the Nicolaevsky Collection, Hoover Institution Archives (HI), box 280, folder 8, 3. The author claims that even though the Germans quickly occupied the area in which he lived, the local people did not hear of atrocities until escaped Red Army prisoners appeared there in the fall of 1941.

8. Roger Reese, "A Note on a Consequence of the Expansion of the Red Army on the Eve of World War II," *Soviet Studies* 41:1 (Jan. 1989), 137.

9. F. B. Komal, "Voennye kadry nakanune voiny," *Voenno-istoricheskii zhurnal* 2 (1990), 27.

10. Reese, "Note on a Consequence," 137.

11. Alvin D. Coox, *Nomonhan: Japan against Russia, 1939* (Stanford, Calif., 1985), 1089–91. Larry W. Moses, "Soviet-Japanese Confrontation in Outer Mongolia: The Battle of Nomonhan-Khalkin Gol," *Journal of Asian History* 1:1 (1967), also leaves an impression of good Soviet performance.

12. Erickson, *Road to Stalingrad,* 13.

13. Anthony F. Upton, *Finland, 1939–1940* (Newark, Del., 1979), 57; Allen F. Chew, *The White Death: The Epic of the Soviet Finnish Winter War* (East Lansing, Mich., 1971), 22.

14. Upton, *Finland,* 69 and 84; Chew, *White Death,* 28 and 55. For a report on the high level of RKKA resistance by a Finnish officer, see V. Zenzinov, *Vstrecha s Rossiei* (New York, 1945), 39–40.

15. Werth, *Russia at War,* 148–49. S. V. Kuleshov et al., *Nashe otechestvo: Opyt politicheskoi istorii,* vol. 2 (Moscow, 1991), 394, notes the same number of new tanks and points out that the RKKA possessed superiority over the Germans in total number of tanks and in the quality of the new Soviet ones compared to the Wehrmacht's vehicles. However, this source does not comment on the quality of the older Soviet tanks or on the fact that in key sectors of the attack the Germans had massed a far larger number of troops, tanks, and planes than the defenders had put into the field. Moreover, the Germans were masters, after their campaigns in France and Poland, of massed tank warfare.

16. Erickson, *Road to Stalingrad,* 46.

17. Werth, *Russia at War,* 149.

18. See Harrison Salisbury, *The 900 Days: The Siege of Leningrad* (New York, 1969), 189–223, on the Baltic fighting; on the day-to-day course of combat throughout the summer, see David M. Glantz and Jonathan M. House, *When Titans Clashed: How the Red Army Stopped Hitler* (Lawrence, Kans., 1995), 49–97.

19. Erickson, *Road to Stalingrad,* 242–43. German field reports mention partisan activity in this and other areas almost from the beginning of the campaign; see, for example, file RH 22/7, Militärarchiv, Freiburg (now at Potsdam), Germany; RH 22/5, 9 Aug. 1941, 335, which mentions "numerous reports" of Red Army stragglers behind the German lines who continued to fight.

20. Carell, *Hitler Moves East,* 44.See also a typical comment by the German invaders in PZ AOKI, Panzergruppe I, National Archives (NA), microfilm series T 313, 16910/27, 22 June–31 Oct. 1941. Morgen u. Abendmeldungen der Abteilung Ic als Anlage zum Tätigkeitsbericht Ic. Panzer AOK 1, Ia/Ic, beilage 5, reel (r.) 9, frame (fr.) 7235656, 22 June 1941: "as long as they [Soviet troops] occupied prepared positions, they fought hard [*zäh*]." But they could not usually put up planned resistance; they had been completely surprised.

21. Streit, *Keine Kameraden,* 83. But see Fischer, *Soviet Opposition,* 3, where he cites German figures that 2,053,000 prisoners were taken before 1 November 1941, and 3.6 million were captured before 1 March 1942.

22. Clark, *Barbarossa,* 142–43.

23. Heeresgruppe Süd, NA, T 311, r. 258, fr. 623, 19.9.41; for a similar report see Pz AOK I, NA, T 313, r. 9, fr. 7235665, 26.6.41.

24. Ibid., fr. 7235758.

25. 6 Div., NA, T 315, r. 308, 26 Infanterie Div. Abt. IC 11 Aug. 41, fr. 165; Pz AOK I Panzergruppe I describes the enemy trying to break out of a cauldron from 21 July to 7 August around Taraschtscha: NA, T 313 r. 9, fr. 7235722–7235764.

26. Harvard Project on the Soviet Social System, Interview Records, "A" schedule protocols and "B" schedule interviews, Widener and Russian Research Center Libraries, Harvard University (HP), respondent no. 118, A series, vol. 9, 39–40.

27. 4 Pz div., NA, T 315, r. 206 fr. 248, interrogation of "Jakob Josifowitsch Dschugaschvilli," 19.7.41.

28. 6 Infanterie Division, NA, T 315, r. 308, fr. 40 (a circular from Generalkommando des VIII Fliegerkorps, Commanding General Richthofen). See also 4 Panzer Division, NA, T 315 r. 206, fr. 226, Interrogation of Russian Captain Markevich, 13.7.41: "Supply situation bad, effectively destroyed by the German airforce."

29. I. Gebirgs Division, NA, T 315, r. 44, fr. 1055, 5.8.41, interview with Colonel Prokol'ev, artillery. The German notes indicate that he spoke of "The newly brought-up reservists, some of whom had not served for ten years, with a one-month refresher course. Very little fighting ability." See also I. Korps. Gen. Kdo. I. AK. (General Staff of the Corps), Anlage zum Kriegstagebuch I.A.K. Tätigkeitsbericht vom 1.2.41–31.3.42, NA, T 314, r. 47, fr. 279, which indicates that Soviet active divisions were stationed along the frontier, suggesting that they planned a defense west of the Dubysa-Venta line.

30. Panzer AOK I, NA, T 313, r. 9, fr. 7235851, 9.9.41. Carell writes that south of Naro-Fominsk many captured soldiers were members of workers battalions raised in Moscow. Carell, *Hitler Moves East*, 152. An army officer born about 1919, whose father was also an officer, remembered that in his unit around Velikie Luki in August most men were reservists fresh from civilian life. He claimed that most did not know Russian. HP, no. 445, A series, vol. 22, 13. See also 7 Panzer Division, Tätigkeitsbericht der 7 Panzer Division, Abt. IC. Russland I. Anlagen zu I. Abschnitt: 1.6.41–7.8.41, NA, T 315, r. 436, fr. 952, 30.7.41 (a report on prisoners, among them deserters, all "older people, who from their statements had no desire to fight").

31. 4 Panzer Division, NA, T 315, r. 206, fr. 343, 5.8.41. Nevertheless, the same diary notes that after encirclement two battalions were "real heroes" and attacked tanks. After at least five days of encirclement, the commissar reported bad morale.

32. HP, no. 1486, A series, vol. 34, 7–8. This was a Russian male born about 1901; he had been a chief engineer in a canning factory.

33. HP, no. 341, A series, vol. 18, 14. This was an ex-Soviet colonel born about 1898.

34. See Mark Von Hagen's chapter in this volume.

35. I. Gebirgs Division, NA, T 315, r. 44, fr. 799, 31.8.41. At the same time a captured Turkman said, "Everyone is afraid of hunger."

36. HP, no. 481, A series, vol. 24, 30–31.

37. 4 Panzer Division, NA, T 315, r. 206, fr. 393, 24.8.41.

38. I. Panzerarmee, NA, T 313, r. 10, fr. 7236204, 1.8.41.

39. I. Gebirgs Division, NA, T 315, r. 44, fr. 184, 27.6.41.

40. Ibid., fr. 535, 18–20.8.41.

41. Franz Halder, *The Private War Journal of Generaloberst Franz Halder* (Nuremberg, 1946), 178–79, entries for 27 and 28 June; Panzer AOK I, NA, T 313, r. 9, fr. 7235722,

21 July; 6 Infanterie Division Ia. Anlegenband II. zum Kriegstagebuch Nr. 4. 17.7.1941–22.8.1941, NA, T 315, r. 308, fr. 165, 11 August 1941, among other examples.

42. For example, HP, no. 379, A series, vol. 19, 27: a female Russian born about 1927, a disadvantaged worker from a family of the same; no. 416, A series, vol. 21, 18: a Don Cossack born about 1908, an electrical lineman from a family of well-off peasants; no. 420, A series, vol. 21, 29: a female of German descent born about 1923, a rank-and-file intellectual whose father was a landowner and officer before the Revolution; no. 373, A series, vol. 19, 58: a Russian female born around 1891, a biologist in charge of a laboratory from a family that was prerevolutionary gentry. The family backgrounds of these respondents may also have inclined them against the Soviet regime from its inception.

43. The Harvard Project interviewees were often from well-educated strata that had good jobs before the war. It was precisely these people who were more likely to be arrested; see Thurston, *Life and Terror*, chap. 5, 137–63. On bias among the Harvard respondents, see Inkeles and Bauer, *Soviet Citizen*, 30–33.

44. I. G. R., "Pochemu ia bezhal iz Sovetskogo Soiuza," in B. M. Kuznetsov, ed., *V ugodu Stalinu: Gody 1945–1946* (New York, 1956), 54; HP, no. 342, 25, and no. 420, A series, vol. 21, 28.

45. See for example Anna Ivanova M., "Why I Did Not Return to the USSR," David Dalin file, Bakhmetieff Archive of Russian and East European History and Culture, Columbia University (BA), 6; Nikolai Borodin, *One Man in His Time* (New York, 1955), 264–69.

46. Inkeles and Bauer, *Soviet Citizen*, 30–33; for an example, see HP, no. 386, A series, vol. 20, 68.

47. Even members of Vlasov's Russian Army of Liberation made this claim. See Andrei Georgevich Aldan, *Armiia obrechennykh* (New York, 1969), 12; "Pis'mo voennoplennykh," in Kuznetsov, ed., *V ugodu Stalinu*, 91. The last source noted that many prisoners had been wounded at the time of capture. See also HP, no. 66, A series, vol. 6, 25–26: a Russian male born in 1906, a bookkeeper from a white-collar family; no. 136, A series, vol. 11, 78: a Russian male born in 1903, a graduate of an NKVD school who became an army officer and whose father was a nobleman and officer; and no. 345, A series, vol. 4, 28: a Belorussian male born in 1928, a poor-average peasant from the same background. Vlasov himself repeatedly fought his way out of encirclements in 1941, only to be captured in yet another one in July 1942.

48. Leonid Reschin, "Psychologische Kriegsführung: Sowjetbürger im Dienst der deutschen Streitkräfte, 1941–1945," in *Kriegsgefangene—Voennoplennye: Sowjetische Kreigsgefangene in Deutschland: Deutsche Kriegsgefangene in der Sowjetunion*, ed. Haus der Geschichte der Bundesrepublik Deutschland (Düsseldorf, 1995), 152.

49. Nicholas Bethell, *The Last Secret: Forcible Repatriation to Russia, 1944–7* (London, 1974), 106–7.

50. Joachim Hoffmann, *Die Ostlegionen, 1941–1942: Turkotataren, Kaukasier und Wolgafinnen im Deutschen Heer* (Freiburg, 1976), 39 and 172.

51. Reschin, "Psychologische Kriegsführung," 152.

52. Little information appears to be available on this issue, but see Viktor Zemskov, "K voprosu o repatriatsii sovetskikh grazhdan, 1944–1951 gody," *Istoriia SSSR* 4 (1990), on the presence of "westerners" in German POW camps.

53. Bernd Bonwetsch, "Die sowjetischen Kriegsgefangenen zwischen Stalin und Hitler," *Zeitschrift für Geschichtswissenschaft* 41 (1993), 138.

54. Mark R. Elliott, *Pawns of Yalta: Soviet Refugees and America's Role in Their Repatriation* (Urbana, Ill., 1982), 15.

55. Earl Ziemke, "Composition and Morale of the Partisan Movement," in *Soviet Partisans in World War II*, ed. John A. Armstrong (Madison, Wis., 1964), 146, 179, and 236. For an example of defection to the partisans, in this case of a "Turk-Battalion" in September 1943, see Josef A. Brodski, "Timor und andere: Sowjetische Zwangsarbeiter im Widerstand und ihr Schicksal nach der Befreiung," in *Europa und der "Reichseinsatz": Ausländische Zivilarbeiter, Kriegsgefangene und KZ-Häftlinge in Deutschland, 1938–1945*, ed. Ulrich Herbert (Essen, 1991), 257.

56. Reschin, "Psychologische Kriegsführung," 153.

57. Catherine Andreyev, *Vlasov and the Russian Liberation Movement: Soviet Reality and Emigré Theories* (London, 1987), 37, 61, 71–77.

58. Dallin, *German Rule in Russia*, 427.

59. Ulrich Herbert, "Zwangsarbeit in Deutschland: Sowjetischer Zivilarbeiter und Kriegsgefangene, 1941–1945," in *Erobern und Vernichtung: Der Krieg gegen die Sowjetunion, 1941–1945*, ed. Peter Jahn and Reinhard Rürup (Berlin, 1991), 111.

60. Dallin, *German Rule in Russia*, 427.

61. Ibid.

62. Streit, *Keine Kamaraden*, 10.

63. Omer Bartov, *Hitler's Army: Soldiers, Nazis, and War in the Third Reich* (New York, 1991), 4, 6; see also Streit, *Keine Kamaraden*, 58.

64. Streit, *Keine Kamaraden*, 31.

65. Dallin, *German Rule in Russia*, 30, 63.

66. Michael Parrish, *The Lesser Terror: Soviet State Security, 1939–1953* (Westport, Conn., 1996), 131.

67. Streit, *Keine Kamaraden*, 69, 72.

68. See the photographs in Haus der Geschichte der Bundesrepublik Deutschland, ed., *Kriegsgefangene—Voennoplennye*, 170–72.

69. For graphic accounts of what it was like to be a Soviet prisoner of the Germans, see Aleksandr I. Solzhenitsyn, *The Gulag Archipelago, 1918–1956: An Experiment in Literary Investigation*, vol. 1, trans. Thomas P. Whitney, (New York, 1973), 218–19. On the harsh rules and working conditions faced by POWs, see Herbert, "Zwangsarbeit in Deutschland," 114–17.

70. Streit, *Keine Kamaraden*, 25.

71. Fischer, *Soviet Opposition*, 110–11; Zemskov, "K voprosu," 27.

72. Zemskov, "K voprosu," 39.

73. Elliot, *Pawns of Yalta*, 1, 32, 88, and 90. Elliot writes that "possibly as many as sev-

eral thousand" nonreturnees took their own lives, but here he cites other scholars' work (173). His own study does not suggest anything like this total, and he rightly expresses doubt about the validity of one such estimate (186n). For reports of the suicides by other POWs who were eyewitnesses, see Kuznetsov, ed., *V ugodu Stalinu*, 36 and 45.

74. At least two veterans who later reached the West expressed the thought that the Vlasovites were enemies of their country. HP, no. 534, A series, vol. 28, 43, and no. 138, A series, vol. 11, 77.

75. Inkeles and Bauer, *Soviet Citizen*, 30–33. On leaving under duress see data from the German *Sicherheitspolizei* (security police) and the SD (security service) in Kiev for 1942. For example, in April and May, 41,900 persons were transported to work in the Reich, of whom only 6,722 were volunteers. Rolf-Dieter Müller, "Die Rekrutierung sowjetischer Zwangsarbeiter für die deutsche Kriegswirtschaft," in Herbert, ed., *Europa und der "Reichseinsatz,"* 240. Given the destruction of the economy in the occupied territory, people typically had the choice of working for the Germans in some way or "fleeing to the underground" (234). The second course was extremely dangerous.

76. "Two Commanders of the Soviet Army," David Dalin file, BA, 116.

77. HP, no. 395, A series, vol. 20, 58.

78. HP, no. 128, A series, vol. 10, 3, 22.

79. Kuznetsov, ed., *V ugodu Stalinu*, 95, quoting a letter from an American lieutenant, Max Semeniuk, of July 1945, regarding conversations with Soviet citizens held prisoner at Fort Dix, New Jersey; these may have been Osttruppen. "Pis'mo DP," in the same source (86), makes the same point, as does "Pis'mo voennoplennykh" (90). See also HP, no. 193, B series, vol. 7, 22.

80. Erickson, *Road to Stalingrad*, 176, notes that the Osobyi Otdel of the NKVD was created on Stalin's orders on 20 July 1941. Its assignment was to deal with retreats and treason within the army. This move, taken a month after the war began in a context of constant defeat, also smacks of desperation.

81. *Voenno-Istoricheskii Zhurnal* 9 (1988), 28.

82. Dmitrii A. Volkogonov, *Triumf i tragediia: Politicheskii portret I. V. Stalina*, vol. 2, pt. 1 (Moscow, 1989), 206.

83. *Voenno-Istoricheskii Zhurnal* 8 (1988), 74–80.

84. Werth, *Russia at War*, 393.

85. Zemskov, "K voprosu," 30, 36, 38.

86. "Rabota na shakhte Donbassa," Nicolaevsky Collection, HI, box 296, folder 13 (marked No. V-1535), 7; and, all A series, HP, no. 332, vol. 17, 44; HP, no. 526, vol. 27, 4; HP, no. 310, vol. 16, 3; HP, no. 80, vol. 6, 3; HP, no. 351, vol. 18, 55. One veteran reported, "If there was no intent of going to the enemy on your part, you were returned to your unit. During the war former prisoners of war were used by the Red Army as agitators and speakers who toured other units." HP, no. 56, A series, vol. 5, 11.

87. Zemskov, "K voprosu," 38–40.

88. *Stalin's Letters to Molotov*, ed. Lars T. Lih, Oleg V. Naumov, and Oleg V. Khlevniuk (New Haven, Conn., 1995), 195, 200, and 230, for example, show that Stalin believed

in the 1920s and early 1930s, the years covered by these documents, that internal enemies posed a grave threat to Soviet rule. Volkogonov, who was able to examine Stalin's personal files, wrote that the *vozhd'* (chief, akin to *Führer*) "always believed" police reports about treason. Volkogonov, *Triumf i tragediia,* vol. 1, pt. 1, 274.

89. HP, no. 1467, A series, vol. 34, 53 (interviewer's comment).

90. "Judge Me!" David Dalin file, BA, 2.

91. HP, no. 528, A series, vol. 27, 4. This Ukrainian male was a poor-average peasant,
born about 1926. See also Mikhail Ivanovich Nil'skii, "Ispoved' leitnanta," 100–102, in
the file "Pobeg" (Ms.) and other papers, BA; Stepan Kurilov, "Why I Did Not Return
to My Country: The Story of a Soviet Waif," David Dalin file, BA, 19.

92. HP, no. 449, A series, vol. 22, 24 A-B. This female Russian respondent was born
about 1922 to a family of well-to-do peasants; she was a rank-and-file worker and then
a student before the war.

93. HP, no. 393, A series, vol. 20, 46: a Russian female disadvantaged worker born
around 1927. Anna Ivanova M., "Why I Did Not Return to the USSR," David Dalin
file, BA, 11.

94. HP, no. 478, A series, vol. 24, 51: a Russian female born about 1922 into the family of a rank-and-file worker; she was a student before the war. See also HP, no. 449, A
series, vol. 22, 24 A–B, who decided not to return after she saw how poor Soviet soldiers in Prague were.

95. HP, no. 446, A series, vol. 22, 85.

96. Alice S. Rossi, "Generational Differences in the Soviet Union," mimeographed
report of the Harvard Project on the Soviet Social System, 1954, available at the Russian Research Center Library, Harvard University, summary, 5.

97. Inkeles and Bauer, *Soviet Citizen,* 265 and 274.

98. HP, no. 421, A series, vol. 22, 70–71.

99. HP, no. 378, A series, vol. 19, 49. This was a Russian male born about 1926; he was
a rank-and-file worker before the war, though his family was from the prerevolutionary middle class. See Elliott's similar conclusion in *Pawns of Yalta,* 167–68 and 171.

Chronology of Major Events Leading to the Soviet-German War and of the War Itself

1914   July to November 1918: World War I in Europe.

1917   February (by the old calendar in use then in Russia, March by the western calendar): the tsarist regime falls to a broad, popular revolution.

1917   October (November in the West): the Bolshevik Revolution or coup d'état brings the Communists, also known as Reds or Bolsheviks, to power in Russia. The country is now called Soviet Russia; from late 1922 on it is known as the Soviet Union or Union of Soviet Socialist Republics (USSR).

1918   Spring to fall 1920: the "Russian Civil War" rages over much of the old Russian Empire. Bolshevik or "Red" forces battle "White" or "counterrevolutionary" forces supported by the western Allies of World War I. The fighting is extremely vicious on all sides. Eventually the Bolsheviks emerge victorious.

1921–22   Famine and peasant revolts against the Soviet government. In March 1921 the regime declares the "New Economic Policy," which allows free trade in grain and many other items. This change is met with great approval by the peasantry.

1924   January: Vladimir Lenin, the Communists' leader for years, dies. Josef Stalin (born Josef Djugashvili) begins his rise to power.

1927   A war scare breaks out; there is fear that the western powers will invade the Soviet Union. An economic crisis begins to develop, including poor harvests, high unemployment, and low grain collections from the peasants by the authorities.

1928–29   The peasants are forced to join collective farms. They continue to live in their old huts but must now farm the land together, something they have never done before. The peasants slaughter millions of farm animals to sell the meat or avoid taking the livestock into the collective farms. Upwards of five million peasants are exiled, arrested, or choose to leave the land voluntarily. Between this point and the German invasion of 1941, millions of peasants migrate to the towns to seek work. Spectacular urban growth occurs in conjunction with the five-year plans to industrialize the country.

1929   October: the American stock market crashes, sending out shock waves that eventually bring on the Great Depression in capitalist countries.

1931   The Japanese invade and occupy Manchuria, putting their troops along the Soviet border in the Far East.

1932–33   Famine in the USSR, especially in Ukraine, South Russia, and Siberia. At least several million die.

1933   January: Adolf Hitler becomes chancellor of Germany. Under his guidance the Germans begin to rebuild their economy and to persecute Jews, Romany ("Gypsies"), Social Democrats, Communists, homosexuals, people with handicaps, and anyone else in the country whom the Nazis deem undesirable.

1936   Germany reoccupies the Rhineland, a demilitarized zone along the Rhine River. The Rhineland had been designated as demilitarized in the treaties ending World War I, so that if another war broke out French troops could quickly occupy it and cripple German war production. Now the western Allies do nothing as Germany builds up its military forces.

1936–38   Terror in the Soviet Union. Millions are arrested, and many of those are shot. Thousands of military officers are removed from their positions.

1938   Summer: fighting occurs between Soviet and Japanese troops along the Manchurian border.

1938   September: the Munich Crisis, in which Britain and France agree that Germany will absorb part of Czechoslovakia; war is averted. The USSR is not invited to Munich.

1939   August 23: the Nazi-Soviet Nonaggression Pact, also known as the Molotov-Ribbentrop Pact. Germany and the USSR do not become allies but agree not to attack one another if war breaks out.

1939   September 1: Germany invades Poland from the west.

1939   September 17: Soviet troops invade Poland from the east. Poland disappears as a country, Germany absorbing the western part and the USSR the eastern section, populated mostly by ethnic Ukrainians and Belorussians.

1939   November to March 1940: the Soviet-Finnish War.

1940   June: France and the Low Countries fall to Germany.

1940   July: The USSR annexes the Baltic states of Latvia, Lithuania, and Estonia.

1941	June 22: Germany invades the Soviet Union. Some 4.6 million troops of Germany and its allies attack 2.9 million troops defending the western border of the USSR.
1941	July 16: Smolensk occupied.
1941	September 8: Leningrad encircled.
1941	September 20: Kiev occupied.
1941	October 14: German victory at Viazma; the road to Moscow seems open.
1941	November 15: German attack on Moscow begins, but stalls within a few days.
1941	December 5: Soviet counterattacks begin, driving the Germans back 100–250 kilometers (66–170 miles) from Moscow.
1942	German victories near Bialystok, Minsk, Smolensk, Uman, and other places. Soviet forces retreat across the Don River in July, falling back toward Stalingrad on the Volga River. The Germans penetrate into the Caucasus Mountains by late summer and threaten Soviet oil supplies from Baku.
1943	January to February: German Sixth Army surrenders at Stalingrad. Soviet troops finish lifting the blockade of Leningrad.
1943	July 5 to late August: Battle of Kursk. Red Army drives back the Germans, liberates Khar'kov, Kiev, much of central Russia and some of Belorussia.
1944	Soviet troops continue to push the Germans back; by late spring the southern front is at the prewar Soviet border.
1944	June 6: D-Day, the invasion of Normandy by the western Allies.
1944	Summer and fall: Soviet troops move into Bulgaria, Romania, part of Yugoslavia and Hungary, and part of prewar Poland.
194	May 1: Soviet troops occupy Berlin.
1945	May 8: Germany surrenders.
1945	August 6 and 8: Americans drop atomic bombs on Hiroshima and Nagasaki.
1945	August 14: Japan surrenders.

Contributors

RICHARD BIDLACK, an associate professor of history at Washington and Lee University, is the author of "Workers at War: Factory Workers and Labor Policy in the Siege of Leningrad," *The Carl Beck Papers in Russian and East European Studies,* no. 902 (Pittsburgh, 1991).

BERND BONWETSCH, a professor of history at the Ruhr-Universität, Bochum, is the author of *Die Russische Revolution 1917: Eine Sozialgeschichte von der Bauernbefreiung 1861 bis zum Oktoberumsturz* (Darmstadt, 1991) and "The Purge of the Military and the Red Army's Operational Capability during the 'Great Patriotic War,'" in *From Peace to War: Germany, Soviet Russia, and the World, 1939–1941,* ed. Bernd Wegner (Providence, R.I., and Potsdam, 1997).

GENNADI BORDIUGOV holds the Russian *kandidat* degree in history and is a *dotsent* (assistant professor) of history at Moscow State University. He is the author of *Istoriia i kon'iunktura: Sub'ektivnye zametki ob istorii sovetskogo obchshestva* (Moscow, 1992), and *Beloe delo: Osnovy, ideologiia, rezhimy vlasti* (Moscow, 1998).

SUSANNE CONZE holds a Ph.D. degree in history from the University of Bielefeld. Her dissertation, entitled "Sowjetische Industriearbeiterinnen in den 40er Jahren: Die Auswirkungen des 2. Weltkrieges auf die Erwerbstätigkeit von Frauen in der UdSSR 1941–1950," will be published by Steiner Verlag, Stuttgart, in 2000.

ANDREI R. DZENISKEVICH holds the Russian *doktor nauk* (doctor of sciences) degree in history and is an affiliate of the Institute of History, Russian Academy of Sciences, St. Petersburg. He is the editor of *Leningrad v osade: Sbornik dokumentov o geroicheskoi oborone Leningrada v gody Velikoi Otechestvennoi voiny, 1941–1944* (St. Petersburg, 1995) and the author of *Nakanune i v dni ispytanii: Leningradskie rabochie v 1938–1945 gg.* (Leningrad, 1990).

BEATE FIESELER, an assistant professor of history at the Ruhr-Universität, Bochum, is the author of *Frauen auf dem Weg in die russische Sozialdemokratie, 1890–1917: Eine kollektive Biographie* (Stuttgart, 1995).

UWE GARTENSCHLÄGER, director of the Russian Office of the German Adult Education Association in St. Petersburg, holds an M.A. degree from the University of Cologne. He is coauthor of *Eine rote Festung wird erobert: National-sozialismus in Oerlingkhausen* (Bielefield, 1986) and "Erwachsenenbildung in Russland," *Osteuropa*, no. 5 (1997): 455–67.

MIKHAIL M. GORINOV holds the Russian *kandidat* degree and is an affiliate of the Institute of History, Russian Academy of Sciences, Moscow. He is coauthor of *Istoriia Otechestva: Kratkii ocherk* (Moscow, 1992) and author of *NEP: Poiski putei razvitiia* (Moscow, 1990).

HANS-HEINRICH NOLTE, a professor in the Historisches Seminar der Universität Hannover, is the author of *Nationenbildung östlich des Bug* (Hannover, 1994) and *Kleine Geschichte Russlands* (Stuttgart, 1998).

AILEEN G. RAMBOW holds a Ph.D. degree in East European and Russian history from the Free University of Berlin and is in charge of external relations in Western Europe for the Civic Education Project, New Haven and Budapest. She is the author of *Überleben mit Worten: Literatur und Ideologie während der Blockade von Leningrad, 1941–1944* (Berlin, 1995).

RICHARD STITES, a professor of history at Georgetown University, is the author of *The Women's Liberation Movement in Russia* (Princeton, 1978 and 1991) and *Russian Popular Culture: Entertainment and Society since 1900* (New York, 1992), among other works.

ROBERT W. THURSTON, a professor of history at Miami University, Oxford, Ohio, is the author of *Liberal City, Conservative State: Moscow and Russia's Urban Crisis, 1906–1914* (New York, 1987) and *Life and Terror in Stalin's Russia, 1934–1941* (New Haven, Conn., 1996).

MARK VON HAGEN, a professor of history and director of the Harriman Institute at Columbia University, is the author of *Soldiers in the Proletarian Dictatorship: The Red Army and the Soviet Socialist State, 1917–1930* (Ithaca, N.Y., 1990) and coeditor of *After Empire: Multiethnic Societies and Nation-Building: The Soviet Union and the Russian, Ottoman, and Habsburg Empires* (Boulder, Colo., 1997).

Index

Typeset in 10.5/13 Minion
with Serifa display
Designed by Dennis Roberts
Composed by Celia Shapland
for the University of Illinois Press

University of Illinois Press
1325 South Oak Street
Champaign, IL 61820-6903
www.press.uillinois.edu